The Critical Reader

AP® English Literature and Composition

Erica L. Meltzer

THE CRITICAL READER
New York

Cover by Tugboat Design

ISBN-13: 978-1-7335895-8-1

For inquiries regarding reprints, translation, bulk orders, and licensing, contact thecriticalreader1@gmail.com.

For Reprints and Permissions, please see p. 213.

ALSO BY ERICA MELTZER

The Ultimate Guide to SAT® Grammar & Workbook

The Critical Reader: The Complete Guide to SAT® Reading

SAT® Vocabulary: A New Approach (with Larry Krieger)

The Complete Guide to ACT® English

The Complete Guide to ACT® Reading

The Complete GMAT® Sentence Correction Guide

GRE® Vocabulary in Practice

How to Write for Class: A Student's Guide to Grammar, Punctuation, and Style

Table of Contents

A Few Notes About This Book

Before you get started, there are just a few points I'd like to call to your attention.

First, if you have not previously used a Critical Reader guide, then let me begin with word of explanation about the content and structure of this book: It is not designed to encourage you to simply crash through lots of practice material but rather to give you an in-depth understanding of the skills and concepts that the AP® English Literature and Composition Exam tests, and of the particular ways in which those things can be assessed. You will undoubtedly notice that the same passages appear multiple times, in different chapters. This is an intentional strategy, designed to emphasize the various angles from which particular textual features can be approached. Narrative voice, for example, can be tested in terms of point of view, but it can also be asked about in terms of tone or function. And even something as seemingly straightforward as literal comprehension can be asked about in terms of vocabulary, paraphrasing, or inference.

If you do happen to have previous experience with Critical Reader guides, you will probably notice that this book is organized in a very similar way and covers many of the same concepts—albeit with examples very explicitly tailored to the AP Literature Exam. This overlap is deliberate. The two AP English Exams essentially form a "set": they are written according to a common template and share the same question types. The fact that one focuses on non-fiction and the other on fiction is in many ways incidental. Furthermore, both the AP exams and the SAT are developed and managed by the College Board (even if the former are still written by ETS), so there are predictable parallels between the concepts tested on SAT Reading and the AP English tests.

Unlike many other AP English Literature guides, this one does not feature long lists of advanced rhetorical devices to memorize (although it does contain a few short ones) for the simple reason that such terms are not the focus of the test. Indeed, they have not been the focus for many years, and they have become even less of one—particularly on the multiple-choice reading section—since the exam was updated in 2020. To be sure, some advanced rhetorical terminology may certainly come in handy on the Prose and Poetry Analysis Essays, but as discussed in the essay section of this book, you are under no obligation to include any particular terms, and you can score very well discussing only more common devices. In terms of essay preparation, you should focus on learning how to effectively integrate textual support into your arguments, and how to draw connections between the specific words and phrases you cite and the larger themes of the works you analyze.

Finally, although one of the hallmarks of great literature is of course that it is open to interpretation, it is advisable—particularly while studying for the reading section—to keep in mind that *literal* meaning is generally not. Passages as well as answer choices may include vocabulary that is both challenging and highly abstract, but the correct options are not subjective, and the arguments you make in your essays must be clearly supported by the specific wording of the text. Otherwise, the test would be invalid, and the College Board would not be allowed to administer it!

Unfortunately, there is no real shortcut for understanding the kind of complex language that characterizes many AP English Literature passages, or for learning to write about literature with nuance and precision. That said, the many explanations provided throughout both the Reading and Essay sections of this book are intended to serve as model textual analyses, whose features you may want to try incorporating into your own writing. Beyond that, this guide is intended to offer you a pathway through the test—to show you its internal logic and patterns, and to turn it from something perplexing and overwhelming into something manageable and perhaps even—dare I say it—interesting.

Erica Meltzer
January 2021

Part I: Reading

Chapter One

Introduction to Multiple-Choice Reading

The reading portion of the Advanced Placement® English Literature and Composition Exam is structured as follows:

- 55 questions total: typically 5 passages, each accompanied by 8-13 questions
- 60 minutes
- Prose Fiction & Poetry passages: at least 2 of each
- 45% of the total exam score

One point is earned for each correct answer, and no points for questions that are skipped or answered incorrectly. **There is no added penalty for wrong answers, so you should not leave questions blank.**

Passages are drawn from both classic and contemporary works, with the highest proportion (around 50%) drawn from 20th century works. The remaining texts are divided between pre-20th century texts and contemporary (21st century) texts.

What Does Multiple-Choice Reading Test?

The reading portion of the AP® Literature and Composition Exam asks you to go beyond *what* a text says to *how* and *why* the text says it. To that end, it tests your ability to do the following:

- Understand the significance of diction (word choice), imagery, and symbols, and how they reveal information about plot, setting, and characters.
- Understand the rhetorical role (e.g., supporting, emphasizing, criticizing) that various pieces of information play within a text.
- "Track" key words and images, and understand when a particular element (e.g., idea, character, object) is referred to in different ways.
- Identify major shifts in style and point of view, and understand their relationship to the structure of the text.
- Make reasonable inferences about meanings not explicitly stated in the text.

The essential skill that the exam requires is something called **"rhetorical reading."** This simply means reading to understand the central idea, relationship, or conflict that a writer is attempting to convey, as well as the rhetorical role, or **function**, that various pieces of information play in conveying that impression to the reader.

You should, however, be aware that while the exam has traditionally tested the identification of advanced rhetorical figures (e.g., synecdoche, onomatopoeia, apostrophe), the focus is now on the identification of more common terms (e.g., abstract language, metaphor) and general purposes (e.g., explaining, criticizing, implying). **If you practice with older exams, keep in mind that the questions do not fully reflect the content of the current test.**

How to Read Passages

As a general rule, you should **read the passage as quickly as you can while still absorbing the content, making sure to focus on the parts you do understand and not wasting time puzzling over confusing details**. The last thing you want to do is get stuck in a loop of reading the same set of lines repeatedly while the clock ticks. (This applies to the poetry and prose essay passages as well.) While you should at least skim through everything upfront, it is usually unnecessary to read every word closely in order to grasp the basics—you can worry about the details as you work through the questions.

Note that effective skimming does not simply involve reading everything quickly, but rather knowing where to move fast and where to slow down. **You should always pay particular attention to the introduction and the conclusion as well as the beginning and end of each stanza or paragraph. These places generally provide the framework for the passage, presenting and commenting on key interactions, attitudes, and events.**

Next, writers are rarely shy about drawing the reader's attention to key points in the action or description, and you must be able to recognize these places: **transitions such as *however, thus,* and *indeed*; "unusual" punctuation such as italics (used for emphasis), dashes and colons (used to signal explanations); strong language such as *only, never,* and *always*; and words such as *important* or any of its synonyms (*key, central, essential*) are all "clues" that tell you to pay attention.** (See the chart on p. 79 for an extensive list.)

If you are able to do so without disrupting your ability to absorb the text, you should **circle these elements as you read**; the information you need to answer many questions will typically be located nearby. That said, if you cannot focus on the meaning of the passage and pay attention to transitions/punctuation simultaneously, then you should not worry about them during your initial read-through. It is far more important that you gain a clear understanding of the text. When you go back to answer the questions, however, you will need to take these textual cues into account.

To be clear, the point is not to just hunt mechanically for transitions and punctuation. You don't need to circle every last *and* or *but* that appears, nor should you do so. Rather, **the real goal is to read actively**—that is, to help yourself understand and think about what the passage is actually saying, not just go through the motions of looking at it line by line because that's what you're supposed to do. Identifying key textual elements can also help you anticipate the questions, and to identify potential answers before you have even finished reading.

Another active-reading strategy is to write 1-2 word paragraph summaries. While writing a sumary for every paragraph is probably too time-consuming (unless, of course, there are only a few paragraphs, or the text is very short), you can choose a few key paragraphs and just jot down their topic to remind you of their main focus. This can be particularly useful for keeping the big picture in mind when paragraphs are very long.

Note: If you feel that you can't read the passages upfront without running out of time, you can try reading short bits and answering the questions as you go. You should, however, keep in mind that some answers may appear after the lines referenced, and that you may need to read ahead to find the necessary information.

Finally, if you are a truly exceptional reader, you may be able to start with the questions and read the passage as you answer them. The major drawback to this approach, no matter how strong your comprehension, is that you will need to jump around to different parts of the passage—not necessarily in order—to obtain the necessary context on some questions. If you are able to read in this fragmented fashion and still come away with a coherent understanding of the passage, then this may be a feasible strategy for you; otherwise, it is best avoided.

Passages drawn from fiction or poetry differ from non-fiction passages because they are not based on arguments but instead revolve around characters' emotions, actions, and relationships. They are more abstract and less straightforward—those traits, particularly when combined with complex, old-fashioned language, can make them quite challenging to follow at times. That said, **AP Literature passages generally serve to convey an essential idea, character trait, or relationship that functions as the "main point"; provided that you can identify that central focus, you should be able to answer many of the questions without too much difficulty.** Thus, it is very much in your interest to actively search for this information as you read, and to note it **in writing**. If it appears directly in the passage, you should circle or underline it; otherwise, you should take a couple of seconds and jot it down yourself. We'll look at how to do this in the following chapter.

Of course, fiction and poetry can be structured in unpredictable ways: sometimes, the main idea or central relationship/conflict will—as is common in other types of writing—be introduced towards the end of the introduction and then reiterated at the end of the conclusion. (You should always pay attention to those places just in case). In other instances, the main idea may be located somewhere else entirely or may only be suggested indirectly. That is why you should not generally skip over sections of the passage outright—the potential for missing key information is too great.

Finally, remember that while you will be asked to identify the basic purpose of symbols and other types of imagery, you cannot engage in too much speculation about their larger meaning. A question cannot be included on the exam unless its answer is directly supported by the specific wording of the passage, so what matters most is your ability to understand literal meaning and how the author's choice of words and use of specific rhetorical devices convey their ideas. If you do go looking for some larger symbolism or start to make assumptions not explicitly suggested by the text, you can easily lose sight of the basics. In fact, most students run into trouble not because there's an esoteric interpretation that can only be perceived through some sort of quasi-mystical process, but rather because they aren't being sufficiently *literal*.

How to Work Through Passage-Based Reading Questions

While the exact approach may vary somewhat depending on the particular question, I generally recommend the following strategy:

1) Read the question slowly.

Put your finger or your pencil on each word of the question as you read it. Otherwise, you may overlook key information.

When you're done, take a second or two to make sure you know exactly what it's asking. If the question is phrased in an even slightly complicated manner, rephrase it in a more straightforward way until you're clear on what you're looking for. If necessary, scribble down the rephrased version.

This is not a minor step. If, for example, the question asks you the purpose of a particular sentence, you must be prepared to reread that sentence with the goal of understanding what role it plays within the argument, or what impression the author is trying to convey. If you reread it with a different goal, e.g., understanding what the sentence is literally saying, you can't do any meaningful work toward answering the question that's actually there.

2) Go back to the passage and reread the lines given in the question. If necessary, read from a sentence or two above to a sentence or two below.

There is unfortunately no surefire way to tell from the wording of a question whether the necessary information is included in the line reference. Most of the time it will be there, but sometimes it will appear either before or after. Very occasionally, it will be located in another paragraph entirely.

Purpose (or "function") questions, which make up a large portion of the exam, often require additional context. As a result, you should be prepared to read both before and after the line reference. In contrast, other detail-based question types are more likely to involve only the information in the line reference itself.

If a line reference begins or ends halfway through a sentence, make sure you back up or keep reading so that you cover the entire sentence in which it appears. Otherwise, you may miss key information. And if a line reference begins close to the beginning of a paragraph, you should automatically back up and read from the first sentence of the paragraph because it will almost always give you the main idea.

If you read the lines referenced and have an inordinate amount of difficulty identifying the answer, or you get stuck between two options and cannot decide between them, that's often a sign that the answer is actually located somewhere other than in the line reference. Go back to the passage and make sure you have the full context for the statement in question.

Note that a long line reference is, paradoxically, often a signal that you don't need to read the entire section. The information necessary to answer the question will usually be located in the first couple of sentences, the last couple of sentences, or in a section with key punctuation (e.g., dashes, italics, colon). Start by focusing on those places; they'll almost always give you enough to go on.

3) Come up with your own answer, and write it down.

The goal is not to write a dissertation or come up with the exact answer. You can be very general and should spend no more than a few seconds on this step. A couple of words scribbled in semi-legible handwriting will suffice. The goal is to identify the essential information or idea that the answer must include, keeping in mind that the correct choice may reword that idea in an unexpected way.

It is, however, important that you write something in your own words because doing so serves to focus you. It reminds you what you're looking for and prevents you from getting distracted by plausible-sounding or confusing answer choices.

Again, make sure you're answering the question that's actually being asked, not just summarizing the passage.

You should take **no more than a few seconds** to do this. If you can't come up with anything, skip to step #4.

4) Read the answers carefully, (A)-(E), in order.

If there's an option that contains the same essential idea you put down, choose it because it's almost certainly right. If it makes you feel better, you can read through the rest of the answers just to be sure, but make sure you don't get distracted by options that sound vaguely possible and start second-guessing yourself.

When you cross out an answer, put a line through the entire thing. Do not just cross out the letter. As far as you're concerned, it no longer exists.

If you can't identify the correct answer…

5) Cross out the answers that clearly don't work; leave <u>everything</u> else.

Try not to spend more than a couple of seconds on each answer choice. If an option clearly does not make sense in context of the question or passage, eliminate it.

Leave any answer that could even slightly work, even if you're not quite sure how it relates to the passage or question. **Remember: your understanding of an answer choice has no bearing whatsoever on whether it's right or wrong, so you should never cross out anything simply because you find it confusing.**

When you get down to two or three answers, go back to the passage again and start checking them out. Whatever you do, do not just sit and stare at them. The information you need to answer the question is in the passage, not in your head.

There are several ways to approach the remaining answers:

First, when you go back to the passage, see whether there are any major transitions or strong language you missed the first time around; you may have been focusing on the wrong part of the line reference. If that is the case, the correct answer may become clear once you identify the appropriate section.

Very often, the correct answer will also contain a synonym for a key word in the passage, so if a remaining choice includes this feature, you should pay very close attention to it.

You can also pick one specific word in each answer to check out when you go back to the passage. For example, if the lines in question focus on a description of a natural setting, then an answer choice about a character's interior life is probably inconsistent with that emphasis. Likewise, if an answer focuses on a specific person, thing, or idea not discussed in the relevant section of the passage, there's also a reasonable chance that it's off-topic.

Remember: the more information an answer contains, the greater the chance that some of that information will be wrong. Correct answers are often shorter and more general than incorrect ones; even a few words can make a difference.

Finally, you can reiterate the main idea of the passage or paragraph, and think about which answer is most consistent with it. That answer will most likely be correct.

6) If you're still stuck, see whether there's a choice that looks like a right answer.

If you still can't figure out the answer, you need to switch from reading the passage to "reading" the test. Working this way will allow you to make an educated guess, even if you're not totally sure what's going on. Does one of the answers you're left with use extremely strong or limiting language (*universally, totally incompatible*)? There's a reasonable chance it's wrong. Does one of them use a common word (e.g., *qualify, conviction*) in its second meaning? There's a reasonable chance it's right. Is one answer very long and detailed and the other shorter and more abstract? You might want to pay closer attention to the latter.

In addition, think about whether all the answers you're left with truly make sense. Incorrect choices may sometimes consist of what is essentially sophisticated-sounding gobbledygook (e.g., "laments the dissolution of his former existence") unrelated to the actual scenario at hand. Don't assume that an answer is right just because it sounds high-minded and important.

7) If you're still stuck, skip it.

You can always come back to it later if you have time, and if you're still not sure, you won't lose extra points for guessing incorrectly. Better to focus on questions you can answer easily first.

Understanding and Marking Line References

Although line references are provided for many questions, they are not always as helpful as many test-takers assume. The most important thing to understand is that a line reference simply tells you where in the passage a particular word, phrase, or set of lines appears. It does not necessarily tell you where the answer is located.

Yes, the information you need to answer a question will frequently appear in the line(s) provided, but sometimes it will also appear in a neighboring line, either before or after. Occasionally, it may appear in a different paragraph entirely. Consider, for example, a question that reads, "The use of the dash in line 27 suggests that…" This question is telling you that a dash appears in line 27; the answer *could* be in line 27, but it could also be in line 25 or line 29 or line 33.

In one strategy, the test-taker goes through the questions and marks all the line references in the passage before reading it so that she or he will "know where to focus." While this can be a very successful strategy for helping people whose minds would otherwise wander—and I would not discourage anyone from using it if they find it helpful—it does have some pitfalls. First, as discussed above, the answer may not actually be located in the lines cited in the question. If it doesn't occur to you to read elsewhere when you can't figure out the answer, you'll often get stuck between two options and have no clear-cut way of figuring out which one is correct. And that's a shame since often the answer will be fairly straightforward; it will simply be somewhere else.

Second, this strategy can drain significant amounts of time that could be better spent answering questions. If you have difficulty finishing sections on time, you probably shouldn't be using it. There's no reason you can't go back to the passage and bracket off the lines as you come to them.

Third, this strategy is to some extent based on a misunderstanding of how the multiple-choice reading section works: **the most important places in the passage, the ones you need to pay the most attention to, are not necessarily the ones indicated by the questions**. Remember: the details are only important in context of the larger relationships or ideas that the author or poet wants to convey. Focusing excessively on a particular set of lines can therefore cause you to lose sight of the big picture—and often it's the big picture you actually need to answer the questions. At the other extreme, only a small part of the line reference may sometimes be important. There's no point in meticulously blocking off eight lines if all you need to focus on is the first sentence or a set of dashes.

Chapter Two

The Big Picture

Although questions asking about passages as a whole typtically make up a relatively small portion of the AP Literature exam, the ability to quickly grasp the general scenario in a given passage is absolutely crucial to your succcess on the multiple-choice portion. Why? Because answers to many questions depend on the larger context of the passage. In fact, if you have a good sense of the passage as a whole, you may even be able to identify answers to some detail-based questions immediately, allowing you to save both time and energy.

What Is the Passage About?

Whenever you read a passage, your first goal is simply to figure out what is literally happening. To establish the essentials, you should consider questions such as the following:

- Who are the characters/narrator?
- What is happening to them, or what topic/situation does the narrator discuss?
- Is the narrator's attitude positive, negative, or neutral? The characters'?
- If there are multiple characters, do they get along, or is there a conflict?
- For poetry: what is the topic, and is there a main theme (e.g., love, longing, envy…)?

Although these are basic questions, the answers will not necessarily be obvious. For that reason, it is important that you know where to look for key information as well as how to identify it.

You must, for example, be able to identify topics of poems because correct answers may state them, either directly or in rephrased form. You also cannot determine whether an answer is off-topic unless you know what the topic is! More seriously, if you misunderstand the basic scenario in a poetry or prose passage, you risk answering multiple questions incorrectly.

You must also try to understand the general **scope** of the passage—that is, how general or specific it is. This is because some incorrect answers may contain statements far broader than what the passage suggests. To avoid this trap, you must know what is and is not discussed.

How to Write a Passage Summary

As mentioned in the previous chapter, although poetry and prose passages are not arguments and do not contain main points per se, **they are generally centered around a central idea, attitude, or relationship that may or may not be directly stated in the text**. In most cases, this information can be condensed into a very short sentence or series of phrases. You should aim to write 5-7 words/symbols at most—the shorter the better. **Note that a summary differs from a topic (e.g., flowers, spring, the sea) or a theme (e.g., love, longing, beauty) in that it expresses a complete thought.**

While this type of hyper-condensed summary can be very challenging to write at first, its usefulness in terms of keeping you focused, and of preventing you from worrying about irrelevant details, cannot be overstated.

As an example, we're going to work with this poem by the nineteenth-century poet John Keats:

> To one who has been long in city pent,
> 'Tis very sweet to look into the fair
> And open face of heaven,—to breathe a prayer
> Full in the smile of the blue firmament.
> Who is more happy, when, with hearts content,
> Fatigued he sinks into some pleasant lair
> Of wavy grass, and reads a debonair
> And gentle tale of love and languishment?
> Returning home at evening, with an ear
> Catching the notes of Philomel,—an eye
> Watching the sailing cloudlet's bright career,
> He mourns that day so soon has glided by:
> E'en like the passage of an angel's tear
> That falls through the clear ether silently.

Although there's a lot of information here, the narrator is nice enough to give us a pretty good idea of what he's talking about, and what he thinks about it, in the first few lines (more about that in the next section). Essentially, he's saying that after being cooped up in the city (*long in city pent*), it's a relief to get away and look into the sky (the *open face of heaven*). He then expands on that idea in the following lines, making clear that he's talking about going into the country, or at least a place with green space (*Fatigued he sinks into some pleasant lair/Of wavy grass*).

What's his attitude? Well, it's extremely positive: words/phrases such as *sweet, happy, hearts content*, and *pleasant lair* indicate that escaping from an urban environment is a pretty amazing thing. And that's all we need to know to write a summary. Some options include:

- **Getting away from city = great!**
- **Country = great escape**
- **Escape to country = amazing**

Notice that we've eliminated all the details, as well as any hint of flowery language. It's the poet's job to be flowery; it's your job to figure out what they're literally saying.

Next, let's look at a prose passage.

It came like a thunder-clap on us all, that the vessel which contained our fortune had been wrecked, and gone to the bottom with all its stores, together with several of the crew, and the unfortunate merchant himself. I was grieved for him; I was grieved for the overthrow of all our air-built castles: but, with the elasticity of youth, I soon recovered the shock.

Though riches had charms, poverty had no terrors for an inexperienced girl like me. Indeed, to say the truth, there was something exhilarating in the idea of being driven to straits, and thrown upon our own resources. I only wished papa, mamma, and Mary were all of the same mind as myself; and then, instead of lamenting past calamities we might all cheerfully set to work to remedy them; and the greater the difficulties, the harder our present privations, the greater should be our cheerfulness to endure the latter, and our vigour to contend against the former.

Mary did not lament, but she brooded continually over the misfortune, and sank into a state of dejection from which no effort of mine could rouse her. I could not possibly bring her to regard the matter on its bright side as I did: and indeed I was so fearful of being charged with childish frivolity, or stupid insensibility, that I carefully kept most of my bright ideas and cheering notions to myself; well knowing they could not be appreciated.

My mother thought only of consoling my father, and paying our debts and retrenching our expenditure by every available means; but my father was completely overwhelmed by the calamity: health, strength, and spirits sank beneath the blow, and he never wholly recovered them. In vain my mother strove to cheer him, by appealing to his piety, to his courage, to his affection for herself and us. That very affection was his greatest torment: it was for our sakes he had so ardently longed to increase his fortune—it was our interest that had lent such brightness to his hopes, and that imparted such bitterness to his present distress. He now tormented himself with remorse at having neglected my mother's advice; which would at least have saved him from the additional burden of debt—he vainly reproached himself for having brought her from the dignity, the ease, the luxury of her former station to toil with him through the cares and toils of poverty. It was gall and wormwood to his soul to see that splendid, highly-accomplished woman, once so courted and admired, transformed into an active managing housewife, with hands and head continually occupied with household labours and household economy. The very willingness with which she performed these duties, the cheerfulness with which she bore her reverses, and the kindness which withheld her from imputing the smallest blame to him, were all perverted by this ingenious self-tormentor into further aggravations of his sufferings. And thus the mind preyed upon the body, and disordered the system of the nerves, and they in turn increased the troubles of the mind, till by action and reaction his health was seriously impaired; and **not one of us could convince him that the aspect of our affairs was not half so gloomy, so utterly hopeless, as his morbid imagination represented it to be.**

Because this passage is so long and contains so many details, it is exactly the type of text that students tend to get lost in. The key to summarizing it, however, is to focus on the introduction and the highlighted topic sentences, which provide the basic framework. The introduction sets up the basic scenario—the narrator's father has lost his fortune—and the various topic sentences outline the different family members' reactions: the narrator is not overly worried; her sister broods; her mother tries to make her father feel better; and her father is deeply depressed. We can take all this information and compress it further into a single statement:

Lose $$, narrator ok BUT family worried.

Using the Introduction

As discussed, you should always pay close attention to the beginning and the end of a passage, but you should particularly focus on the beginning during your first read-through. The purpose of an introduction, after all, is to provide the big picture: to orient the reader within a text by presenting the characters, their situations, and their attitudes. In general, you should **read the passage slowly and deliberately until you have a good sense of what it's about**—once you've established the basics, you can move more quickly through the rest of the text.

Let's look at some examples of how initial paragraphs can present key information for making sense out of a text.

Poetry Introduction #1

> I acknowledge my status as a stranger:
> Inappropriate clothes, odd habits
> Out of sync with wasp and wren.

In just three lines, the narrator establishes a clear framework for the poem: it will focus on outsider status, someone who is slightly out of step with the world.

Poetry Introduction #2

> The words are what I know,
> but they are no comfort.
> The comfort is in the music
> that says what I cannot know.

Even though we only have four lines here, they provide quite a bit of information. They suggest that the poem focuses on the relationship between words and music, and that music will be praised for its ability to provide comfort in a way that words cannot.

Poetry Introduction #3

> April this year, not otherwise
> Than April of a year ago,
> Is full of whispers, full of sighs,
> Of dazzling mud and dingy snow;
> Hepaticas* that pleased you so
> Are here again, and butterflies.

*Flowers that bloom in the spring

In this case, the poem is not actually separated into stanzas, so we're going to work with the first sentence. It's less direct and more suggestive, but we can still get a reasonable idea of the issues at play. Essentially, the narrator is comparing April of the present year to the same month last year; that fact, combined with the direct address to a person (*Hepaticas that pleased you so*) and the reference to April being *full of sighs*, suggests that the person is absent and that the narrator misses them very much. The theme might be described as "longing."

Poetry Introduction #4

We **could** deny our winter, refuse to cut
our hands mining the sharp ores of grief.
Whenever the cold comes, we **could** follow

the arrowheads of geese shafting south
to an azure place where whales sing offshore
and otters frolic in the wanton surf.

This is a much subtler example than the others; however, if we look at the wording very closely, we can see that it provides a clue about how the poem might be structured. The key word here is *could*: it indicates that the speaker is discussing something that people *might* do to avoid difficulty or pain but will not necessarily do. This word suggests that at some point in the poem, the speaker will shift course and focus on an alternate possibility, or on the result of that decision.

Now let's look at some prose passages.

Prose Introduction #1

As I remember, Giffen's appeared at the beginning of the twenties, and I am sure I am not alone in associating its emergence with that change of mood within our profession—that change which came to push the polishing of silver to the position of central importance it still by and large maintains today. The shift was, I believe, like some many other major shifts around this period, a generational matter; it was during these years that our generation of butlers 'came of age', and figures like Mr Marshall, in particular, played a crucial part in making silver-polishing so central.

Although the very beginning of the first sentence provides little helpful information, the information after the dash indicates that silver polishing is of *central importance,* and the reference to *major shifts* and *our generation of butlers* in the following sentence reveals the speaker's profession and implies that the following paragraphs will focus on the impact of silver polish on the narrator's job.

Prose Introduction #2

She was one of those children possessed by a desire to have the world just so. Whereas her big sister's room was a stew of unclosed books, unfolded clothes, umade bed, unemptied ashtrays, Briony's was a shrine to her controlling demon: the model farm spread across a deep window ledge consisted of the usual animals, but all facing one way—toward their owner—as if about to break into song, and even the farmyard hens were neatly corralled. In fact, Briony's was the only tidy upstairs room in the house. Her straight-backed dolls in their many-roomed mansion appeared to be under strict instructions not to touch the walls; the various thumb-sized figures to be found standing about her dressing table—cowboys, deep-sea divers, humanoid mice—suggested by their even ranks and spacing a citizen's army awaiting orders.

In this paragraph—indeed, in the very first sentence—we essentially have a miniature and highly revealing psychological portrait. We learn that Briony is deeply attached to order and neatness; essentially, she is something of a control freak. We can reasonably assume that the rest of the passage will go into more detail about these qualities, and/or illustrate how they influence her interactions with others.

Prose Introduction #3

In nothing—as the expert on whose advice families moved to new neighborhoods to live there for a generation—was Babbitt more splendidly innocent than in the science of sanitation. He did not know a malaria-bearing mosquito from a bat; he knew nothing about tests of drinking water; and in the matters of plumbing and sewage he was as unlearned as he was voluble. He often referred to the excellence of the bathrooms in the houses he sold. He was fond of explaining why it was that no European ever bathed. Some one had told him, when he was twenty-two, that all cesspools were unhealthy, and he still denounced them. If a client impertinently wanted him to sell a house which had a cesspool, Babbitt always spoke about it—before accepting the house and selling it.

Like the previous example, this paragraph reveals a lot in relatively few lines. We learn that Babbitt knows very little about sanitation but that he nevertheless takes care to present himself as a great expert on the topic. We get the impression of a person whose ignorance is matched only by his confidence, and we can expect that the rest of the passage will illustrate this quality. Let's look at how to work through a couple of big-picture questions.

Big-Picture: Poetry

We could deny our winters, refuse to cut
Our hands mining the sharp ores of grief
Whenever the cold comes, we could follow

the arrowheads of geese shafting south
to an azure place where whales sing offshore
and otters frolic in the wanton surf.

We could grow soft as children in the arms
of leisure, but we might never learn in time
how to stoke the cold fire of the will

in that winter we cannot refuse, when we must glean
from the icy fields the last scattered grains
we once disdained, with only the luminous pallor

of the moon scarfed in clouds to light our way,
rising above the outstretched arms of the trees
in its long slow journey through the night.

1. In the poem, the speaker is most concerned with representing the

(A) beauty of the natural world
(B) inability to appreciate the power of nature
(C) desire to attain a more authentic mode of living
(D) consequences of a life devoid of genuine challenges
(E) dire consequences of failing to protect the environment

Explanation: Recall that when we looked at the beginning of this poem, we focused on the word *could* and the possibility that the poem might at some point address the result of *deny(ing) our winters/refus(ing) to cut our hands/mining the sharp ores of grief*— that is, refusing to deal with extreme hardship or grief.

In fact, that is what happens: in line 8, the word *but* signals a change in direction, after which the poem lays out the "consequences" of leading such a life: *we might never learn in time/how to stoke the cold fire of the will/in that winter we cannot refuse...*

Essentially, the speaker is suggesting that people whose lives have been too easy, who have always evaded genuine difficulties ("a life devoid of real challenges"), will be unprepared for serious hardship. That corresponds directly to (D).

Big-Picture: Prose

In nothing—as the expert on whose advice families moved to new neighborhoods to live there for a generation—was Babbitt more splendidly innocent than in the science of sanitation. He did not know a malaria-bearing mosquito from a bat; he knew nothing about tests of drinking water; and in the matters of plumbing and sewage he was as unlearned as he was voluble. He often referred to the excellence of the bathrooms in the houses he sold. He was fond of explaining why it was that no European ever bathed. Some one had told him, when he was twenty-two, that all cesspools were unhealthy, and he still denounced them. If a client impertinently wanted him to sell a house which had a cesspool, Babbitt always spoke about it—before accepting the house and selling it.

When he laid out the Glen Oriole acreage development, when he ironed woodland and dipping meadow into a glenless, orioleless, sunburnt flat prickly with small boards displaying the names of imaginary streets, he righteously put in a complete sewage-system. It made him feel superior; it enabled him to sneer privily at the Martin Lumsen development, Avonlea, which had a cesspool; and it provided a chorus for the full-page advertisements in which he announced the beauty, convenience, cheapness, and supererogatory healthfulness of Glen Oriole. The only flaw was that the Glen Oriole sewers had insufficient outlet, so that waste remained in them, not very agreeably, while the Avonlea cesspool was a Waring septic tank.

The whole of the Glen Oriole project was a suggestion that Babbitt, though he really did hate men recognized as swindlers, was not too unreasonably honest. Operators and buyers prefer that brokers should not be in competition with them as operators and buyers themselves, but attend to their clients' interests only. It was supposed that the Babbitt-Thompson Company were merely agents for Glen Oriole, serving the real owner, Jake Offutt, but the fact was that Babbitt and Thompson owned sixty-two per cent. of the Glen, the president and purchasing agent of the Zenith Street Traction Company owned twenty-eight per cent., and Jake Offutt (a gang-politician, a small manufacturer, a tobacco-chewing old farceur who enjoyed dirty politics, business diplomacy, and cheating at poker) had only ten per cent., which Babbitt and the Traction officials had given to him for "fixing" health inspectors and fire inspectors and a member of the State Transportation Commission. But Babbitt was virtuous. He advocated, though he did not practise, the prohibition of alcohol; he praised, though he did not obey, the laws against motor-speeding; he paid his debts; he contributed to the church, the Red Cross, and the Y. M. C. A.; he followed the custom of his clan and cheated only as it was sanctified by precedent; and he never descended to trickery.

1. The passage primarily suggests that

(A) when Babbitt reflects on his professional actions, he often regrets his behavior
(B) despite his public displays of virtue, Babbitt behaves in an unscrupulous manner
(C) although Babbitt often misleads his clients, he does so reluctantly
(D) Babbitt's professional success is attributable to his virtuous behavior
(E) Babbitt's tendancy to distort the truth places him at odds with his colleagues

Explanation: As we saw when we looked at the introduction to this passage, Babbitt is presented as someone who happily and unapologetically presents himself as an expert on topics he knows nothing about, and indeed that characterization is confirmed in the rest of the passage, particularly the conclusion. There the narrator emphasizes the gap between the virtuous way in which Babbitt attempts to present himself (he is in favor of prohibition and against speeding; he donates to charity) and his willingess to behave dishonestly when that behavior is shared by those around him. That corresponds directly to (B); all the other answers are directly contradicted by the description of Babbitt in the passage.

What Type of Passage Is It?

Some questions may directly ask you to categorize a passage—most likely a poem—in terms of its general rhetorical form. You should be familiar with the terms below:

Positive	Negative	Neutral
Allegory, Parable – story in which each element serves as a specific symbol, typically to convey a moral **Celebration, Ode** – enthusiastic praise **Eulogy, Tribute** – Text praising a person or thing that is no longer alive/present **Justification, Vindication** – defense **Reminiscence** – memory (usually happy)	**Admonition, Rebuke** – scolding **Apology** – expression of regret **Diatribe** – furious rant **Elegy, Lament** – expression of grief/mourning **Invocation** – summoning of or appeal to a person, often a deity **Parody, Satire** – mockery **Plea** – desperate appeal	**Account** – description of events; narrative **Anecdote** – brief story **Commentary** – expression of opinion or explanation **Explication** – Detailed explanation **Meditation** – extended reflection **Speculation** – consideration of a hypothetical situation

Let's look at some sample questions.

Passage Type #1

Slow, slow, fresh fount, keep time with my salt tears;
Yet slower, yet, O faintly, gentle springs!
List to the heavy part the music bears,
Woe weeps out her division, when she sings.
Droop herbs and flowers;
Fall grief in showers;
Our beauties are not ours.
O, I could still,
Like melting snow upon some craggy hill,
Drop, drop, drop, drop,
Since nature's pride is now a withered daffodil.

1. The poem as a whole is best understood as

(A) a lament
(B) an ode
(C) a parody
(D) a vindication
(E) a diatribe

Explanation: The reference to *tears* in the first line, followed by *weeps* (line 4), *droop* (line 5), *grief* (line 6), and a *withered daffodil* (line 11) make it quite clear that the narrator is extremely sad. "Ode" and "vindication" are both positive, so (B) and (D) can be eliminated immediately. (C) can likewise be crossed out because there is no mockery here, as "parody" would imply—the sadness is quite literal. "Diatribe" is negative, but the speaker is sad, not angry, so (E) does not fit either. That leaves (A), which is correct: this poem is the essence of a "lament."

Passage Type #2

I heard the trailing garments of the Night
Sweep through her marble halls!
I saw her sable skirts all fringed with light
From the celestial walls!

I felt her presence, by its spell of might,
Stoop o'er me from above;
The calm, majestic presence of the Night,
As of the one I love.

I heard the sounds of sorrow and delight,
The manifold, soft chimes,
That fill the haunted chambers of the Night,
Like some old poet's rhymes.

From the cool cisterns of the midnight air
My spirit drank repose;
The fountain of perpetual peace flows there, —
From those deep cisterns flows.

O holy Night! from thee I learn to bear
What man has borne before!
Thou layest thy finger on the lips of Care,
And they complain no more.

Peace! Peace! Orestes*-like I breathe this prayer!
Descend with broad-winged flight,
The welcome, the thrice-prayed for, the most fair,
The best-beloved Night!

*Character in Greek mythology

1. The poem as a whole is best understood as

(A) a lament about the fear induced by the night
(B) an account of a memorable night
(C) a plea to be released from the night
(D) a defense of the influence of the night
(E) a celebration of the tranquility of the night

Explanation: Words and phrases throughout the poem indicate that the speaker has an extremely positive view of the night; in fact, the entire poem is devoted to praising it. "Lament" is straightforwardly negative, so (A) can be eliminated right away. The speaker clearly does not want to be "released" from the night—just the opposite, in fact—so (C) can be crossed out as well. (D) does not fit: "defense" implies a pushback against criticism, but although the night is often associated with negative events, there is no indication that the speaker is refuting that conception here. (B) does not work either because its scope is too narrow: the speaker is talking about night in general rather than one particular night.

That leaves (E), which is correct. *Tranquility* means "calm," and this word directly corresponds to phrases such as *calm, majestic presence* and *perpetual peace.*

Passage Type #3

Love is not all: it is not meat nor drink
Nor slumber nor a roof against the rain;
Nor yet a floating spar to men that sink
And rise and sink and rise and sink again;
Love can not fill the thickened lung with breath,
Nor clean the blood, nor set the fractured bone;
Yet many a man is making friends with death
Even as I speak, for lack of love alone.
It well may be that in a difficult hour,
Pinned down by pain and moaning for release,
Or nagged by want past resolution's power,
I might be driven to sell your love for peace,
Or trade the memory of this night for food.
It well may be. I do not think I would.

1. The poem as a whole is best understood as

(A) a lament about the pains of love
(B) a eulogy for a former love
(C) a meditation on the value of love
(D) an ode to the healing power of love
(E) an apology for the burdens of love

Explanation: Because this is a big-picture question, start by summing up what the poem is literally about. Clearly, the topic is love—the speaker announces that in the very first line. The first section (lines 1-6) focuses on all the things that love cannot do (substitute for food, save people from drowning, heal people who are sick or injured…). In line 7, however, the word *yet* signals a shift in focus, to the importance of love and what might induce the speaker to give it up.

The fact that the poet discusses love's benefits as well as its shortcomings indicates that the poem is a reflection, or a "meditation," on the topic, a fact that corresponds only to (C). Choices (B) and (D) are positive, whereas (A) and (E) are negative. The second part of the answer is supported by the statement *I might be driven to sell your love for peace,* which indicates that the speaker is mulling what love is worth, i.e., its "value."

Exercises: The Big Picture

1. We could deny our winters, refuse to cut
Our hands mining the sharp ores of grief
Whenever the cold comes, we could follow

the arrowheads of geese shafting south
to an azure place where whales sing offshore
and otters frolic in the wanton surf.

We could grow soft as children in the arms
of leisure, but we might never learn in time
how to stoke the cold fire of the will

in that winter we cannot refuse, when we must glean
from the icy fields the last scattered grains
we once disdained, with only the luminous pallor

of the moon scarfed in clouds to light our way,
rising above the outstretched arms of the trees
in its long slow journey through the night.

1. Taken as a whole, this poem is best understood to be

(A) an ironic commentary
(B) a tribute
(C) an elegy
(D) an admonition
(E) an apology

2. Mr. Ralph Nickleby was not, strictly speaking, what you would call a merchant, neither was he a banker, nor an attorney, nor a special pleader, nor a notary. He was certainly not a tradesman, and still less could he lay any claim to the title of a professional gentleman; for it would have been impossible to mention any recognised profession to which he belonged. Nevertheless, as he lived in a spacious house in Golden Square, which, in addition to a brass plate upon the street-door, had another brass plate two sizes and a half smaller upon the left hand door-post, surrounding a brass model of an infant's fist grasping a fragment of a skewer, and displaying the word 'Office,' it was clear that Mr. Ralph Nickleby did, or pretended to do, business of some kind; and the fact, if it required any further circumstantial evidence, was abundantly demonstrated by the diurnal attendance, between the hours of half-past nine and five, of a sallow-faced man in rusty brown, who sat upon an uncommonly hard stool in a species of butler's pantry at the end of the passage, and always had a pen behind his ear when he answered the bell.

1. The passage as a whole primarily suggests that Mr. Ralph Nickleby

(A) acquired his house through illicit means
(B) is unsuited to practice any profession
(C) appears to have achieved immense success
(D) possesses few practical skills
(E) may be involved in unethical activities

3. Announced by all the trumpets of the sky,
Arrives the snow, and, driving o'er the fields,
Seems nowhere to alight: the whited air
Hides hills and woods, the river, and the heaven,
And veils the farm-house at the garden's end.
The sled and traveller stopped, the courier's feet
Delayed, all friends shut out, the housemates sit
Around the radiant fireplace, enclosed
In a tumultuous privacy of storm.

Come see the north wind's masonry.
Out of an unseen quarry evermore
Furnished with tile, the fierce artificer
Curves his white bastions with projected roof
Round every windward stake, or tree, or door.
Speeding, the myriad-handed, his wild work
So fanciful, so savage, nought cares he
For number or proportion. Mockingly,
On coop or kennel he hangs Parian wreaths;
A swan-like form invests the hidden thorn;
Fills up the farmer's lane from wall to wall,
Maugre the farmer's sighs; and, at the gate,
A tapering turret overtops the work.
And when his hours are numbered, and the world
Is all his own, retiring, as he were not,
Leaves, when the sun appears, astonished Art
To mimic in slow structures, stone by stone,
Built in an age, the mad wind's night-work,
The frolic architecture of the snow.

1. In the poem, the speaker primarily presents

(A) a request to be spared from a destructive force
(B) a dramatization of the creative power of nature
(C) a comparison between human and natural inventions
(D) a celebration of a beloved tradition
(E) a eulogy for a vanished way of life

4. My cousin Mary came in on the freight train one morning, with nothing but an old blue keepsake box full of worthless pins and buttons. My father picked her up in his arms and carried her down the hallway into the kitchen. He sat her down, then my mother said, "Go clean the counters, Sita." So I don't know what lies she told them after that.

Later on that morning, my parents put her to sleep in my bed. When I objected to this, saying that she could sleep on the trundle, my mother said, "Cry sakes, you can sleep there too, you know." And that is how I ended up that night, crammed in the trundle, which is too short for me. I slept with my legs dangling out into the cold air. I didn't feel welcoming toward Mary the next morning, and who can blame me?

1. This passage primarily concerns

(A) an ongoing conflict
(B) a dramatic confrontation
(C) a long-awaited moment
(D) an unpleasant recollection
(E) a new experience

5. There is a change—and I am poor;
Your love hath been, nor long ago,
A fountain at my fond heart's door,
Whose only business was to flow;
And flow it did; not taking heed
Of its own bounty, or my need.

What happy moments did I count!
Blest was I then all bliss above!
Now, for that consecrated fount
Of murmuring, sparkling, living love,
What have I? shall I dare to tell?

A comfortless and hidden well.
A well of love—it may be deep—
I trust it is,—and never dry:
What matter? if the waters sleep
In silence and obscurity.
—Such change, and at the very door
Of my fond heart, hath made me poor.

2. In the poem, the speaker presents

(A) a diatribe against love's false promises
(B) a wistful longing for a happier time
(C) a plea for the restoration of an idyllic world
(D) a discredited illusion of renewal and regeneration
(E) a celebration of water's healing properties

6. Thomas Gradgrind, sir. A man of realities. A man of facts and calculations. A man who proceeds upon the principle that two and two are four, and nothing over, and who is not to be talked into allowing for anything over. Thomas Gradgrind, sir peremptorily Thomas Thomas Gradgrind. With a rule and a pair of scales, and the multiplication table always in his pocket, sir, ready to weigh and measure any parcel of human nature, and tell you exactly what it comes to. It is a mere question of figures, a case of simple arithmetic. You might hope to get some other nonsensical belief into the head of George Gradgrind, or Augustus Gradgrind, or John Gradgrind, or Joseph Gradgrind (all supposititious, non-existent persons), but into the head of Thomas Gradgrind—no, sir!

In such terms Mr. Gradgrind always mentally introduced himself, whether to his private circle of acquaintance, or to the public in general. In such terms, no doubt, substituting the words "boys" and "girls," for "sir," Thomas Gradgrind now presented Thomas Gradgrind to the little pitchers before him, who were to be filled so full of facts.

Indeed, as he eagerly sparkled at them from the cellarage before mentioned, he seemed a kind of cannon loaded to the muzzle with facts, and prepared to blow them clean out of the regions of childhood at one discharge. He seemed a galvanizing apparatus, too, charged with a grim mechanical substitute for the tender young imaginations that were to be stormed away.

1. Taken as a whole, this passage is best understood to be

(A) a sincere tribute
(B) a biting satire
(C) a moralistic parable
(D) a sharp rebuke
(E) an inspiring ode

7. From Cairo to Baton Rouge, when the river is over its banks, you have no particular trouble in the night, for the thousand-mile wall of dense forest that guards the two banks all the way is only gapped with a farm or wood-yard opening at intervals, and so you can't 'get out of the river' much easier than you could get out of a fenced lane; but from Baton Rouge to New Orleans it is a different matter. The river is more than a mile wide, and very deep—as much as two hundred feet, in places. Both banks, for a good deal over a hundred miles, are shorn of their timber and bordered by continuous sugar plantations, with only here and there a scattering sapling or row of ornamental China-trees. The timber is shorn off clear to the rear of the plantations, from two to four miles. When the first frost threatens to come, the planters snatch off their crops in a hurry. When they have finished grinding the cane, they form the refuse of the stalks (which they call BAGASSE) into great piles and set fire to them, though in other sugar countries the bagasse is used for fuel in the furnaces of the sugar mills. Now the piles of damp bagasse burn slowly, and smoke like Satan's own kitchen.

An embankment ten or fifteen feet high guards both banks of the Mississippi all the way down that lower end of the river, and this embankment is set back from the edge of the shore from ten to perhaps a hundred feet, according to circumstances; say thirty or forty feet, as a general thing. Fill that whole region with an impenetrable gloom of smoke from a hundred miles of burning bagasse piles, when the river is over the banks, and turn a steamboat loose along there at midnight and see how she will feel. And see how you will feel, too! You find yourself away out in the midst of a vague dim sea that is shoreless, that fades out and loses itself in the murky distances; for you cannot discern the thin rib of embankment, and you are always imagining you see a straggling tree when you don't. The plantations themselves are transformed by the smoke, and look like a part of the sea. All through your watch you are tortured with the exquisite misery of uncertainty. You hope you are keeping in the river, but you do not know. All that you are sure about is that you are likely to be within six feet of the bank and destruction, when you think you are a good half-mile from shore. And you are sure, also, that if you chance suddenly to fetch up against the embankment and topple your chimneys overboard, you will have the small comfort of knowing that it is about what you were expecting to do. One of the great Vicksburg packets darted out into a sugar and had to stay there a week. But there was no novelty about it; it had often been done before.

1. In the passage, the speaker presents

    (A) an arduous undertaking
    (B) a thrilling adventure
    (C) an unavoidable tragedy
    (D) a brief diversion
    (E) an unforeseeable predicament

8. The bridesmaids were here, and yet the bridegroom had not come. Ursula wondered if something was amiss, and if the wedding would yet all go wrong. She felt troubled, as if it rested upon her. The chief bridesmaids had arrived. Ursula watched them come up the steps. One of them she knew, a tall, slow, reluctant woman with a weight of fair hair and a pale, long face. This was Hermione Roddice, a friend of the Criches. Now she came along, with her head held up, balancing an enormous flat hat of pale yellow velvet, on which were streaks of ostrich feathers, natural and grey. She drifted forward as if scarcely conscious, her long blanched face lifted up, not to see the world. She was rich. She wore a dress of silky, frail velvet, of pale yellow colour, and she carried a lot of small rose-coloured cyclamens. Her shoes and stockings were of brownish grey, like the feathers on her hat, her hair was heavy, she drifted along with a peculiar fixity of the hips, a strange unwilling motion. She was impressive, in her lovely pale-yellow and brownish-rose, yet macabre, something repulsive. People were silent when she passed, impressed, roused, wanting to jeer, yet for some reason silenced. Her long, pale face, that she carried lifted up, somewhat in the Rossetti fashion, seemed almost drugged, as if a strange mass of thoughts coiled in the darkness within her, and she was never allowed to escape.

Ursula watched her with fascination. She knew her a little. She was the most remarkable woman in the Midlands. Her father was a Derbyshire Baronet of the old school, she was a woman of the new school, full of intellectuality, and heavy, nerve-worn with consciousness. She was passionately interested in reform, her soul was given up to the public cause. But she was a man's woman, it was the manly world that held her.

Hermione knew herself to be well-dressed; she knew herself to be the social equal, if not far the superior, of anyone she was likely to meet in Willey Green. She knew she was accepted in the world of culture and of intellect. She was a Kulturtrager, a medium for the culture of ideas. With all that was highest, whether in society or in thought or in public action, or even in art, she was at one, she moved among the foremost, at home with them. No one could put her down, no one could make mock of her, because she stood among the first, and those that were against her were below her, either in rank, or in wealth, or in high association of thought and progress and understanding. So, she was invulnerable. All her life, she had sought to make herself invulnerable, unassailable, beyond reach of the world's judgment.

1. Taken as a whole, the passage indicates that Hermione

(A) views all the inhabitants of Willey Green with disdain
(B) is ostracized by the other wedding guests
(C) is oblivious to how others perceive her
(D) rejects ordinary class distinctions
(E) seeks to present herself as aloof and impenetrable

2. This passage can best be described as

(A) a critique
(B) a satire
(C) a portrait
(D) an apology
(E) a rebuke

Explanations: The Big Picture

1.1 D

The poem focuses on the dangers that can arise when people shield themselves excessively from difficulties (*We could deny our winters, refuse to cut/Our hands mining the sharp ores of grief*) —namely, they end up unprepared to cope with real challenges when they occur (*we might never learn in time how to stoke the cold fire of the will…*). Essentially, the piece serves as a warning or a scolding about avoiding difficulties. An "admonition" (synonym for "rebuke" and "chastisement," which could also appear as answers) is most consistent with this description. There is nothing ironic about the poem, eliminating (A), nor does it pay homage to someone, eliminating (B). (C) is incorrect because an "elegy" is a lament, and (E) does not fit because the poem is the opposite of an apology.

2.1 E

The passage focuses on Nickleby's less savory qualities, suggesting that he is not an honest person—i.e., that he may be involved in "unethical activities." The narrator emphasizes that he engages in some sort of profession despite NOT practicing *any recognised profession* (line 7), and that he perhaps only *pretended to do, business of some kind* (lines 15-16). Furthermore, the description of a *sallow-faced man in rusty brown* (lines 19-20) gives an impression of something vaguely unhealthy and perhaps slightly sinister. That corresponds directly to (E). (A), (B), and (D) all fall into the category of "could be true but not explicitly supported by the passage." These answers also do not capture the main idea of the passage, which is that Nickleby is an extremely shady figure. (C) is a bit too extreme: the passage indicates that Nickleby lives in a *spacious house* with two brass plates, suggesting a reasonable but not "immense" amount of success.

3.1 B

If you think in terms of the topic and play positive/negative, you can narrow down the options fairly quickly. Line 2 states the topic (*snow*), and the phrase *Announced by all the trumpets of the sky* suggests that the presentation will be generally positive—negative events are not normally greeted with this type of fanfare. In (A), the phrase "spared from a destructive force" is negative, and "vanished way of life" is most likely inconsistent with the topic, so you can assume that (A) and (E) are incorrect. Although the idea of a "tradition" in (D) might seem to be supported by the description of housemates sitting around the fire in lines 7-9, this image is restricted to the first stanza. If you look at the second stanza, where the bulk of the text occurs, you can see that it focuses on nature itself and that the speaker describes its handiwork in very dramatic terms (*speeding, so fanciful, so save, nought cares he/For number or proportion*). In contrast, there is no mention of "human inventions." That eliminates (C) and makes (B) correct.

4.1 D

The narrator clearly displays a negative attitude throughout the passage: she describes her cousin's only possession as *worthless*, states that she doesn't *know what lies* her cousin told her parents and that she *didn't feel welcoming toward Mary*. Based on these statements, (C) and (E) can be eliminated. (A) does not fit either because the narrator is recounting a single incident—her cousin's arrival—not an "ongoing" situation. (B) does not make sense either since the passage says nothing about a "confrontation" between the narrator and her cousin. (D) is correct because the narrator is looking back on the events of the passage (as indicated by the use of the past tense) with displeasure.

5.1 B

If you read carefully, you can answer this question using only the beginning of the poem. The first stanza indicates that the speaker is sad or depressed (*poor*) because *your love hath been* (note the past tense), *nor long ago, a fountain at my fond heart's door*. In other words, the speaker got dumped and is now depressed. That idea is reinforced at the beginning of the second stanza, where the lines *What happy moments did I count!/Blest was I then all bliss above* indicates that the speaker is looking back on a happier time in sadness—that is, expressing "a wistful longing for a happier time." (A) does not fit because a "diatribe" is characterized by anger, and the speaker is merely sad; (C) is overly broad, and (D) and (E) are off topic.

6.1 B

This passage is the essence of a satire—the characterization and language are deliberately and ridiculously over-the-top. Throughout the excerpt, the exaggerated military diction and imagery, e.g., the cannon, phrases such as *blowing them clean out of the water*, and the repetition of the word *sir*, indicate that the narrator is mocking Thomas Gradgrind's overly harsh approach to education. (B) is the only possible answer.

7.1 A

Although the passage is quite dense, the first sentence provides an important clue. The narrator contrasts the process of getting "out of the river" from Cairo to Baton Rouge (*no particular trouble*) with that from Baton Rouge to New Orleans (*a different matter*)—the implication is that the latter is much more difficult, an impression confirmed by the description of the river that follows (*more than a mile wide, and very deep*). Based on that information alone, "a thrilling adventure" and "a brief diversion" do not make sense, eliminating (B) and (D). The description of the river conditions also suggests that any difficulties are entirely predictable, so they are hardly "unforeseen." This impression is confirmed by the last sentence, which states that *there was no novelty about it; it had often been done before*. (E) can thus be eliminated as well. (C) is too extreme—trying to navigate a gloomy, smoky river is not a "tragedy"—but it is an "arduous (very difficult) undertaking." (A) is thus correct.

8.1 E

This is an excellent example of a big-picture question whose answer is found in the conclusion. In fact, the last sentence provides the answer almost word-for-word, indicating that Hermione had *sought to make herself invulnerable, unassailable* ("impenetrable"), *beyond reach of the world's judgment* ("aloof"). That corresponds directly to (E).

8.2 C

The passage is dedicated to providing a physical and psychological description of Hermione Roddice—in other words, a "portrait." (B), (D), and (E) do not fit at all; although the narrator does describe the negative reactions Hermione provokes, the primary goal of the passage is not to analyze her shortcomings or to provide an academic evaluation. (A) can thus be eliminated as well.

Chapter Three

Defining Words and Phrases

The AP English Literature Exam can test your understanding of words and phrases from a variety of angles:

In some cases, you may be asked to determine the literal meaning of a phrase or a figure of speech (e.g., a metaphor) based on the context of the passage.

In other instances, you may be given a word or phrase and asked what or whom it refers to.

It is also possible that you will be given a word or phrase and asked to identify an earlier word/phrase with the same meaning. Essentially, these questions target your ability to "track" a concept or image over an extended portion of the text.

Questions may be phrased in the following ways:

- In context, "living temples"(most probably) refer to...
- In context, "living temples" most nearly means...
- The concept of "second morn" is most like/analogous to...
- The pronoun "it" (line 11) refers to the speaker's...
- The word "snow" (line 17) most clearly echoes which earlier line from the poem?

Although these questions are generally asked in a fairly straightforward way, they may target sections of the text that are potentially confusing or dense with abstract/figurative language. So while they can be asked about prose passages, particularly ones with more complex or antiquated wording, you should not be surprised to find them accompanying poetry passages.

To emphasize, though, these are the most literal of comprehension questions: you must focus only on the specific words in the text, and not speculate about anything beyond what is directly stated or suggested.

Pronouns

If you've taken the SAT or the ACT, or are currently studying for one of those exams, you might be familiar with questions that look like this:

The blue whale, which measures nearly a hundred feet long, is one of the largest animals on Earth, and their "songs" are among the loudest sounds in the animal kingdom.	A) NO CHANGE B) they're C) its D) it's

To determine the answer, you must not only know the rules for apostrophes, but you must also determine whether the pronoun should be singular or plural. To do that, it is necessary to identify the noun to which the pronoun refers—that is, its **antecedent**, or its **referent**. Here, you must back up to the beginning of the sentence to find that noun (*The blue whale*).

(**Note:** While the noun-before-pronoun construction is most common, in some cases nouns may actually come after the pronouns that refer to them. Becaue the prefix *ante-* means "before," I use the term *referent* rather than *antecedent* in order to avoid confusion.)

Why this detour into grammar? Because the AP Literature Exam can test a version of pronoun agreement, albeit in a somewhat different way and at a much higher level. Although you do not have to worry about identifying grammatical errors, you do need to be able to match pronouns to their referents. In some cases, the noun may appear in the same sentence. In other cases, however, it may appear a sentence (or even two) before. And because there may be quite a bit of information between the pronoun and the noun, you will need to think very carefully about what logically refers to what.

Even if you are not explicitly asked to match nouns and pronouns on the actual test, the ability to make these connections is also crucial to understanding many passages. Words like *it(s)* and *they/their* allow you to follow the action or a character's thought process, and understand who is doing what to whom. But given the amount of information a passage can present in a very short space, pronouns can also be often be confusing. So why rely on them?

Let's start with the fact that authors use pronouns for the sake of readability; using the same noun over and over again would make their writing wordy and awkward. Compare, for instance, these two versions of the opening of Marianne Moore's poem "The Jellyfish":

Version 1	**Version 2**
Visible, invisible, A fluctuating charm, An amber-colored amethyst Inhabits **it**; your arm Approaches, and **It** opens and **It** closes; You have meant To catch **it**, And **it** shrivels...	Visible, invisible, A fluctuating charm, An amber-colored amethyst Inhabits **the jellyfish**; your arm Approaches, and **the jellyfish** opens and **the jellyfish** closes; You have meant To catch **the jellyfish**, And **the jellyfish** shrivels...

In the first version, the use of the pronoun *it* results in a text that is simple and clear; in the second, the repeated use of the noun makes the piece dull and unnecessarily repetitive.

As a general rule, the easiest way to answer pronoun questions is to be able to identify the nouns they refer to yourself, without having to check each answer individually. While this can be challenging at first, it is also a skill that can be developed with practice.

In many cases, pronouns will be placed close to their referents, and the relationship will be fairly obvious—even in passages that are otherwise very challenging.

For instance:

The <u>winged seeds</u>, where **they** lie cold and low,
Each like a <u>corpse</u> within **its** grave, until
Thine azure sister of the Spring shall blow…

Despite the antiquated language, the placement of *they* and *its* next to their relative referents make the poem relatively easy to follow. In other cases, however, pronouns may be separated from their referents by multiple lines; the two may not even appear within the same sentence.

One important thing to remember is that pronouns often—although by no means always—refer to the subject of a sentence. Indeed, authors use pronouns specifically to avoid repeating the subject. As a result, if you are unsure where to look for the referent, a good place to start is the beginning of the sentence. If that doesn't work, back up to the sentence before that—and if necessary, the sentence before that. Do not keep reading!

Let's start with a poetry example:

Thou who didst waken from his summer dreams,
The blue Mediterranean, where he lay,
Lulled by the coil of his crystalline streams,
Beside a pumice isle in Baiae's bay,
And saw in sleep old palaces and towers
Quivering within the wave's intenser day,
All overgrown with azure <u>moss and flowers</u>
So sweet, the sense faints picturing **them**!

Them appears at the end of a very long sentence, so there are theoretically many places where the referent could be located. The easiest way to identify it, however, is to think about the meaning—what could be *so sweet* that it causes the senses to faint? Logically, *moss and* (especially) *flowers*, which are mentioned in the line immediately above the pronoun. Though the poem contains other plural nouns (*summer dreams, crystalline streams, palaces and towers*), *moss and flowers* makes the most sense.

Now let's look at a slightly more challenging excerpt:

> As if some little Arctic flower,
> Upon the polar hem,
> Went wandering down the latitude
> Until **it** puzzled came
> To continents of summer,
> To firmaments of sun,
> To strange, bright crowds of flowers,
> And birds of foreign tongue.

Even if the sentence is somewhat confusing, the pronoun-referent relationship is still structured according to the most common pattern: *Some little Arctic flower* appears right at the beginning of the sentence, acting as its subject, and the pronoun *it* is later used to refer back to the subject. Making that relationship allows you to understand that Dickinson is literally describing the puzzlement felt by a cold-weather flower upon journeying into a warmer region.

Next we're going to look at a prose sample. It's from George Eliot's 1859 novel, *Adam Bede*:

> Mr. Casson's person was by no means of that common type which can be allowed to pass without description. On a front view **it** appeared to consist principally of two spheres, bearing about the same relation to each other as the earth and the moon: that is to say, the lower sphere might be said, at a rough guess, to be thirteen times larger than the upper which naturally performed the function of a mere satellite and tributary.

Here again, the sentence in which the bolded pronoun (*it*) appears, is quite long: seven full lines, in fact. And just as in the previous example, if you aren't sure what the pronoun refers to, you could potentially waste a lot of time trying to understand what the author is describing.

If, however, you know that referents typically come before pronouns, you can begin by backing up. Notice that *it* appears close to the beginning of the second sentence, and that there isn't a noun in that part of the sentence to which the pronoun could logically refer. (Grammatically, *it* cannot refer to *a front view*.) As a result, you must back up even farther and read from the sentence before, with a focus on the first words: *Mr. Casson's person*, i.e., his physical appearance. And indeed, that is what *it* most logically refers to: the information after the pronoun consists of an extended description of Mr. Casson's strikingly large, round body.

Now try one one on your own. See if you can ignore the multiple-choice answer format and focus on identifying the referent without relying on the choices.

My long two-pointed ladder's sticking through a tree
Toward heaven still,
And there's a barrel that I didn't fill
Beside it, and there may be two or three
Apples I didn't pick upon some bough.
But I am done with apple-picking now.
Essence of winter sleep is on the night,
The scent of apples: I am drowsing off.
I cannot rub the strangeness from my sight
I got from looking through a pane of glass
I skimmed this morning from the drinking trough
And held against the world of hoary grass.
It melted, and I let it fall and break.
But I was well
Upon my way to sleep before it fell,
And I could tell
What form my dreaming was about to take.

1. In line 15, "it" refers to what earlier phrase from the passage?

(A) "the scent of apples" (line 8)
(B) "the strangeness" (line 9)
(C) "a pane of glass" (line 10)
(D) "the drinking trough" (line 11)
(E) "hoary grass" (line 12)

The answer is at the end of the chapter, on p. 54.

The Former and the Latter

One pair of terms that often gives students difficulty is *the former* and *the latter*. Like pronouns, they are used to refer back to words or ideas mentioned earlier in the same sentence or in a previous sentence. *The former* is used to refer back to the noun or phrase mentioned first, and *the latter* is used to refer back to the noun or phrase mentioned second. Even if you are not tested on them directly (although questions targeting them have appeared in the past), you are likely to encounter them in passages, and confusion about them may affect your overall comprehension.

Let's look at a typical example:

> **(1) Mr. Darcy** said very little, and **(2) Mr. Hurst** nothing at all. **(1) <u>The former</u>** was divided between admiration of the brilliancy which exercise had given to [Elizabeth's] complexion, and doubt as to the occasion's justifying her coming so far alone. **(2) <u>The latter</u>** was thinking only of his breakfast. (Austen, *Pride and Prejudice*)

The first sentence refers to two individuals: Mr. Darcy and Mr. Hurst. In the following sentence, *the former* refers to Mr. Darcy because his name appears first, while *the latter* refers to Mr. Hurst because his name appears second (*latter* is like *later).*

Note that in some instances, *the latter* appears before *the former*. In such cases, *the former* still refers to the noun that comes first, and *the latter* still refers to the noun that comes second.

Defining Nouns

You may also be asked to identify what specific nouns, or in some cases short phrases, refer to. These questions come in two forms:

1) "Refers to" Questions

"Definition" questions require you to identify what a particular word or phrase "refers to," or "most likely refers to." Note that in the case of the latter, the answer will still be clearly supported by the text; for practical purposes, the questions are identical, no matter how poetic or figurative the language may be.

The answers to these questions are **not directly stated in the passage**—you must connect the specific wording of the text to the rephrased answer choices based on context.

2) "Matching" questions

"Matching" questions require you to identify when a noun (or phrase) refers to the same person, object, idea, etc. as a noun in an earlier part of the passage.

The responses to these questions **are literally stated in the passage**—answer choices consist of words or phrases from the passage, along with their line numbers. That does not necessarily make these questions easier, though. Often, they involve complex syntax and/or highly figurative language, and answer choices may be drawn from a very substantial section of the passage (40 lines or more).

"Refers to" and "Means"

Let's start with a poetry example:

Slow, slow, fresh fount, keep time with my salt tears;
Yet slower, yet, O faintly, gentle springs!
List to the heavy part the music bears,
Woe weeps out her division, when she sings.
Droop herbs and flowers;
Fall grief in showers;
Our beauties are not ours.

1. The "heavy part" (line 3) refers to a

(A) piercing sound
(B) sense of anguish
(C) dawning hope
(D) bitter feud
(E) sudden storm

Explanation: If you look at line 3, you might notice that the "heavy part" has something to do with music and assume that the answer is (A) because it mentions a sound. In reality, though, this is exactly the kind of trap you want to avoid. A more effective approach is to think about the big picture. Phrases like *salt tears*, *woe* (sadness) *weeps out*, and *Fall grief in showers* clearly convey the speaker's sadness, and so you can assume the answer will reflect that emotion.

Given that information, you might be able to jump to (B): *anguish* means "extreme sadness." Otherwise, you can eliminate (C) because there is nothing in the poem to suggest that the speaker is hopeful. (A) is fairly negative but not directly related to sadness, and (E) doesn't make much sense: there's nothing about a storm in that part of the passage. (D) is extremely negative: the reference to a "feud" is entirely off topic. Only (B) logically indicates that the music reflects the speaker's grief.

Now let's try something longer:

Come live with me, and be my love,
And we will some new pleasures prove
Of golden sands, and crystal brooks,
With silken lines, and silver hooks.

There will the river whispering run
Warm'd by thy eyes, more than the sun;
And there the 'enamour'd fish will stay,
Begging themselves they may betray.

When thou wilt swim in that live bath,
Each fish, which every channel hath,
Will amorously to thee swim,
Gladder to catch thee, than thou him.

If thou, to be so seen, be'st loth,
By sun or moon, thou dark'nest both,
And if myself have leave to see,
I need not their light having thee.

Let others freeze with angling reeds,
And cut their legs with shells and weeds,
Or treacherously poor fish beset,
With strangling snare, or windowy net.

Let coarse bold hands from slimy nest
The bedded fish in banks out-wrest;
Or curious traitors, sleeve-silk flies,
Bewitch poor fishes' wand'ring eyes.

For thee, thou need'st no such deceit,
For thou thyself art thine own bait:
That fish, that is not catch'd thereby,
Alas, is wiser far than I.

1. The word "others" in line 17 most likely refers to

(A) bodies of water in faraway lands
(B) swimmers who find themselves trapped in the water
(C) aquatic creatures that inhabit rivers and brooks
(D) people less enticing than the object of the speaker's affections
(E) fish that become ensared in fishermen's nets

Explanation: In this case, the word being asked about provides an important clue about both the meaning and the location of the answer. The word *others* is really only used to develop a contrast—*some people do x, but others do y*—and it is reasonable to assume that that is the case here. To find out what or whom *others* are being contrasted with, you must therefore focus on the information before that word.

Although your instinct may be to check each answer, in order, that is not necessarily the most efficient way to determine the answer. A more effective strategy is to think about the general scenario being described and then consider the question in that context. The poem is relatively short, so unless you understood it perfectly the first time through and are certain of the answer, you should go back and reread it from the beginning. The language is sufficiently challenging that if you start somewhere in the middle, you are likely to get confused.

What's going on? Essentially, the speaker is in love with someone so extraordinary and seductive that if that person were to simply stand in a brook, fish would swim up to them and happily let themselves be caught. That is the focus of lines 1-16; line 17 marks a shift, from a description of how the speaker's beloved would catch fish to describing how other people—people who are not the speaker's beloved—would catch them.

What does the poet tell us about these "others"? That they would struggle: they would *freeze, cut their legs with shells and weeds*, and succeed in catching only *treacherously poor fish*. Why? Because they are less attractive (i.e., enticing) than the speaker's beloved (i.e., the object of his affections). That corresponds directly to (D).

Next let's look at a fiction example:

One evening of late summer, before the nineteenth century had reached one-third of its span, a young man and woman, the latter carrying a child, were approaching the large village of Weydon-Priors, in Upper Wessex, on foot. They were plainly but not ill clad, though the thick hoar of dust which had accumulated on their shoes and garments from an obviously long journey lent a disadvantageous shabbiness to their appearance just now.

The man was of fine figure, swarthy, and stern in aspect; and he showed in profile a facial angle so slightly inclined as to be almost perpendicular. He wore a short jacket of brown corduroy, newer than the remainder of his suit, which was a fustian waistcoat with white horn buttons, breeches of the same, tanned leggings, and a straw hat overlaid with black glazed canvas. At his back he carried by a looped strap a rush basket, from which protruded at one end the crutch of a hay-knife, a wimble* for hay-bonds being also visible in the aperture. His measured, springless walk was the walk of the skilled countryman as distinct from the desultory shamble of the general labourer; while in the turn and plant of each foot there was, further, a dogged and cynical indifference personal to himself, showing its presence even in the regularly interchanging fustian folds, now in the left leg, now in the right, as he paced along.

What was really peculiar, however, in this couple's progress, and would have attracted the attention of any casual observer otherwise disposed to overlook them, was the perfect silence they preserved. They walked side by side in such a way as to suggest afar off the low, easy, confidential chat of people full of reciprocity; but on closer view it could be discerned that the man was reading, or pretending to read, a ballad sheet which he kept before his eyes with some difficulty by the hand that was passed through the basket strap. Whether this apparent cause were the real cause, or whether it were an assumed one to escape an intercourse that would have been irksome to him, nobody but himself could have said precisely; but his taciturnity was unbroken, and the woman enjoyed no society whatever from his presence. Virtually she walked the highway alone, save for the child she bore.

*Marbleworker's brace for drilling

1. In context, "an assumed one" (lines 41-42) is best understood to mean one that was

(A) feigned
(B) reasoned
(C) controlled
(D) defined
(E) explained

Explanation: The narrator contrasts *an assumed one* with *the real cause,* implying that the phrase in question must mean the opposite of real, i.e., fake. That is the definition of "feigned," so (A) is correct. Essentially, the narrator is saying that it is unclear whether the man truly needed to look at the ballad sheet as he walked, or whether he was merely doing so as an excuse to avoid speaking.

"Matching" Questions

In this next section, we're going to look at questions that ask you to match a phrase from later in the passage to one that appears earlier. Unlike pronoun questions, matching questions may be phrased in ways that are not completely straightforward. For example, you may be asked to identify a word or phrase that "echoes" an earlier section of the passage. Don't get distracted by the vaguely poetic wording! All you need to do is identify two words/phrases that are talking about the same thing.

Matching questions also differ from other definition questions in the sense that the answer choices themselves can be much more helpful. In some cases, you may even be able to identify the most likely answer by using only the wording of the choices — that is, without looking back at the passage at all. (You should, of course, go back to the passage and double-check before bubbling in your response.)

Think of it this way: the correct answer must mean something similar to the word or phrase in question, and that relationship may very well exist outside the passage. Even when it is not entirely obvious, there will sometimes be just enough of a connection to point you in the right direction and save you the time of meticulously considering the pros and cons of each option. To illustrate, we're going to look at the following question without the accompanying passage:

1. The word "shock" most clearly echoes which earlier word from the passage?

   (A) "thunder-clap" (line 1)
   (B) "fortune" (line 2)
   (C) "stores" (line 3)
   (D) "castles" (line 7)
   (E) "youth" (line 7)

Explanation: Let's start by rephrasing the question: In the passage, which one of these words has a meaning most similar to "shock"? If you're not sure right away, don't worry — if the answer were perfectly straightforward, the question wouldn't be asked in the first place. Our first goal is just to narrow things down.

Let's start by eliminating options that don't make a lot of sense. Right away, (D) and (E) seem like too much of a stretch: even in the context of a poem, it seems unlikely that "youth" and "castles" would convey the idea of shock. (C) seems like a poor choice as well: when it is used in a literary sense, "stores" typically refers to items put away for future use (e.g., stores of canned food for the winter), but this definition has no evident connection to shock either.

(A) and (B) seem like better candidates: a "thunder-clap" seems pretty consistent with a shock in that it's loud and upsetting and can come out of absolutely nowhere. A "fortune" seems like something that, given the right context, maybe possibly could be connected to the idea of a shock. It doesn't seem nearly as good a choice as (A), but we'll keep it just in case.

On the next page, we're going to look at the question with the passage. Remember to focus on (A) and (B). If you're certain that neither one fits, you can always re-consider options you've eliminated, but there's no sense in doing a lot of work upfront if you ultimately ignore it and start by checking all the answers.

It came like a thunder-clap on us all, that the vessel which contained our fortune had been wrecked, and gone to the bottom with all its stores, together with several of the crew, and the unfortunate merchant himself. I was grieved for him; I was grieved for the overthrow of all our air-built castles: but, with the elasticity of youth, I soon recovered the shock.

1. The word "shock" most clearly echoes which earlier word from the passage?

(A) "thunder-clap" (line 1)
(B) "fortune" (line 2)
~~(C) "stores" (line 3)~~
~~(D) "castles" (line 7)~~
~~(E) "youth" (line 7)~~

Explanation: Even though there are only eight lines, it quickly becomes clear that the author is describing a very negative situation: statements like *all the vessels that contained our fortune had been wrecked* and *I was grieved for him* convey an obvious tragedy. In that context, *I soon recovered the shock* indicates that the word in the question refers to an abrupt loss of money, not the "fortune" itself. So (B) does not fit.

Although the passage does not explicitly define the "shock" anywhere, the structure confirms that (A) is in fact the answer: the first sentence introduces the tragedy that the narrator experienced suddenly (i.e., *like a thunderclap*), and the final sentence reinforces that idea.

One more prose example:

Mr Nickleby closed an account-book which lay on his desk, and, throwing himself back in his chair, gazed with an air of abstraction through the dirty window. Some London houses have a melancholy little plot of ground behind them, usually fenced in by four high whitewashed walls, and frowned upon by stacks of chimneys: in which there withers on, from year to year, a crippled tree, that makes a show of putting forth a few leaves late in autumn when other trees shed theirs, and, drooping in the effort, lingers on, all crackled and smoke-dried, till the following season, when it repeats the same process, and perhaps, if the weather be particularly genial, even tempts some rheumatic sparrow to chirrup in its branches. People sometimes call these dark yards "gardens"; it is not supposed that they were ever planted, but rather that they are pieces of unreclaimed land, with the withered vegetation of the original brick-field. No man thinks of walking in this desolate place, or of turning it to any account.

1. "This desolate place" (line 20) is most clearly like

(A) "Some London houses" (line 4)
(B) "a melancholy little plot of ground (lines 4-5)
(C) "a crippled tree" (line 8)
(D) "the following season" (line 12)
(E) "the original brick field" (19)

Explanation: Start with the phrase in question, "this desolate (isolated, bare) place," and check the wording of the answers for similarities. While (A), (B), (C), and (E) all refer to places, (B) and (C) contain negative language ("melancholy" and "crippled" respectively), so focus on them. The sentence in which they appear, and indeed the whole passage, focuses on the "melancholy little plot of ground"—that is, the backyard area behind some homes. The "crippled tree" is merely present. If you read through the rest of the passage, you can see that the "melancholy plot" is later referred to in different ways: *these dark yards* (line 16), *pieces of unreclaimed land* (lines 17-18), and finally *this desolate place* (line 20). That makes (B) correct.

And finally, a poetry example. It's a bit more challenging than the previous questions, so we're going to approch it in steps. **Before you look at the question, take a moment and read through the text carefully enough to get a general sense of what the poet is describing.**

O wild West Wind, thou breath of Autumn's being,
Thou, from whose unseen presence the leaves dead
Are driven, like ghosts from an enchanter fleeing,
Yellow, and black, and pale, and hectic red,
Pestilence-stricken multitudes: O thou,
Who chariotest to their dark wintry bed
The winged seeds, where they lie cold and low,
Each like a corpse within its grave, until
Thine azure sister of the Spring shall blow
Her clarion o'er the dreaming earth, and fill
(Driving sweet buds like flocks to feed in air)
With living hues and odours plain and hill:
Wild Spirit, which art moving everywhere;
Destroyer and preserver; hear, O hear!

1. "Wild Spirit" (line 13) most clearly echoes which earlier phrase from the passage?

Don't look at the answers quite yet. Right now, our focus is on defining the "Wild Spirit." What do lines 13-14 tell us about it? That it's *moving everywhere*, that it's a *Destroyer and preserver*. That's nice, but unfortunately it doesn't help us answer the question.

If you've read the passage and gotten the gist, you might be able to recognize that it essentially consists of one long description of the West Wind. That might seem like a very general piece of knowledge, but in fact it's the main piece of information you need to answer the question.

If you read the poem and got confused—which would be understandable, since the language is quite challenging—go back to the very first line and just focus on that: *O wild West Wind, thou breath of Autumn's being*. What does the wind do? It blows things around, i.e., makes them *[move] everywhere*. So the beginning and the end of this excerpt are talking about the same thing.

Now look at the full question:

O wild West Wind, thou breath of Autumn's being,
Thou, from whose unseen presence the leaves dead
Are driven, like ghosts from an enchanter fleeing,
Yellow, and black, and pale, and hectic red,
Pestilence-stricken multitudes: O thou,
Who chariotest to their dark wintry bed
The winged seeds, where they lie cold and low,
Each like a corpse within its grave, until
Thine azure sister of the Spring shall blow
Her clarion o'er the dreaming earth, and fill
(Driving sweet buds like flocks to feed in air)
With living hues and odours plain and hill:
Wild Spirit, which art moving everywhere;
Destroyer and preserver; hear, O hear!

1. "Wild spirit" (line 13) most clearly echoes which earlier phrase from the passage?

   (A) "the leaves dead" (line 2)
   (B) "ghosts from an enchanter fleeing" (line 3)
   (C) "winged seeds" (line 7)
   (D) "Thine azure sister of the Spring" (line 9)
   (E) "odours plain and hill" (line 12)

Explanation: Unfortunately, the description in line 1 isn't among the answer choices. But that doesn't mean you can't narrow things down by looking at the wording of the options. Remember that the correct choice must refer to the West Wind in some way.

(A): This answer is off-topic. Dead leaves have nothing to do with the wind.

(B): "Ghosts from an enchanter fleeing" seems like it could refer to the wind. Leave it.

(C): This choice doesn't quite fit. The "winged" part makes sense, but the wind doesn't consist of seeds. Assume it's wrong.

(D): This answer isn't clearly right or wrong. It might work. Leave it.

(E): The wind isn't an "odour." Assume it's wrong.

Now we're down to (B) and (D). If we go back to line 3, we can see that "ghosts from an enchanter fleeing" actually refers to dead leaves as well. (*Thou, from whose unseen presence the leaves dead/ Are driven, like ghosts from an enchanter fleeing*). That leaves (D), which is correct. The key word in line 9 is *blow*: even if you find the rest of the description confusing, this verb indicates that the poet is indeed referring to the wind.

Exercises: Defining Words and Phrases

In the following exercises, underline in the passage the word or phrase to which the pronoun in question refers. The goal is to practice backing up as far as necessary to identify the referent. (Multiple-choice questions can be answered as usual.)

Example:

Bright and pleasant was the sky, balmy the air, and beautiful the appearance of every object around, as Mr. Pickwick leaned over the balustrades of Rochester Bridge, contemplating nature, and waiting for breakfast. **The scene (#1)** was indeed one which might well have charmed a far less reflective mind, than that to which it was presented.

On the left of the spectator lay the **ruined wall (#2)**, broken in many places, and in some, overhanging the narrow beach below in rude and heavy masses. Huge knots of seaweed hung upon the jagged and pointed stones, trembling in every breath of wind; and the green ivy clung mournfully round the dark and ruined battlements. Behind it rose the **ancient castle (#3)**, its towers roofless, and its massive walls crumbling away, but telling us proudly of its old might and strength, as when, seven hundred years ago, it rang with the clash of arms, or resounded with the noise of feasting and revelry.

1. In line 6, the word "it" refers to

2. In line 14, the word "it" refers to

3. In line 15, the word "its" refers to

Now try some on your own.

1. A noiseless patient spider,
I mark'd where on a little promontory it stood isolated,
Mark'd how to explore the vacant vast surrounding,
It launch'd forth filament, filament, filament, out of itself,
Ever unreeling them, ever tirelessly speeding them.

And you O my soul where you stand,
Surrounded, detached, in measureless oceans of space,
Ceaselessly musing, venturing, throwing, seeking the spheres to connect them,
Till the bridge you will need be form'd, till the ductile anchor hold,
Till the gossamer thread you fling catch somewhere, O my soul.

1. In line 4, the word "it" refers to

2. In line 5, the repeated word "them" refers to

3. In line 8, the word "them" refers to

4. In line 9, the speaker uses the word "you" to address

(A) "my soul" (line 6)
(B) "oceans of space" (line 7)
(C) "the spheres" (line 8)
(D) "the bridge" (line 9)
(E) "the gossamer thread" (line 10)

2. I am a little world made cunningly
Of elements, and an angelic spright,
But black sin hath betrayed to endless night
My worlds both parts, and oh! both parts must die.
You, which beyond that heaven which was most high
Have found new spheres and of new lands can write,
Pour new seas in mine eyes, that so I might
Drown my world with my weeping earnestly,
Or wash it, if it must be drowned no more:
But oh! it must be burnt; alas the fire
Of lust and envy burnt it heretofore,
And made it fouler; Let their flames retire,
And burn me, O Lord, with a fiery zeal
Of thee and thy house, which doth in eating heal.

1. In line 10, the word "it" refers to

2. In line 11, the word "it" refers to

3. In line 12, the word "their" refers to

3. As I remember, Giffen's appeared at the beginning of the twenties, and I am sure I am not alone in associating its emergence with that change of mood within our profession—that change which came to push the polishing of silver to the position of central importance it still by and large maintains today. The shift was, I believe, like some many other major shifts around this period, a generational matter; it was during these years that our generation of butlers 'came of age', and figures like Mr Marshall, in particular, played a crucial part in making silver-polishing so central.

1. In line 3, the word "its" refers to

2. The phrase "the shift" (lines 6-7) most clearly echoes which other phrase from the passage?

(A) "our profession" (line 4)
(B) "that change of mood" (line 3)
(C) "the position of central importance" (lines 5-6)
(D) "during these years" (lines 8-9)
(E) "a crucial part" (lines 10-11)

4. There is a change—and I am poor;
Your love hath been, nor long ago,
A fountain at my fond heart's door,
Whose only business was to flow;
And flow it did; not taking heed
Of its own bounty, or my need.

What happy moments did I count!
Blest was I then all bliss above!
Now, for that consecrated fount
Of murmuring, sparkling, living love,
What have I? shall I dare to tell?

A comfortless and hidden well.
A well of love—it may be deep—
I trust it is,—and never dry:
What matter? if the waters sleep
In silence and obscurity.
—Such change, and at the very door
Of my fond heart, hath made me poor.

1. In line 5, the word "it" refers to

2. The phrase "the waters" (line 15) most clearly echoes which earlier phrase from the passage?

(A) "a change" (line 1)
(B) "my fond heart's door" (line 3)
(C) "my need" (line 6)
(D) "happy moments" (line 7)
(E) "that consecrated fount" (line 9)

5. Travelling northward from the township of Otis, the road leads for twenty or thirty miles towards Windsor, lengthwise upon that long broken spur of heights which the Green Mountains of Vermont send into Massachusetts. For nearly the whole of the distance, you have the continual sensation of being upon some terrace in the moon. The feeling of the plain or the valley is never yours; scarcely the feeling of the earth. Unless by a sudden precipitation of the road you find yourself plunging into some gorge, you pass on, and on, and on, upon the crests or slopes of pastoral mountains, while far below, mapped out in its beauty, the valley of the Housatonic lies endlessly along at your feet.

1. The phrase "crests or slopes" (line 11) is most analagous to which earlier phrase from the passage?

   (A) "long broken spur of heights" (line 3)
   (B) "the continual sensation" (line 6)
   (C) "The feeling of the plain" (lines 7)
   (D) "a sudden precipitation" (line 9)
   (E) "some gorge" (line 10)

2. In line 12, the word "its" refers to

6. Come live with me, and be my love,
And we will some new pleasures prove
Of golden sands, and crystal brooks,
With silken lines, and silver hooks.

There will the river whispering run
Warm'd by thy eyes, more than the sun;
And there the 'enamour'd fish will stay,
Begging themselves they may betray.

When thou wilt swim in that live bath,
Each fish, which every channel hath,
Will amorously to thee swim,
Gladder to catch thee, than thou him.

If thou, to be so seen, be'st loth,
By sun or moon, thou dark'nest both,
And if myself have leave to see,
I need not their light having thee.

Let others freeze with angling reeds,
And cut their legs with shells and weeds,
Or treacherously poor fish beset,
With strangling snare, or windowy net.

Let coarse bold hands from slimy nest
The bedded fish in banks out-wrest;
Or curious traitors, sleeve-silk flies,
Bewitch poor fishes' wand'ring eyes.

For thee, thou need'st no such deceit,
For thou thyself art thine own bait:
That fish, that is not catch'd thereby,
Alas, is wiser far than I.

1. In line 12, the word "him" refers to

2. In line 16, the word "their" refers to

3. "That fish, that is not catched" (line 27) most likely refers to a person who

   (A) refuses to engage in deceit
   (B) resists the charms of the speaker's loved one
   (C) is not easily deceived by trickery
   (D) considers the water a source of danger
   (E) fails to attract the speaker's attention

7. It stood upon a low hill, above the river—the river being the Thames at some forty miles from London. A long gabled front of red brick, with the complexion of which time and the weather had played all sorts of pictorial tricks, only, however, to improve and refine it, presented to the lawn its patches of ivy, its clustered chimneys, its windows smothered in creepers. The house had a name and a history; the old gentleman taking his tea would have been delighted to tell you these things: how it had been built under Edward the Sixth, had offered a night's hospitality to the great Elizabeth* (whose august person had extended itself upon a huge, magnificent and terribly angular bed which still formed the principal honour of the sleeping apartments), had been a good deal bruised and defaced in Cromwell's* wars, and then, under the Restoration, repaired and much enlarged; and how, finally, after having been remodelled and disfigured in the eighteenth century, it had passed into the careful keeping of a shrewd American banker, who had bought it originally because (owing to circumstances too complicated to set forth) it was offered at a great bargain: bought it with much grumbling at its ugliness, its antiquity, its incommodity, and who now, at the end of twenty years, had become conscious of a real aesthetic passion for it, so that he knew all its points and would tell you just where to stand to see them in combination and just the hour when the shadows of its various protuberances—which fell so softly upon the warm, weary brickwork—were of the right measure.

1. In line 1, the word "it" refers to

2. In line 20, the word "it" refers to

3. In line 29, the word "them" refers to

4. In context, "of the right measure" (lines 32-33) is best understood to mean

   (A) sharply defined
   (B) properly sized
   (C) moderately constrained
   (D) most flattering
   (E) mildly askew

*Queen Elizabeth I (1533-1603)

** Seventeenth-century English general and politician

8. As late I rambled in the happy fields,
What time the sky-lark shakes the tremulous dew
From his lush clover covert;—when anew
Adventurous knights take up their dinted shields:
I saw the sweetest flower wild nature yields,
A fresh-blown musk-rose; 'twas the first that threw
Its sweets upon the summer: graceful it grew
As is the wand that queen Titania wields.
And, as I feasted on its fragrancy,
I thought the garden-rose it far excell'd:
But when, O Wells! thy roses came to me
My sense with their deliciousness was spell'd:
Soft voices had they, that with tender plea
Whisper'd of peace, and truth, and friendliness unquell'd.

1. In line 9, the word "its" refers to

2. In line 13, the word "they" refers to

9. An embankment ten or fifteen feet high guards both banks of the Mississippi all the way down that lower end of the river, and this embankment is set back from the edge of the shore from ten to perhaps a hundred feet, according to circumstances; say thirty or forty feet, as a general thing. Fill that whole region with an impenetrable gloom of smoke from a hundred miles of burning bagasse piles, when the river is over the banks, and turn a steamboat loose along there at midnight and see how she will feel. And see how you will feel, too! You find yourself away out in the midst of a vague dim sea that is shoreless, that fades out and loses itself in the murky distances; for you cannot discern the thin rib of embankment, and you are always imagining you see a straggling tree when you don't. The plantations themselves are transformed by the smoke, and look like a part of the sea. All through your watch you are tortured with the exquisite misery of uncertainty. You hope you are keeping in the river, but you do not know. All that you are sure about is that you are likely to be within six feet of the bank and destruction, when you think you are a good half-mile from shore. And you are sure, also, that if you chance suddenly to fetch up against the embankment you will have the small comfort of knowing that it is about what you were expecting to do. One of the great Vicksburg packets darted out into a sugar plantation one night, at such a time, and had to stay there a week. But there was no novelty about it; it had often been done before.

1. In line 10, the word "she" refers to

2. In line 13, the word "itself" refers to

3. In lines 28-29, "One of the great Vicksburg packets" most closely echoes which earlier phrase from the passage?

(A) "burning bagasse piles" (line 8)
(B) "a steamboat" (line 9)
(C) "the thin rib of embankment" (lines 14-15)
(D) "The plantations" (line 16)
(E) "the exquite misery of uncertainty" (line 19)

10. It came like a thunder-clap on us all, that the vessel which contained our fortune had been wrecked, and gone to the bottom with all its stores, together with several of the crew, and the unfortunate merchant himself. I was grieved for him; I was grieved for the overthrow of all our air-built castles: but, with the elasticity of youth, I soon recovered the shock.

Though riches had charms, poverty had no terrors for an inexperienced girl like me. Indeed, to say the truth, there was something exhilarating in the idea of being driven to straits, and thrown upon our own resources. I only wished papa, mamma, and Mary were all of the same mind as myself; and then, instead of lamenting past calamities we might all cheerfully set to work to remedy them; and the greater the difficulties, the harder our present privations, the greater should be our cheerfulness to endure the latter, and our vigour to contend against the former.

Mary did not lament, but she brooded continually over the misfortune, and sank into a state of dejection from which no effort of mine could rouse her. I could not possibly bring her to regard the matter on its bright side as I did: and indeed I was so fearful of being charged with childish frivolity, or stupid insensibility, that I carefully kept most of my bright ideas and cheering notions to myself; well knowing they could not be appreciated.

1. In line 16, the word "them" refers to

2. In lines 19-20, the words "the latter" and "the former" refer to

3. In line 28, "cheering notions" refers to

(A) sudden insights
(B) clever strategems
(C) staunch opinions
(D) optimistic viewpoints
(E) impulsive foolishness

Explanations: Defining Words and Phrases

"Apple Picking" question (p. 41): C

1.1 it = a noiseless patient spider (line 1)

1.2 them = filament, filament, filament (line 4)

1.3 them = (measureless) oceans of space (line 7)

1.4 A: you = my soul (line 6)

2.1 it = my world (line 8)

2.2 it = my world (line 8)

2.3 their = lust and envy (line 11)

3.1 its = Giffen's (line 1)

3.2 B: The "shift" refers to the new importance placed on silver polishing, a transformation that accompanied a "change of mood" with the butlering profession. Shift = change, so (B) is correct.

4.1 it = a fountain (line 3)

4.2 E: "The waters" refers to the main image of the poem, the *fountain at my fond heart's door*. "Fount" is another word for "fountain," so (E) is correct.

5.1 A: The phrase "crests (peaks) or slopes" literally refers to parts of mountains, as indicated in the sentence where the phrase appears, so the correct answer must refer to the same thing. If you look at the wording of the answer choices, the only word that clearly fits this requirement is "heights" in (A). Plains are flat, eliminating (C); precipitations are drops, eliminating (D); and gorges are canyons or ravines, found below mountains, eliminating (E). (B) does not fit either because a "sensation" (feeling) has nothing to do with a height either.

5.2 its = the valley of the Housatonie (line 13); note that the referent follows the pronoun.

6.1 him = each fish (line 10)

6.2 sun or moon (line 14)

6.3 B: Throughout the poem, the speaker uses the fishing metaphor to convey the nearly irresistible charms of the beloved; in that context, a fish "that is not catched" refers to a person who is not ensnared by the speaker's beloved, i.e. who "resists [their] charms." That corresponds to (B). (A), (D), and (E) are entirely off-topic, and (C) does not fit because the speaker implies that the beloved naturally attracts people by being innately appealing rather than by any sort of tricks.

7.1 it = the house (line 8); another instance of the referent following the pronoun

7.2 it = the house (line 8)

7.3 them = its points (line 28)

7.4 D: Under normal circumstances, you should make sure to read the entire sentence in which the word or phrase referenced in a question appears; however, in this case, the sentence is so long (it begins in line 8) that that is not a reasonable approach. Instead, focus on the information that appears after the colon in line 24. In that section, the narrator indicates that the American banker who bought the house *had become conscious of a real aesthetic passion for it.* The word *aesthetics* means "relating to beauty," and so in that context, "the right measure" must convey the idea that the owner knows how to show the house off in a way that emphasizes its attractiveness, i.e., to present it in the "most flattering" light. (D) is thus correct.

8.1 its = A fresh-blown musk-rose (line 6)

8.2 they = thy roses (line 11)

9.1 she = a steamboat (line 9)

9.2 itself = a vague dim sea (line 12)

9.3 B: On its own, the phrase in question provides virtually no information—to understand what a Vicksburg packet refers to, you must consider the context of the passage. In lines 20-27, the narrator evokes the experience of running a steamboat into the riverbanks because of low visibility. Given that information, the final sentence is logically providing an example of a specific steamboat that went aground this way, with "[o]ne of the great Vicksburg packets" referring to the boat in question. (B) is the only option that fits.

10.1 them = past calamities (line 15)

10.2 the latter = our present privations; the former = the difficulties

10.3 D: The key information appears at the beginning of the sentence, before the colon. There, the narrator states that she *could not possibly bring [Mary] to regard the matter on the bright side* (i.e., to view things more positively). In that context, the narrator's "cheering notions" are logically "optimistic viewpoints," making (D) correct.

Chapter Four

Literal Comprehension and Inference

In the previous chapter, we looked at how to summarize full passages in order to answer big-picture questions; here, we're going to focus on the same skill but on a smaller scale. The most straightforward and common multiple-choice questions—the ones that directly test your comprehension of a given section of a passage—also require you to understand the relevant portion of the text well enough to recognize a summary of it.

That summary, however, will not be written using the same wording as that in the passage—**the test is whether you understand the literal meaning or direct implication of the text well enough to recognize it when it's stated using different, often more general, language.** Correct answers thus require you to recognize **paraphrased** versions of statements from the passage. If you can grasp the essential ideas expressed in the passage, there's a good chance you'll be fine. If, however, you do not know the meanings of key words and/or try to interpret beyond what the text directly suggests, you're likely to go off track.

To reiterate: correct answer choices will typically contain synonyms for key words in the passage but rarely the words themselves. Or, said otherwise: same idea, different words.

Questions of this type may be phrased in a variety of ways.

- Lines x-y indicate/reveal that...
- In lines x-y, the author suggests/implicitly acknowledges that...
- In the third paragraph, the author draws a distinction between...
- In line x, the metaphor of the sea chiefly serves to emphasize

Note that questions can be phrased either in terms of what the passage conveys/reveals or in terms of what it suggests or implies. Despite this, **there is little practical difference between inference and literal comprehension questions, and both can be approached the same way**.

Note also that **in some cases, literal comprehension questions may "pose" as function/rhetorical strategy questions** (as in the last example above). They are discussed here rather than in Chapter 5, however, because they are truly designed to test your understanding of literal meaning, with the function or rhetorical technique cited in the question having little effect on the answer.

Paraphrasing

At the most straightforward level, you may be asked to literally "translate" a phrase or sentence that includes some sort of linguistic challenge (e.g., figurative or old-fashioned language, complex syntax) into clear, modern English. Although questions worded in terms of paraphrasing are not a major component of the exam, they do sometimes appear.

For example, consider the opening stanza from the John Donne poem *The Good Morrow* (1633):

I wonder by my troth, what thou and I
Did, till we loved? Were we not wean'd till then?
But suck'd on country pleasures, childishly?
Or snorted we in the Seven Sleepers' den*?
'Twas so; but this, all pleasures fancies be;
If ever any beauty I did see,
Which I desired, and got, 'twas but a dream of thee.

*Cave in which a group of ancient youths hid to escape persecution.

1. What is the best paraphrase of lines 6-7?

(A) I dreamed of your beauty before I met you.
(B) Because of your beauty, I wished to meet you as from the moment I saw you.
(C) The beauty that I saw before I met you could not compare to your beauty.
(D) No other person could possibly be as beautiful as you.
(E) I believe that you are beautiful because you appear so in my dreams.

Explanation: Although this question can be answered using only lines 6-7, it is nevertheless helpful to consider the context of the stanza. Essentially, the speaker is addressing his beloved and suggesting that they were mere children before they met each other—that their lives had not really begun yet, or were not quite real. Lines 6-7 serve to support that idea.

Let's look at them piece by piece. Notice that the lines are not divided according to where the speaker would logically pause:

If ever any beauty I did see/Which I desired and got

If ever I saw any beauty that I wanted and obtained,

'twas but a dream of thee

What makes this line challenging is that there are two non-literal meanings here:

First, *but* is used to mean "only" (its common second meaning): *but a dream* = only a dream.

Second, *dream* means something like *shadow* or *poor imitation*—the speaker is basically saying that the beauty he saw elsewhere only hinted at the beauty he would eventually encounter in his beloved. In other words, it "could not compare." That corresponds to (C).

Otherwise, (A), (B), and (E) can be eliminated because the speaker is talking about seeing beauty in sources *other* than the beloved. Be careful with (D): it might be true, but it doesn't rephrase lines 6-7. The speaker only mentions beauty he saw in the past—there is nothing about whether another person could ever possibly match the beauty of his beloved.

Starting on the next page, we're going to look at some additional questions. Keep in mind that although they're phrased in different ways, they are all testing your ability to understand the literal meaning of the information in question.

I wonder by my troth, what thou and I
Did, till we loved? Were we not wean'd till then?
But suck'd on country pleasures, childishly?
Or snorted we in the Seven Sleepers' den*?
'Twas so; but this, all pleasures fancies be;
If ever any beauty I did see,
Which I desired, and got, 'twas but a dream of thee.

And now good-morrow to our waking souls,
Which watch not one another out of fear;
For love all love of other sights controls,
And makes one little room an everywhere.
Let sea-discoverers to new worlds have gone;
Let maps to other, worlds on worlds have shown;
Let us possess one world; each hath one, and is one.

My face in thine eye, thine in mine appears,
And true plain hearts do in the faces rest;
Where can we find two better hemispheres
Without sharp north, without declining west?
Whatever dies, was not mix'd equally;
If our two loves be one, or thou and I
Love so alike that none can slacken, none can die.

*Cave in which a group of ancient youths hid to escape persecution.

1. In context, "Which watch not one another out of fear" (line 9) is best understood to convey the speaker's

(A) concern that his loved one will betray him
(B) insistence that love is a form of control
(C) worry that he will not remain faithful
(D) belief in a relationship based on mutual trust
(E) desire for a spiritual rebirth

2. Which best describes the speaker's implication in lines 19-21?

(A) Love cannot endure when it is distributed unequally.
(B) People who love deeply can retain their youth indefinitely.
(C) Love fortifies the soul so that people are not overwhelmed by their losses.
(D) Even when people love each other equally, the intensity of their feelings eventually wanes.
(E) People's memories of their loved ones often grow stronger with time.

Explanation #1: Throughout the poem, the speaker describes an ideal relationship, one in which two people complement each other perfectly. In that context, the negation in line 9 is very important: *And now good-morrow to our waking souls/Which watch* not *each other out of fear.* Essentially, the speaker is saying that he and his beloved will find it unnecessary to monitor each other's faithfulness because they will not be afraid that either of them will stray—their love is that strong.

That meaning is exactly the opposite of (A), (B), and (C), and has nothing to do with (E). (D) correctly states the idea expressed in line 9, albeit in very different language: the speaker's assertion that a good relationship is one in which neither party feels any need to control the other reveals a belief in the importance of mutual trust.

Explanation #2: Although this question is phrased in terms of implication (meaning that it is technically an inference question), it is effectively identical to the literal paraphrase question we worked through on the previous page. The correct answer merely restates the meaning of the passage in a more straightforward way and from a slightly different angle; there is no need to speculate about any sort of symbolism or the larger meaning of the poem. Lines 19-21 emphasize the importance of equality in love, indicating that love only comes to an end ("cannot endure") if it is not *mix'd equally* ("distributed unequally"). That corresponds directly to (A).

My long two-pointed ladder's sticking through a tree
Toward heaven still,
And there's a barrel that I didn't fill
Beside it, and there may be two or three
Apples I didn't pick upon some bough.
But I am done with apple-picking now.
Essence of winter sleep is on the night,
The scent of apples: I am drowsing off.
I cannot rub the strangeness from my sight
I got from looking through a pane of glass
I skimmed this morning from the drinking trough
And held against the world of hoary grass.
It melted, and I let it fall and break.
But I was well
Upon my way to sleep before it fell,
And I could tell
What form my dreaming was about to take.
Magnified apples appear and disappear,
Stem end and blossom end,
And every fleck of russet showing clear.
My instep arch not only keeps the ache,
It keeps the pressure of a ladder-round.
I feel the ladder sway as the boughs bend.
And I keep hearing from the cellar bin
The rumbling sound.
Of load on load of apples coming in.
For I have had too much
Of apple-picking: I am overtired
Of the great harvest I myself desired.
There were ten thousand thousand fruit to touch,
Cherish in hand, lift down, and not let fall.
For all
That struck the earth,
No matter if not bruised or spiked with stubble,
Went surely to the cider-apple heap
As of no worth.
One can see what will trouble
This sleep of mine, whatever sleep it is.
Were he not gone,
The woodchuck could say whether it's like his
Long sleep, as I describe its coming on,
Or just some human sleep.

1. In context of the passage, the speaker's reaction to "the rumbling sound" (line 25) can best be described as one of

(A) awe and excitement
(B) displeasure and dismay
(C) curiosity and inquisitiveness
(D) fear and loathing
(E) anxiety and befuddlement

2. According to the passage, apples have "no worth" (line 36) if they

(A) are harvested too late
(B) are bruised or damaged
(C) have flecks of russet
(D) interfere with sleep
(E) have fallen to the ground

Explanation #1: If you understand the big picture, then the question is quite straightforward. The "rumbling sound" signals that *loads on loads* more apples are arriving, but the entire point of the poem is that the speaker is tired of picking apples and wants only to rest. The correct answer must be negative, eliminating (A) and (C). "Fear and loathing" is too extreme—the speaker is irritated but not outright furious—so (D) can be eliminated. In (E), "anxiety" could plausibily fit, but there is nothing in the passage to suggest "befuddlement" (confusion). That leaves (B): "displeasure and dismay" clearly conveys the speaker's disappointment at the appearance of yet more apples.

Explanation #2: Don't fall into the trap and pick (B), which would seem to be the logical answer. In fact, lines 31-36 indicate the speaker could not let the apples fall, *for all that struck the earth* (i.e., that fell to the ground) were put into the cider-heap and considered worthless even if they were not *bruised or spiked with stubble*. So in fact, the answer is (E).

One evening of late summer, before the nineteenth century had reached one-third of its span, a young man and woman, the latter carrying a child, were approaching the large village of Weydon-Priors, in Upper Wessex, on foot. They were plainly but not ill clad, though the thick hoar of dust which had accumulated on their shoes and garments from an obviously long journey lent a disadvantageous shabbiness to their appearance just now.

The man was of fine figure, swarthy, and stern in aspect; and he showed in profile a facial angle so slightly inclined as to be almost perpendicular. He wore a short jacket of brown corduroy, newer than the remainder of his suit, which was a fustian waistcoat with white horn buttons, breeches of the same, tanned leggings, and a straw hat overlaid with black glazed canvas. At his back he carried by a looped strap a rush basket, from which protruded at one end the crutch of a hay-knife, a wimble* for hay-bonds being also visible in the aperture. His measured, springless walk was the walk of the skilled countryman as distinct from the desultory shamble of the general labourer; while in the turn and plant of each foot there was, further, a dogged and cynical indifference personal to himself, showing its presence even in the regularly interchanging fustian folds, now in the left leg, now in the right, as he paced along.

What was really peculiar, however, in this couple's progress, and would have attracted the attention of any casual observer otherwise disposed to overlook them, was the perfect silence they preserved. They walked side by side in such a way as to suggest afar off the low, easy, confidential chat of people full of reciprocity; but on closer view it could be discerned that the man was reading, or pretending to read, a ballad sheet which he kept before his eyes with some difficulty by the hand that was passed through the basket strap. Whether this apparent cause were the real cause, or whether it were an assumed one to escape an intercourse that would have been irksome to him, nobody but himself could have said precisely; but his taciturnity was unbroken, and the woman enjoyed no society whatever from his presence. Virtually she walked the highway alone, save for the child she bore.

*Marbleworker's brace for drilling

1. The description in lines 5-9 ("They were . . . now") suggests that the family's clothes

(A) were poorly made
(B) lacked any semblance of style
(C) were of better quality than they seemed
(D) had been thoroughly ruined by their journey
(E) made them appear sickly

2. The sentence in lines 20-28 ("His . . . along") reveals that the narrator

(A) disapproves of the man's conduct
(B) is respectful of manual labor
(C) disdains contemporary fashions
(D) refrains from making judgments
(E) is attuned to social distinctions

3. Lines 33-40 ("They walked . . . strap") primarily serve to emphasize the couple's

(A) deep conection
(B) mutual respect
(C) self-sufficiency
(D) weak morale
(E) deceptive appearance

4. The use of "apparent" in line 40 implies that the narrator believes the man

(A) was using the ballad sheet as a pretext for avoiding an interaction
(B) lacked the ability to communicate with his family
(C) was incapable of understanding the ballad sheet
(D) felt ashamed of his shodddy appearance
(E) would have preferred to be speaking to traveling companions

Explanation #1: Lines 5-9 provide two important pieces of information: first, the family was *plainly but not ill-* (poorly) *clad*; and second, that they were covered in dust that *lent a disadvantageous shabbiness to their appearance*. In other words, the clothes were actually of decent quality, but they appeared run-down because of the dust from the road. That corresponds to (C). (A) is contradicted by the passage; (B) is not addressed; (D) is too extreme—the clothes appear shabby, not destroyed; and (E) plays on the literal meaning of *ill* (sick) but is unsupported by the passage.

Explanation #2: Although this question asks about the sentence in lines 20-28 as a whole, the answer is based only on the first half (the information before the semi-colon). What does the narrator focus on there? The fact that the man walks in the more deliberate manner of a *skilled countryman* (higher class) as opposed to that of a *general labourer* (lower class). The fact that he is able to make this distinction suggests that he is someone who is sensitive to (i.e., "is attuned to") social distinctions. That makes the answer (E).

Explanation #3: If you just scan through lines 33-40, you can noticed that halfway through the word *but* appears (line 35), signaling the introduction of contradictory information. The first half of the sentence indicates that from a distance, the couple appeared to engage in the type of conversation typical of people who are close to one another, whereas the second half of the sentence (the information after the semicolon) reveals that the man is not interacting with the woman and child at all. In other words, their superficial appearance is deceptive, making the answer (E).

Explanation #4: Although the question technically asks about the implication of a word, in reality the answer simply sums up the meaning of the following lines. The narrator speculates that the man may have been staring at the ballad sheet in order to avoid speaking to the woman and child. The phrase *apparent cause* literally refers to the fact that the man's focus on the ballad sheet prevented him from interacting with the others. In that context, *apparent* serves to draw the reader's attention to the idea of appearances: the man only gave the appearance of having to look at the ballad sheet but was really staring at it in order to avoid speaking. In other words, he was using it as a "pretext (justification or excuse) for avoiding an interaction."

NOT, LEAST, and EXCEPT

Among literal comprehension questions, those that ask you to identify something that the passage is NOT can be the most resistant to shortcuts. Oftentimes, you will simply need to hunt back through the passage in order to see whether particular pieces of information are in fact mentioned. But that said, you can sometimes eliminate several answers by using the main point or your overall knowledge of the passage. Then, you can go back and check the other two or three options carefully. In some cases, you can even use the main point to identify the answer immediately. So while these questions may appear time-consuming, they do have the potential to be solved fairly quickly in certain instances.

Important: Whenever you encounter one of these questions, circle or underline NOT, LEAST, or EXCEPT. It is very easy to forget that the right answer will be false, and marking this key word will keep you on track so that you do not accidentally resort to the default strategy of looking for statements that the passage supports.

For example:

Love is not all: it is not meat nor drink
Nor slumber nor a roof against the rain;
Nor yet a floating spar to men that sink
And rise and sink and rise and sink again;
Love can not fill the thickened lung with breath,
Nor clean the blood, nor set the fractured bone;
Yet many a man is making friends with death
Even as I speak, for lack of love alone.
It well may be that in a difficult hour,
Pinned down by pain and moaning for release,
Or nagged by want past resolution's power,
I might be driven to sell your love for peace,
Or trade the memory of this night for food.
It well may be. I do not think I would.

1. The poem deals with all of the following EXCEPT the

(A) limits of love
(B) consequences of a lack of love
(C) importance the speaker places on love
(D) vulnerability required to love
(E) inability of love to alter physical reality

Explanation: Although you could check each answer individually, in order, against the poem, a simpler way to approach the question is to think of it in terms of the big picture.

As we saw in Chapter 2, it's divided into two sections, with the first (lines 1-6) focusing on the things love cannot do ("the limits of love") and the second (7-14) focusing on the value of love for the speaker ("the importance the speaker places on love"). That eliminates both (A) and (C).

Given that the first section emphasizes the fact that love cannot literally heal sickness, provide food, etc., (E) can be eliminated as well.

The major risk at this point is that you'll start to scan the poem randomly, unsure of how to decide between (B) and (D). One way of avoiding that trap is to look for shifts in the text since correct answers are most likely to be located near them. Here, the most significant change is signaled by the word *yet* in line 7. That line (*Yet many a man is making friends with death/Even as I speak, for lack of love alone*) indicates that people can die from lack of love—that is, the "consequences of a lack of love." (B) can thus be eliminated, leaving (D) as the answer.

Comparing and Contrasting

You may also be asked to compare or (more likely) contrast/distinguish between the focus in various parts of the passage. In some cases, you may be able to use the main point to answer these questions, while in other cases you may need to consider the details on their own terms.

This time we're going to work with a prose passage:

It came like a thunder-clap on us all, that the vessel which contained our fortune had been wrecked, and gone to the bottom with all its stores, together with several of the crew, and the unfortunate merchant himself. I was grieved for him; I was grieved for the overthrow of all our air-built castles: but, with the elasticity of youth, I soon recovered the shock.

Though riches had charms, poverty had no terrors for an inexperienced girl like me. Indeed, to say the truth, there was something exhilarating in the idea of being driven to straits, and thrown upon our own resources. I only wished papa, mamma, and Mary were all of the same mind as myself; and then, instead of lamenting past calamities we might all cheerfully set to work to remedy them; and the greater the difficulties, the harder our present privations, the greater should be our cheerfulness to endure the latter, and our vigour to contend against the former.

Mary did not lament, but she brooded continually over the misfortune, and sank into a state of dejection from which no effort of mine could rouse her. I could not possibly bring her to regard the matter on its bright side as I did: and indeed I was so fearful of being charged with childish frivolity, or stupid insensibility, that I carefully kept most of my bright ideas and cheering notions to myself; well knowing they could not be appreciated.

1. Which best describes the difference in the way the narrator and Mary are characterized in the second and third paragraph?

(A) Graceful acceptance versus profound melancholy
(B) Intense disquiet versus mild complacency
(C) Fierce determination versus staunch defensiveness
(D) Tacit excitement versus staid resignation
(E) Unexpected fortitude versus giddy playfulness

Explanation: To answer this question, focus on the beginning of each paragraph, and work through the answers one side at a time.

In the second paragraph, the first two sentences describe the narrator's reaction: poverty had *no terrors* for her, and there was even *something exhilarating* about it. So her reaction was positive. Now, check only the first half of each answer. (A), (C), (D), and (E) all contain positive words, but "intense disquiet (worry)" is firmly negative, so (B) can be eliminated.

Next, look at the first sentence of the second paragraph: Mary *brooded continually over the misfortune, and sank into a state of dejection* that the narrator could not shake her out of. In other words, she was deeply depressed. The only option that fits is "profound melancholy" ("resignation" is acceptance). So (A) is correct.

Exercises: Literal Comprehension

1. He stepped into the foyer, impeccably suited and scarved, with a silk tie knotted at his collar. Each evening he appeared in ensembles of plums, olives, and chocolate browns. He was a compact man, and though his feet were perpetually splayed, and his belly slightly wide, he nevertheless maintained an efficient posture, as if balancing in either hand two suitcases of equal weight. His ears were insulated by tufts of graying hair that seemed to block out the unpleasant traffic of life. He had thickly lashed eyes shaded with a trace of camphor, a generous mustache that turned up playfully at the ends, and a mole shaped like a flattened raisin in the very center of his left cheek. On his head he wore a black fez* made from the wool of Persian lambs, secured by bobby pins, without which I was never to see him. Though my father always offered to fetch him in our car, Mr. Pirzada preferred to walk from his dormitory to our neighborhood, a distance of about twenty minutes on foot, studying trees and shrubs on his way, and when he entered our house his knuckles were pink with the effects of crisp autumn air.

*A fez is a traditional Turkish hat

1. The description in lines 1-9 ("He stepped . . . life") primarily emphasizes Mr. Pirzada's

(A) generosity and sincerity
(B) impulsivity and excitability
(C) thoughtfulness and circumspection
(D) aloofness and reticence
(E) elegance and composure

2. The narrator mentions the "ensembles" (line 3) and the "black fez" (line 14) in order to highlight the

(A) eccentricity of Mr. Pirzada's style
(B) consistency of Mr. Pirzada's appearance
(C) contrast between Mr. Pirzada's behavior and that of the narrator's family
(D) peculiarity of Mr. Pirzada's clothing
(E) narrator's discomfort with Mr. Pirzada

2. As late I rambled in the happy fields,
What time the sky-lark shakes the tremulous dew
From his lush clover covert;—when anew
Adventurous knights take up their dinted shields:
I saw the sweetest flower wild nature yields,
A fresh-blown musk-rose; 'twas the first that threw
Its sweets upon the summer: graceful it grew
As is the wand that queen Titania* wields.
And, as I feasted on its fragrancy,
I thought the garden-rose it far excell'd:
But when, O Wells! thy roses came to me
My sense with their deliciousness was spell'd:
Soft voices had they, that with tender plea
Whisper'd of peace, and truth, and friendliness unquell'd.

*Mythological queen of the fairies

1. What is the best paraphrase of line 9 ("And, as . . . fragrancy")?

(A) And as I ate and grew full
(B) And as I sniffed its odor deeply
(C) And as I drank from its petals
(D) And as I looked at its shape
(E) And as I listened intently to its music

2. In the poem, the speaker evokes all of the following senses EXCEPT

(A) sight
(B) taste
(C) touch
(D) sound
(E) smell

3. Samuel Michael had never been a talkative man, but his calm, steady habits had brought a sense of security and consistency to their home. Mattie had been the only child of his autumn years, and so for as long as she could remember, he had been an old man with set and exacting ways. Unlike her mother he never raised his voice, and when the two had a difference of opinion, her mother would charge around the house, mumbling and banging pans, while he would just sit on the porch rocker and read his Bible.

1. Throughout the passage, Samuel Michael is characterized as

(A) warm and tender
(B) sharp and perceptive
(C) meek and retiring
(D) harsh and demanding
(E) unflappable and taciturn

4. Announced by all the trumpets of the sky,
Arrives the snow, and, driving o'er the fields,
Seems nowhere to alight: the whited air
Hides hills and woods, the river, and the heaven,
And veils the farm-house at the garden's end.
The sled and traveller stopped, the courier's feet
Delayed, all friends shut out, the housemates sit
Around the radiant fireplace, enclosed
In a tumultuous privacy of storm.

Come see the north wind's masonry.
Out of an unseen quarry evermore
Furnished with tile, the fierce artificer
Curves his white bastions with projected roof
Round every windward stake, or tree, or door.
Speeding, the myriad-handed, his wild work
So fanciful, so savage, nought cares he
For number or proportion. Mockingly,
On coop or kennel he hangs Parian wreaths;
A swan-like form invests the hidden thorn;
Fills up the farmer's lane from wall to wall,
Maugre the farmer's sighs; and, at the gate,
A tapering turret overtops the work.
And when his hours are numbered, and the world
Is all his own, retiring, as he were not,
Leaves, when the sun appears, astonished Art
To mimic in slow structures, stone by stone,
Built in an age, the mad wind's night-work,
The frolic architecture of the snow.

1. Which of the following best states the contrast in focus between lines 1-5 and lines 6-9?

(A) exterior vs. interior
(B) detached vs. personal
(C) exaggerated vs. understated
(D) urban vs. bucolic
(E) lofty vs. base

2. The metaphor of "masonry" (line 10) primarily serves to emphasize the

(A) mystery of creation
(B) wonder of a season
(C) brute force of nature
(D) solidity of a structure
(E) unpredictability of winter storms

5. Their house was in Wickham Place, and fairly quiet, for a lofty promontory of buildings separated it from the main thoroughfare. One had the sense of a backwater, or rather of an estuary, whose waters flowed in from the invisible sea, and ebbed into a profound silence while the waves without were still beating. Though the promontory consisted of flats*— expensive, with cavernous entrance halls, full of concierges and palms—it fulfilled its purpose, and gained for the older houses opposite a certain measure of peace. These, too, would be swept away in time, and another promontory would arise upon their site, as humanity piled itself higher and higher on the precious soil of London.

*apartments

1. Based on the last sentence (lines 11-14), which of the following can be reasonably inferred regarding the narrator's belief about the "flats" (line 8)?

(A) They are looked down on by the inhabitants of the older houses.
(B) Their gaudy décor reflects their owners' social pretensions.
(C) They fail to provide a sufficiently peaceful atmosphere for the older houses.
(D) They were constructed in a shoddy and haphazard fashion.
(E) Their luxurious trapping cannot protect them from eventual collapse.

6. Mr. Ralph Nickleby sat in his private office one morning, ready dressed to walk abroad. He wore a bottle-green spencer over a blue coat; a white waistcoat, grey mixture pantaloons, and Wellington boots drawn over them. The corner of a small-plaited shirt-frill struggled out, as if insisting to show itself, from between his chin and the top button of his spencer; and the latter garment was not made low enough to conceal a long gold watch-chain, composed of a series of plain rings, which had its beginning at the handle of a gold repeater in Mr. Nickleby's pocket, and its termination in two little keys: one belonging to the watch itself, and the other to some patent padlock. He wore a sprinkling of powder upon his head, as if to make himself look benevolent; but if that were his purpose, he would perhaps have done better to powder his countenance also, for there was something in its very wrinkles, and in his cold restless eye, which seemed to tell of cunning that would announce itself in spite of him. However this might be, there he was; and as he was all alone, neither the powder, nor the wrinkles, nor the eyes, had the smallest effect, good or bad, upon anybody just then, and are consequently no business of ours just now.

1. In lines 14-20, Mr. Nickleby is characterized as

(A) slyly charming
(B) mildly reclusive
(C) vaguely sinister
(D) thoroughly menacing
(E) coolly indifferent

2. The narrator indicates that Mr. Nickleby's attempt to make himself appear "benevolent" (line 16) was

(A) haphazard
(B) fruitless
(C) determined
(D) thorough
(E) uninentional

7. We could deny our winters, refuse to cut
Our hands mining the sharp ores of grief
Whenever the cold comes, we could follow

the arrowheads of geese shafting south
to an azure place where whales sing offshore
and otters frolic in the wanton surf.

We could grow soft as children in the arms
of leisure, but we might never learn in time
how to stoke the cold fire of the will

in that winter we cannot refuse, when we must glean
from the icy fields the last scattered grains
we once disdained, with only the luminous pallor

of the moon scarfed in clouds to light our way,
rising above the outstretched arms of the trees
in its long slow journey through the night.

1. The fourth stanza suggests that the "winter" is

(A) inevitable
(B) revelatory
(C) exquisite
(D) intoxicating
(E) exhilarating

8. An embankment ten or fifteen feet high guards both banks of the Mississippi all the way down that lower end of the river, and this embankment is set back from the edge of the shore from ten to perhaps a hundred feet, according to circumstances; say thirty or forty feet, as a general thing. Fill that whole region with an impenetrable gloom of smoke from a hundred miles of burning bagasse* piles, when the river is over the banks, and turn a steamboat loose along there at midnight and see how she will feel. And see how you will feel, too! You find yourself away out in the midst of a vague dim sea that is shoreless, that fades out and loses itself in the murky distances; for you cannot discern the thin rib of embankment, and you are always imagining you see a straggling tree when you don't. The plantations themselves are transformed by the smoke, and look like a part of the sea. All through your watch you are tortured with the exquisite misery of uncertainty. You hope you are keeping in the river, but you do not know. All that you are sure about is that you are likely to be within six feet of the bank and destruction, when you think you are a good half-mile from shore. And you are sure, also, that if you chance suddenly to fetch up against the embankment and topple your chimneys overboard, you will have the small comfort of knowing that it is about what you were expecting to do.

*Sugar-cane residue, used as fuel

1. In lines 11-27, the speaker suggests that "you will feel"

(A) newly appreciative of life on the water
(B) refreshed by the briskness of the fresh air
(C) disoriented and distrustful of your own perceptions
(D) humbled by the immensity of the river
(E) capable of grasping previously unthinkable situations

2. What is the best paraphrase of the phrase "if you chance suddenly to fetch up against the embankment" in lines 23-24?

(A) if you are lucky enough to retrieve something from the embankment
(B) if you are eager to arrive at the embankment
(C) if you risk heading toward the embankment
(D) if perhaps you collide with the embankment
(E) if you consider yourself fortunate to glimpse the embankment

9. With what deep murmurs through time's silent stealth
Doth thy transparent, cool, and wat'ry wealth
Here flowing fall,
And chide, and call,
As if his liquid, loose retinue stay'd
Ling'ring, and were of this steep place afraid;
The common pass
Where, clear as glass,
All must descend
Not to an end,
But quicken'd by this deep and rocky grave,
Rise to a longer course more bright and brave.

Dear stream! dear bank, where often I
Have sate and pleas'd my pensive eye,
Why, since each drop of thy quick store
Runs thither whence it flow'd before,
Should poor souls fear a shade or night,
Who came, sure, from a sea of light?
Or since those drops are all sent back
So sure to thee, that none doth lack,
Why should frail flesh doubt any more
That what God takes, he'll not restore?

O useful element and clear!
My sacred wash and cleanser here,
My first consigner unto those
Fountains of life where the Lamb goes!
What sublime truths and wholesome themes
Lodge in thy mystical deep streams!
Such as dull man can never find
Unless that Spirit lead his mind
Which first upon thy face did move,
And hatch'd all with his quick'ning love.
As this loud brook's incessant fall
In streaming rings restagnates all,
Which reach by course the bank, and then
Are no more seen, just so pass men.
O my invisible estate,
My glorious liberty, still late!
Thou art the channel my soul seeks,
Not this with cataracts and creeks.

1. In line 23, the "element" refers to both

(A) night and air
(B) water and purification
(C) freedom and regeneration
(D) flesh and spirit
(E) light and truth

2. In lines 33-36, the "brook's" movement is characterized as

(A) frantic
(B) tranquil
(C) meandering
(D) perpetual
(E) torpid

3. In line 38, the use of the phrase "still late" indicates that the narrator

(A) is concerned that time is running out
(B) perceives the brook as a source of ultimate freedom
(C) has grown tired of listening to the brook
(D) no longer wishes to be cleansed by the brook
(E) has not yet achieved salvation

10. From the oval-shaped flower-bed there rose perhaps a hundred stalks spreading into heart-shaped or tongue-shaped leaves half way up and unfurling at the tip red or blue or yellow petals marked with spots of colour raised upon the surface; and from the red, blue or yellow gloom of the throat emerged a straight bar, rough with gold dust and slightly clubbed at the end. The petals were voluminous enough to be stirred by the summer breeze, and when they moved, the red, blue and yellow lights passed one over the other, staining an inch of the brown earth beneath with a spot of the most intricate colour. The light fell either upon the smooth, grey back of a pebble, or, the shell of a snail with its brown, circular veins, or falling into a raindrop, it expanded with such intensity of red, blue and yellow the thin walls of water that one expected them to burst and disappear. Instead, the drop was left in a second silver grey once more, and the light now settled upon the flesh of a leaf, revealing the branching thread of fibre beneath the surface, and again it moved on and spread its illumination in the vast green spaces beneath the dome of the heart-shaped and tongue-shaped leaves. Then the breeze stirred rather more briskly overhead and the colour was flashed into the air above, into the eyes of the men and women who walk in Kew Gardens in July.

The figures of these men and women straggled past the flower-bed with a curiously irregular movement not unlike that of the white and blue butterflies who crossed the turf in zig-zag flights from bed to bed. The man was about six inches in front of the woman, strolling carelessly, while she bore on with greater purpose, only turning her head now and then to see that the children were not too far behind. The man kept this distance in front of the woman purposely, though perhaps unconsciously, for he wished to go on with his thoughts.

"Fifteen years ago I came here with Lily," he thought. "We sat somewhere over there by a lake and I begged her to marry me all through the hot afternoon. How the dragonfly kept circling round us: how clearly I see the dragonfly and her shoe with the square silver buckle at the toe. All the time I spoke I saw her shoe and when it moved impatiently I knew without looking up what she was going to say: the whole of her seemed to be in her shoe. And my love, my desire, were in the dragonfly; for some reason I thought that if it settled there, on that leaf, the broad one with the red flower in the middle of it, if the dragonfly settled on the leaf she would say 'Yes' at once. But the dragonfly went round and round: it never settled anywhere, of course not, happily not, or I shouldn't be walking here with Eleanor and the children."

1. In the first paragraph, the narrator discusses all of the following aspects of the light EXCEPT

(A) Its effect on different objects
(B) The various colors it generates
(C) Its continual movement
(D) Its warmth
(E) Its brilliance

2. In the second paragraph (lines 28-38), the narrator draws a distinction between

(A) aimless and deliberate movement
(B) reluctant and eager action
(C) solitude and social interaction
(D) equivocation and decisiveness
(E) childish fantasy and adult reality

3. Based on the third paragraph (lines 39-55), it can be reasonably inferred that Lily

(A) avoided providing a direct response
(B) was enthralled by the dragonfly
(C) declined the man's proposal
(D) had a restless and irritable personality
(E) based her response on the dragonfly's movements

Explanations: Literal Comprehension

1.1 E

In lines 1-9, the narrator portrays Mr. Pirzada as someone who is well dressed (*impeccably suited and scarved, with a silk tie knotted at his collar*) and not easily disturbed either physically or mentally (he *maintained an efficient posture* and had ears that were *insulated by tufts of graying hair that seemed to block out the unpleasant traffic of life*). In other words, he is described as being both elegant and composed.

1.2 B

Make sure you read the entire sentence in which each of the phrases referenced appears. In line 3, the narrator states that Mr. Pirzada arrived in his "ensembles" *each evening*, and in lines 15-16, the black fez is mentioned in context of the fact that the narrator *was never to see him* without it. Those two statements indicate that Mr. Pirzada was always dressed the same way. In other words, they emphasize the "consistency of [his] appearance." There is nothing to indicate that the narrator found his clothing eccentric or peculiar, eliminating (A) and (D), and (C) and (E) are entirely unsupported by the passage.

2.1 B

Fragrancy is another word for *odor*, and logically, a person who receives roses will smell them. In that context, the word *feasted* (ate abundantly) cannot be taken literally; rather, it refers to the act of "sniffing [an] odor deeply." (B) is thus correct.

2.2 C

Remember that this is an EXCEPT question, so the correct answer is the option that is NOT mentioned in the poem. In line 5, the speaker refers to sight (*I saw the sweetest flower*). In lines 9 and 12, the speaker alludes to taste (*I feasted on its fragrancy; My sense with their deliciousness was spelld*). Note that although these lines do not refer to literal taste, these answers can be eliminated because the question asks which senses are "evoked" (called up, suggested). In line 13, the speaker mentions *soft voices*, indicating hearing. In line 9, the reference to *fragrancy* evokes smell. Only touch is not mentioned, either directly or indirectly, so (C) is correct.

3.1 E

Although the question asks about the passage as a whole, the first sentence provides sufficient information to answer it. The reader is told that Samuel Michael *had never been a talkative man* (taciturn = using few words) and that he had *calm, steady habits* (unflappable = calm, not easily flustered). This characterization is confirmed in the last sentence, which contrasts Samuel's habit of sitting quietly in his rocker while his wife banged pots and pans. (A), (B), and (C) do not fit this description at all, but don't get fooled by (D): although line 6 describes Samuel as *with set and exacting ways*, the passage does not imply that he behaved harshly, or that he was demanding of others. (E) is thus correct.

4.1 A

What is the focus of lines 1-5? *The sky, the fields, the whited air, hills, woods, river*, etc. All things associated with the outdoors ("exterior"). What is the focus of lines 6-9? *The housemates sit[ting] around the radiant fireplace*, very clearly indoors ("interior"). That corresponds directly to (A).

4.2 C

Although you are given line 10 as a reference, the answer is located later on in the stanza. In addition, note that you do not need to know what masonry (building, construction) is to answer the question. The north wind's handiwork is described as *fierce, speeding, wild, so fanciful, so savage, nought cares he/For number or proportion*. Essentially the image is that of an immensely powerful and unrestrained (i.e., "brute") force of nature, a description that corresponds to (C). None of the other answers is supported by the specific language in the passage.

5.1 E

What do we know about the "flats" mentioned in line 8? They have *cavernous entrance halls, full of concierges and palms*. In other words, they're pretty high class. What do we learn from the last sentence? That everything will eventually be swept away and replaced in time. The logical implication is that the flats will not be protected by their "luxuries," an idea that corresponds directly to (E). All the other answers could be true, but there is nothing in the passage to directly support them.

6.1 C

Make sure you read the full line reference provided. In particular, the semicolon followed by the word *but* signals the presence of important information. Indeed, the key information follows: Mr. Nickleby is described as having a *cold restless eye, which seemed to tell of cunning that would announce itself in spite of him*. The overall impression is of someone who is "vaguely sinister," making the answer (C). Don't get fooled by (D): although Mr. Nickleby may appear "menacing," the point is that the impression is indirect and only hinted at. The word "thoroughly" is too strong and not supported by the passage. The opposite is true for (A): Mr. Nickleby may appear "sly," but the narrator does not directly suggest that he is "charming."

6.2 B

The narrator indicates that Mr. Nickleby's efforts to seem benevolent failed—his cunning *announce[s] itself in spite of him*. Saying that an attempt was "fruitless" is another way of saying that it was not successful.

7.1 A

In line 10, the winter is described as something *we cannot refuse*. In other words, it is "inevitable." Don't get distracted by the imagery in the following stanzas; the question asks about the fourth stanza only.

8.1 C

Lines 11-20 emphasize the sense of overwhelming uncertainty and perceptual distortion one experiences on the river. Phrases such as *vague dim sea* (line 12), *murky distances* (lines 13-14), and *you are always imagining you see a straggling tree when you don't* (lines 15-16) emphasize this sense of confusion and unreality, and correspond directly to (C).

8.2 D

The primary challenge in this question is that the words *chance* (verb) and *fetch up against* are not used in their normal ways—that is, *chance* is used as a verb, and *fetch* does not mean "retrieve" (as (A) incorrectly implies). The meaning of the phrase in question is suggested by the word *destruction* (line 22) in the previous sentence and the phrase *topple your chimneys overboard* (line 25) in the following sentence. What would cause the boat's destruction and cause its chimney to fall overboard? Logically, that would happen if the boat (captained by "you") crashed into, or "collide[d]" with it. The only answer to convey this meaning is (D).

9.1 B

If you read the poem from the beginning and are able to generally follow it, then you can probably infer that the "element" refers to water—the overall topic of the poem. If you start reading at line 23, you must back up to the beginning of the previous stanza, in which the speaker addresses the stream (*Dear stream! dear bank, where often I/Have sate and pleas'd my pensive eye*). The third stanza, where the line referenced appears, continues that monologue. You could also make an educated guess based on the phrase *My sacred wash and cleanser here* (line 24), which provides the second half of the answer: cleanser = purification. Note, however, that if you can identify that the "element" refers to water, then (B) must be the answer by default.

9.2 D

The phrase *incessant* (unending) *fall* indicates that the brook never stops moving. Something that occurs perpetually is something that occurs without end, so (D) is correct. "Frantic" (hysterical), "tranquil" (very calm), "meandering" (wandering), and "torpid" (sluggish) all do not fit. Note that you do not need to worry about the definition of "torpid" as long as you can identify the correct answer.

9.3 E

An important clue to the meaning of "still late" appears in the following line (39), when the speaker announces that *Thou art the channel my soul seeks*—essentially, this line serves to clarify/expand on the previous statement. If the speaker is still seeking the desired channel, then it can only be because they have not yet achieved their goal, i.e., salvation. That corresponds to (E). Be careful with (B): the brook, unlike the true channel being sought (God), has *cataracts and creeks* and is NOT the "ultimate source of freedom."

10.1 D

This is an "all of the following EXCEPT" question, so the correct answer will be the option that does NOT appear in the passage. Throughout the first paragraph, the narrator describes the movement of the light and its effects on various objects (pebble, snail, leaf), eliminating (A) and (C). Lines 4-18 describe the colors the light produces, eliminating (B). (E) can be eliminated as well because the statement that the light *expanded with such intensity of red, blue and yellow the thin walls of water* conveys the idea of brilliance. Only warmth is not mentioned anywhere in the paragraph, making the answer (D).

10.2 A

Lines 28-33 describe people *with curiously irregular movement…who crossed the turf in zig-zag flights* and a man who *[strolls] carelessly*, whereas lines 33-36 characterize the woman as *bor[ing] on with greater purpose, only turning her head now and then to see that the children were not too far behind*. Irregular and careless = aimless; with greater purpose = deliberate. That makes the answer (A).

10.3 C

In the third paragraph, the man describes his attempt to propose to Lily, explaining how her restlessness and impatience mirrored that of the dragonfly—the implication is that he was unable to persuade her to say yes. In addition, the statement that *[the dragonfly] never settled anywhere, of course not…or I shouldn't be walking here with Eleanor and the children* indicates that he married Eleanor after Lily "declined [his] proposal."

Chapter Five

Reading for Function

"Function" questions ask you to determine not what a particular section of text is literally saying but rather what **rhetorical purpose** it serves within the larger passage (e.g., emphasize, define, introduce). These questions have traditionally been only a minor part of the AP Literature test; however, the 2020 course redesign turned them into a much more prominent feature of the exam. As a result, you can expect to encounter at least one question of this sort accompanying most reading passages.

Function questions can target a wide range of textual features:

- Individual words
- Rhetorical devices and images
- Sentences
- Paragraphs or multiple paragraphs
- Full passages (unlikely but possible)

They can be phrased in the following ways:

- The main purpose of the repetition in lines x-y is to...
- The function of the passive voice in line x is to...
- In relation to the first two paragraphs, the final paragraph serves primarily to...
- Which of the following best conveys the effect of the sentences in lines x-y?

Note that while some questions are phrased in terms of "purpose" or "function" whereas others are phrased in terms of "effect," there is no meaningful difference between them, and they can be approached in exactly the same way.

Note also that while function questions may ask about specific rhetorical devices, sometimes in ways that may seem confusing (e.g., "What is the main effect of the repetition of positive adjectives in line 51?"), in most cases you do not need to worry about the specific devices or technical terms themselves. Provided that you have a solid grasp of what is being literally conveyed in the relevant section, you should generally be able to determine the answer to these questions without too much difficulty. That said, in some cases rhetorical terms may serve as a shortcut to the answer (more about that in the following chapter).

Function questions fall into two main groups:

1) Those that can be answered only by looking at the specific wording in the lines cited in the question. In such cases, the lines will typically contain punctuation, phrasing, or an important transition that points to a particular answer.

2) Those that cannot be obtained by looking at the lines cited in the question, but that instead depend on contextual information located either before or after.

To reiterate: line references on their own simply tell you where the relevant information is located—they do not necessarily tell you the relationship of those lines to anything else in the passage. **The information you need to determine the answer may appear either before the line(s) referenced in the question or, less frequently, after**.

While "effect" questions can generally be answered based on the lines themselves, for other question types there is no fixed formula. If you read the lines in question closely, understand them, and still have no idea how to choose among multiple answers, that's a sign that you might not be looking in the right place. Go back to the passage and read from a sentence or two above to a sentence or two below. **If you are asked about an individual word or phrase, always make sure to read the entire sentence in which it appears.**

Remember also that **if the lines cited in the question are relatively close to the beginning of a paragraph, you should back up and begin reading from there**—first sentences will nearly always introduce the focus of a paragraph, making it easier for you to understand the role of a particular word or phrase within it. When you are working with poetry, be aware that you may need to back up several stanzas or, if the poem is relatively short, all the way to the beginning. Information in the first line or two may provide crucial context.

Understanding "Function" Answer Choices

The main difficulty posed by function questions is that unlike literal comprehesion questions, their answers do not merely rephrase the content of the passage. Rather, they recast it in the more general language of rhetorical purpose—language that may not always have a clear relationship to the wording of the text. When test-takers approach these questions in terms of what the passage is saying, they are inevitably surprised to discover that the answers bear little resemblance to the text's literal meaning and are unsure of how to proceed.

This confusion is based on a misunderstanding of what function questions are about. In reality, they test not only the ability to grasp the literal sense of a given word, phrase, etc., but also to move beyond it into a more abstact understanding of its role within the text or its relationship to another part of the passage.

While answers to function questions are based on the specific wording in the passage, they are not stated directly in the passage. Typically, each choice will be begin with a function word (e.g., "illustrate," "call into question," "define"), followed by a reference to the relevant aspect of the passage (e.g., "the excitement mentioned in the previous sentence"). Less frequently, the function word will appear in the question itself, and the answers will simply refer to what is being emphasized, illustrated, etc.

Possible "Function" Answers

Positive	Negative	Neutral
Support Assert Illustrate Provide an example Provide evidence Exemplify Bolster Substantiate Advance (a claim) Affirm Defend Claim Prove* **Praise** Celebrate **Acknowledge** Recognize **Emphasize** Highlight Call attention to Dramatize Reinforce Reiterate Stress Underscore **Explain** Account for Qualify Clarify Articulate Specify Define Justify **Promote** Encourage Advocate Persuade **Engage** Draw in	**Refute** Counter Criticize Challenge Discredit* Dismiss Disparage Decry Contradict Deny Imply skepticism Debate Dispel Limit Question Rebuff Rebut Undermine Discredit Attack* Condemn* Disprove* **Warn** Raise concern **Make fun of** Satirize Mock Scoff at Jeer at* **Exaggerate** **Downplay** Minimize* Trivialize* **Lament** Bemoan **Concede**	**Describe** Discuss Present Characterize Portray Depict Represent Evoke Trace Show **Indicate** Identify Offer Point out Provide **Suggest** Imply **Introduce** **Shift** Change Digress* **Restate** Summarize Paraphrase **Hypothesize** Speculate **Analyze** Consider Develop Examine Explore Explicate Meditate Ponder Reflect on **Attribute** Cite Allude

*Indicates an answer that is likely to be incorrect.

For a glossary of selected terms, please see p. 94.

Because literature passages are so varied, it is difficult to make generalizations about the wording of correct vs. incorrect answer choices; however, there are some broad patterns.

First, literature passage are, well, literary. **They are not arguments and, as a result, you should be careful with answers involving arguing, claiming, (dis)proving, discrediting, etc.**

Second, correct answers must be consistent with the scope of the passage. If the poet or author is not making sweeping statements about human nature or eternal truths, the correct answer will not do so either. **As a result, choices with overly extreme language, e.g., "always," "never," "thoroughly impossible," should be treated with caution.**

Third, **certain rhetorical strategies typically correspond to specific rhetorical functions:** the purpose of repetition, for example, is to emphasize. So if a question asks about a section of the passage involving this technique, answer choices that involve emphasizing, reinforcing, highlighting, or underscoring typically merit careful consideration. Likewise, quotation marks frequently indicate that a word or phrase is not intended to be taken literally. This is a technique frequently used to convey irony and mockery, and to call appearances into question.

Playing Positive and Negative with Function Questions

One of the simplest ways to approach function questions and eliminate answer choices quickly is to play positive/negative. Positive passages (or sections of passages) are more likely to have positive answers, whereas negative passages are more likely to have negative answers. You should however, **keep in mind that correct answers may contain language more neutral than that used in the passage**. And obviously, this strategy is of limited use if a question dealing with a clearly positive section of a passage has no negative answers or vice versa. Nevertheless, it can be a useful tool for narrowing down your options. For example:

He admired each district along his familiar route to the office: The bungalows and shrubs and winding irregular drive ways of Floral Heights. The one-story shops on Smith Street, a glare of plate-glass and new yellow brick; groceries and laundries and drug-stores to supply the more immediate needs of East Side housewives. The market gardens in Dutch Hollow, their shanties patched with corrugated iron and stolen doors. Billboards with crimson goddesses nine feet tall advertising cinema films, pipe tobacco, and talcum powder. The old "mansions" along Ninth Street, S.E., like aged dandies in filthy linen; wooden castles turned into boarding-houses, with muddy walks and rusty hedges, jostled by fast-intruding garages, cheap apartment-houses, and fruit-stands conducted by bland, sleek Athenians. Across the belt of railroad-tracks, factories with high-perched water-tanks and tall stacks-factories producing condensed milk, paper boxes, lighting-fixtures, motor cars. Then the business center, the thickening darting traffic, the crammed trolleys unloading, and high doorways of marble and polished granite.

1. Which of the following statements best conveys the effect of the sentences in lines 7-15 ("The market ...Athenians").

(A) The frank tone suggests the narrator's sympathy for the residents of Floral Heights.
(B) The imagery conveys the derelict state of of certains sections of Floral Heights.
(C) The florid diction reveals the destructive effects of the factories on Floral Heights
(D) The adjectives indicate the narrator's affection for Floral Heights.
(E) The parallel structure reinforces the monotony of Floral Heights.

Explanation: At first glance, the complexity of the answer choices can make this question seem overwhelming. In reality, however, it is relatively manageable—provided that you start with the passage itself.

What is described in lines 7-15? Essentially, the narrator focuses on a not-so-nice part of Floral Heights: it contains *shanties* (shacks) with *stolen doors*, run-down structures with *muddy walks and rusty hedges*, *cheap apartment houses*, etc. This is clearly a negative description, so it can very reasonably be assumed that the correct answer will be either negative or neutral. (A) and (D) are both positive, as indicated by the words "sympathy" and "affection," so these answers can be eliminated right away, leaving you additional time to focus on more plausible candidates.

To decide among the remaining options, you can simplify even further. Don't worry about the references to the various rhetorical strategies, e.g., parallel structure, adjectives, diction—they essentially serve to make the answers appear more complicated than they actually are. (Note that answers containing highly technical or exotic-sounding terms are, if anything, more likely to be wrong.) What really counts is the information that comes after.

As a case in point, consider our general summary of lines 7-15: part of Floral Heights is run down. Run down = derelict state. That corresponds directly to (B).

(C) does not work because the text does not make an explicit link between the factories and the condition of the neighborhoods described; the two descriptions are merely placed close to one another in the text. (E) is directly contradicted by the text, which emphasizes the variety of the neighborhoods in Floral Heights.

Transitions, Punctuation, and Key Words and Phrases

For obvious reasons, questions accompanying AP English Literature passages tend to focus on the most significant parts of each text—that is, ones where there is particularly strong use of imagery or descriptive language; where ideas are introduced or contradicted; where there are shifts in tone or focus/point of view; or where key aspects of characters' relationships or emotions are revealed.

Important moments are often indicated through the use of specific words and phrases (particularly transitions) as well as certain kinds of punctuation. As mentioned earlier, these elements often correlate in turn with particular rhetorical functions.

The chart on the next page lists some of the more common key words, phrases, rhetorical figures, and types of punctuation, along with the functions to which they correspond.

Functions of Key Words, Punctuation, and Rhetorical Figures

<table>
<tr><th colspan="2">Continuers</th><th>Contradictors</th></tr>
<tr>
<td>Support, Illustrate
Also
And
As well as
Furthermore
In addition
Moreover

Indicate Sequence of Events
First/In the first place
Next
Then
Formerly
Previously
Subsequently
Finally

Explain, Clarify, Define
Effectively
Essentially
In other words
That is (to say)
Colon
Dash
Parentheses

Cause and Effect
As a result
As such
Because
Consequently
For
Hence
So
Therefore
Thus
Thereby</td>
<td>Compare
(Just) as
Much as/like
More/Less...than

Hypothesize, Speculate
If
May
Maybe
Might
Could
Perhaps
Would

Emphasize, Highlight,
Call Attention to, Underscore
In fact
Indeed
Italics
Capital letters
Exclamation point
Repetition (of a word, phrase)
Hyperbole (exaggeration)

Indicate Importance
Important
Significant
Essential
Fundamental
Central
Key</td>
<td>Refute, Criticize, Challenge, Dispute, Contrast
(Al)though
But
Despite
However
In contrast
In spite of
Instead
Meanwhile
Nevertheless
On the contrary
On one hand/On the other hand
Otherwise
Still
Regardless
Rather than
Whereas
While
Yet

Question, Imply Skepticism
Question mark
Quotation marks

Qualify
Dashes
Parentheses</td>
</tr>
</table>

Now let's look at some examples, starting with the passage we worked with earlier.

#1: Purpose of Diction

He admired each district along his familiar route to the office: The bungalows and shrubs and winding irregular drive ways of Floral Heights. The one-story shops on Smith Street, a glare of plate-glass and new yellow brick; groceries and laundries and drug-stores to supply the more immediate needs of East Side housewives. The market gardens in Dutch Hollow, their shanties patched with corrugated iron and stolen doors. Billboards with crimson goddesses nine feet tall advertising cinema films, pipe tobacco, and talcum powder. The old "mansions" along Ninth Street, S.E., like aged dandies in filthy linen; wooden castles turned into boarding-houses, with muddy walks and rusty hedges, jostled by fast-intruding garages, cheap apartment-houses, and fruit-stands conducted by bland, sleek Athenians. Across the belt of railroad-tracks, factories with high-perched water-tanks and tall stacks-factories producing condensed milk, paper boxes, lighting-fixtures, motor cars. Then the business center, the thickening darting traffic, the crammed trolleys unloading, and high doorways of marble and polished granite.

1. The main purpose of the adjectives "filthy" (line 12) "muddy," and "rusty" (line 13) is primarily to

(A) call attention to the general decrepitude of Floral Heights
(B) explain how the "mansions" deteriorated into their present state
(C) suggest that Floral Heights is in a persistent state of decline
(D) emphasize the contrast between the structures' former grandeur and their present state
(E) introduce humor into an otherwise morose description

Explanation: The first thing to notice about this question is that "filthy," "muddy," and "rusty" are all extremely negative words, so presumably the answer will reflect that fact. There is nothing in the passage to suggest that these words are not meant literally, or that they are intended to be funny, so (E) can be eliminated right away.

Next, the description in question occurs in the middle of the passage and concerns only a particular section of Floral Heights (*Ninth Street, S.E.*). This is important because it defines the **scope** of the answer: the correct response cannot involve the town/city as a whole. Both (A) and (C) involve generalizations about Floral Heights and are therefore incorrect. Furthermore, these answers are contradicted by information at both the beginning and the end of the passage indicating that Floral Heights is a perfectly nice place: it has *bungalows and shrubs and winding irregular drive ways* (lines 2-3); shops with *plate-glass and new yellow brick* (lines 4-5); and a business center with *high doorways of marble and polished granite* (lines 21-22).

(B) is incorrect because the adjectives in question do nothing to "explain" why the structures in question are in such poor condition; they merely describe the structures.

That leaves (D), which is consistent with lines 12-13: this section highlights the contrast between the grand intentions behind these structures (*mansions, castles*) and the ramshackle state they have fallen into (they are now *boarding-houses* and *cheap apartment-houses*). Note that to make full sense out of the lines referenced in the question, you must back up to the beginning of the sentence in line 11 and read all the way through to its end in line 16.

#2: Purpose of Punctuation

He admired each district along his familiar route to the office: The bungalows and shrubs and winding irregular drive ways of Floral Heights. The one-story shops on Smith Street, a glare of plate-glass and new yellow brick; groceries and laundries and drug-stores to supply the more immediate needs of East Side housewives. The market gardens in Dutch Hollow, their shanties patched with corrugated iron and stolen doors. Billboards with crimson goddesses nine feet tall advertising cinema films, pipe tobacco, and talcum powder. The old "mansions" along Ninth Street, S.E., like aged dandies in filthy linen; wooden castles turned into boarding-houses, with muddy walks and rusty hedges, jostled by fast-intruding garages, cheap apartment-houses, and fruit-stands conducted by bland, sleek Athenians. Across the belt of railroad-tracks, factories with high-perched water-tanks and tall stacks-factories producing condensed milk, paper boxes, lighting-fixtures, motor cars. Then the business center, the thickening darting traffic, the crammed trolleys unloading, and high doorways of marble and polished granite.

1. The quotation marks around the word "mansions" in line 11 primarily serve to

(A) suggest that Floral Heights is incapable of returning to its former glory
(B) criticize the residents of Floral Heights for their moral laxity
(C) trace the decline of a section of Floral Heights
(D) suggest that the residents of Floral Heights are indifferent to the poor condition of their city
(E) call attention to a contrast between appearance and reality

Explanation: Don't get fooled by the seeming complexity of the answer choices; in reality, the question is fairly straightforward. What does the word "mansion" imply? A structure that's grand, elegant, rich… Not something filthy, or rusty, or cheap. So why use quotation marks? To draw attention to the fact that the buildings being described do not at all resemble the typical conception of a mansion. In other words, they "call attention to a contrast between appearance and reality." That makes (E) correct. It is not even necessary to consider the other answers.

#3: Purpose of a Rhetorical Strategy

I am a little world made cunningly
Of elements, and an angelic spright,
But black sin hath betrayed to endless night
My worlds both parts, and oh! both parts must die.
You, which beyond that heaven which was most high
Have found new spheres and of new lands can write,
Pour new seas in mine eyes, that so I might
Drown my world with my weeping earnestly,
Or wash it, if it must be drowned no more:
But oh! it must be burnt; alas the fire
Of lust and envy burnt it heretofore,
And made it fouler; Let their flames retire,
And burn me, O Lord, with a fiery zeal
Of thee and thy house, which doth in eating heal.

1. The repetition of the word "new" in lines 6-7 primarily serves to

(A) convey the speaker's disillusionment with religion
(B) reinforce the speaker's desire for regeneration
(C) celebrate the speaker's angelic qualities
(D) call attention to a longing for artistic expression
(E) call the speaker's contradictory nature into question

Explanation: Although lines 6-7 provide the essential information, it's still helpful to consider the preceding sentence. There, the speaker sets up the essential drama of the poem: he is made up of two conflicting parts—good and bad—and must be destroyed because the bad outweighs the good. In lines 5-8, he describes how that destruction might come about. The phrase *beyond that heaven which was most high* indicates that the speaker is addressing God and asking him to destroy his world so that he can achieve a state of rebirth, free from the sin weighing him down. Given that, the repeated use of the word *new* serves to emphasize (i.e., "reinforce") his desire to achieve a state of regeneration. That makes (B) correct.

#4: Purpose of a Paragraph

One evening of late summer, before the nineteenth century had reached one-third of its span, a young man and woman, the latter carrying a child, were approaching the large village of Weydon-Priors, in Upper Wessex, on foot. They were plainly but not ill clad, though the thick hoar of dust which had accumulated on their shoes and garments from an obviously long journey lent a disadvantageous shabbiness to their appearance just now.

The man was of fine figure, swarthy, and stern in aspect; and he showed in profile a facial angle so slightly inclined as to be almost perpendicular. He wore a short jacket of brown corduroy, newer than the remainder of his suit, which was a fustian waistcoat with white horn buttons, breeches of the same, tanned leggings, and a straw hat overlaid with black glazed canvas. At his back he carried by a looped strap a rush basket, from which protruded at one end the crutch of a hay-knife, a wimble* for hay-bonds being also visible in the aperture. His measured, springless walk was the walk of the skilled countryman as distinct from the desultory shamble of the general labourer; while in the turn and plant of each foot there was, further, a dogged and cynical indifference personal to himself, showing its presence even in the regularly interchanging fustian folds, now in the left leg, now in the right, as he paced along.

What was really peculiar, however, in this couple's progress, and would have attracted the attention of any casual observer otherwise disposed to overlook them, was the perfect silence they preserved. They walked side by side in such a way as to suggest afar off the low, easy, confidential chat of people full of reciprocity; but on closer view it could be discerned that the man was reading, or pretending to read, a ballad sheet which he kept before his eyes with some difficulty by the hand that was passed through the basket strap. Whether this apparent cause were the real cause, or whether it were an assumed one to escape an intercourse that would have been irksome to him, nobody but himself could have said precisely; but his taciturnity was unbroken, and the woman enjoyed no society whatever from his presence. Virtually she walked the highway alone, save for the child she bore.

1. The final paragraph primarily serves to

   (A) describe a puzzling lack of interaction between two characters
   (B) depict a relationship characterized by confidentiality and mutual understanding
   (C) assert that the man remained focused on the ballad sheet in order to avoid an uncomfortable discussion
   (D) document the dissolution of a previously close relationship
   (E) justify the man's lack of interest in his traveling companion

*Marbleworker's brace for drilling

Explanation: When long line references appear, don't fall into the trap of rereading more than is absolutely necessary. Instead, try to identify the key places. Although your first instinct may be to reread the full paragraph, in reality the first sentence provides all the necessary information. What does it reveal? That the couple's relationship is *really peculiar* (i.e., "puzzling") because the man is completely ignoring his companion, even though she is right beside him. Completely ignoring = lack of interaction. That corresponds directly to (A).

While it is possible to answer some purpose-of-a-paragraph questions by focusing only on the paragraph in question, as in the example we just looked at, in certain cases the answer in fact may be located elswhere.

For example, consider this question:

One evening of late summer, before the nineteenth century had reached one-third of its span, a young man and woman, the latter carrying a child, were approaching the large village of Weydon-Priors, in Upper Wessex, on foot. They were plainly but not ill clad, though the thick hoar of dust which had accumulated on their shoes and garments from an obviously long journey lent a disadvantageous shabbiness to their appearance just now.

The man was of fine figure, swarthy, and stern in aspect; and he showed in profile a facial angle so slightly inclined as to be almost perpendicular. He wore a short jacket of brown corduroy, newer than the remainder of his suit, which was a fustian waistcoat with white horn buttons, breeches of the same, tanned leggings, and a straw hat overlaid with black glazed canvas. At his back he carried by a looped strap a rush basket, from which protruded at one end the crutch of a hay-knife, a wimble* for hay-bonds being also visible in the aperture. His measured, springless walk was the walk of the skilled countryman as distinct from the desultory shamble of the general labourer; while in the turn and plant of each foot there was, further, a dogged and cynical indifference personal to himself, showing its presence even in the regularly interchanging fustian folds, now in the left leg, now in the right, as he paced along.

What was really peculiar, however, in this couple's progress, and would have attracted the attention of any casual observer otherwise disposed to overlook them, was the perfect silence they preserved. They walked side by side in such a way as to suggest afar off the low, easy, confidential chat of people full of reciprocity; but on closer view it could be discerned that the man was reading, or pretending to read, a ballad sheet which he kept before his eyes with some difficulty by the hand that was passed through the basket strap. Whether this apparent cause were the real cause, or whether it were an assumed one to escape an intercourse that would have been irksome to him, nobody but himself could have s aid precisely; but his taciturnity was unbroken, and the woman enjoyed no society whatever from his presence. Virtually she walked the highway alone, save for the child she bore.

*Marbleworker's brace for drilling

1. In relation to the first paragraph, the second paragraph serves primarily to

(A) suggest that the man's clothing was poorly suited to his social station
(B) emphasize the eccentric nature of the man's appearance
(C) explain the importance of the couple's journey to Weydon-Priors
(D) illustrate the statement that the travelers were dressed plainly but not poorly
(E) convey to readers the historical context of the family's journey

Explanation: Pay no attention to the long second paragraph or the wordy answer choices. The answer is almost directly stated in the last sentence of the **first** paragraph: *They were plainly but not ill clad* (dressed)., i.e., "plainly but not poorly." The entire second paragraph, which focuses on the man's clothing, serves to support that statement. (D) is thus correct.

#5: Purpose of a Passage

Although questions asking about the purpose of an entire prose passage are unlikely to make up a significant portion of the exam, they do sometimes appear.

It came like a thunder-clap on us all, that the vessel which contained our fortune had been wrecked, and gone to the bottom with all its stores, together with several of the crew, and the unfortunate merchant himself. I was grieved for him; I was grieved for the overthrow of all our air-built castles: but, with the elasticity of youth, I soon recovered the shock.

Though riches had charms, poverty had no terrors for an inexperienced girl like me. Indeed, to say the truth, there was something exhilarating in the idea of being driven to straits, and thrown upon our own resources. I only wished papa, mamma, and Mary were all of the same mind as myself; and then, instead of lamenting past calamities we might all cheerfully set to work to remedy them; and the greater the difficulties, the harder our present privations, the greater should be our cheerfulness to endure the latter, and our vigour to contend against the former.

Mary did not lament, but she brooded continually over the misfortune, and sank into a state of dejection from which no effort of mine could rouse her. I could not possibly bring her to regard the matter on its bright side as I did: and indeed I was so fearful of being charged with childish frivolity, or stupid insensibility, that I carefully kept most of my bright ideas and cheering notions to myself; well knowing they could not be appreciated.

My mother thought only of consoling my father, and paying our debts and retrenching our expenditure by every available means; but my father was completely overwhelmed by the calamity: health, strength, and spirits sank beneath the blow, and he never wholly recovered them. In vain my mother strove to cheer him, by appealing to his piety, to his courage, to his affection for herself and us. That very affection was his greatest torment: it was for our sakes he had so ardently longed to increase his fortune—it was our interest that had lent such brightness to his hopes, and that imparted such bitterness to his present distress. He now tormented himself with remorse at having neglected my mother's advice; which would at least have saved him from the additional burden of debt—he vainly reproached himself for having brought her from the dignity, the ease, the luxury of her former station to toil with him through the cares and toils of poverty. It was gall and wormwood to his soul to see that splendid, highly-accomplished woman, once so courted and admired, transformed into an active managing housewife, with hands and head continually occupied with household labours and household economy. The very willingness with which she performed these duties, the cheerfulness with which she bore her reverses, and the kindness which withheld her from imputing the smallest blame to him, were all perverted by this ingenious self-tormentor into further aggravations of his sufferings. And thus the mind preyed upon the body, and disordered the system of the nerves, and they in turn increased the troubles of the mind, till by action and reaction his health was seriously impaired; and not one of us could convince him that the aspect of our affairs was not half so gloomy, so utterly hopeless, as his morbid imagination represented it to be.

1. The primary purpose of the passage is to

(A) convey the narrator's fortitude in confronting a calamitious event
(B) assert the importance of maintaining one's equilibrium in the face of tragedy
(C) depict a family's varying reactions to a dramatic change in circumstances
(D) portray a dramatic conflict between members of a family faced with an unprecedented loss
(E) criticize the narrator's father for his recklessness and self-indulgence

Explanation: To reiterate, when you encounter a question based on a large amount of information, the most counterproductive approach is to attempt to reread everything—that will only waste time and, more likely than not, lead to confusion. Instead, start by focusing on the place where the general scenario of the passage is presented: the introduction, which in this case comprises roughly the first two paragraphs. Note that there is no fixed rule: you may be able to answer some questions based on only one paragraph, while in other cases you may need to consider three. If a purpose-of-a-passage question appears first, however, then you can assume that the necessary information will be located close to the beginning.

What does the narrator tell us in this section? That her father has abruptly lost his entire fortune, plunging her family into poverty. The key information occurs in the second paragraph, where the presence of major transitions (*though, indeed*) and extreme language (*only*) serve as signals to pay close attention. Indeed, the narrator's statement that she *only wished papa, mama, and Mary were of the same mind as myself; and then, instead of lamenting past calamaties, we might all cheerfully set to work to remedy them* essentially provides the answer, or at least narrows the options down to two. The fact that the other members of the narrator's family were not *of the same mind as [her]self* is another way of saying that they had "varying reactions" to her father's loss. (A), (B), and (E) are all inconsistent with this idea, eliminating those possiblities.

The phrase "dramatic conflict" in (D) is well, dramatic, suggesting that this answer is incorrect, whereas (C) is worded in a manner more consistent with a right answer. In addition, the second paragraph suggests nothing about an intense clash between the family members; it merely indicates that they had a tendency to wallow in their unhappiness. If you're not sure, though, the third paragraph indicates that the narrator *kept most of [her] bright ideas and cheering notions to [her]self* for fear of provoking a conflict with her sister (lines 27-29). That eliminates (D) and makes (C) correct.

Exercises: Reading for Function

1. Travelling northward from the township of Otis, the road leads for twenty or thirty miles towards Windsor, lengthwise upon that long broken spur of heights which the Green Mountains of Vermont send into Massachusetts. For nearly the whole of the distance, you have the continual sensation of being upon some terrace in the moon. The feeling of the plain or the valley is never yours; scarcely the feeling of the earth. Unless by a sudden precipitation of the road you find yourself plunging into some gorge, you pass on, and on, and on, upon the crests or slopes of pastoral mountains, while far below, mapped out in its beauty, the valley of the Housatonie lies endlessly along at your feet.

1. The primary purpose of lines 5-8 is to

(A) illustrate the beauty of the landscape
(B) emphasize the length of the journey
(C) explain some motivations for travel
(D) convey a sense of alienation
(E) establish an informal tone to amuse the reader

2. Love is not all: it is not meat nor drink
Nor slumber nor a roof against the rain;
Nor yet a floating spar to men that sink
And rise and sink and rise and sink again;
Love can not fill the thickened lung with breath,
Nor clean the blood, nor set the fractured bone;
Yet many a man is making friends with death
Even as I speak, for lack of love alone.
It well may be that in a difficult hour,
Pinned down by pain and moaning for release,
Or nagged by want past resolution's power,
I might be driven to sell your love for peace,
Or trade the memory of this night for food.
It well may be. I do not think I would.

1. Which of the following statements best conveys the effect of the sentences in lines 1-6 ("Love is . . . bone")?

(A) The active verbs emphasize the speaker's reverence for love.
(B) The lamenting tone reveals the speaker's sense of regret.
(C) The exaggerated language conveys the speaker's disdain for those carried away by love.
(D) The negative diction emphasizes the limits of love's power.
(E) The formal style creates a sense of detachment from the reader.

3. As I remember, Giffen's appeared at the beginning of the twenties, and I am sure I am not alone in associating its emergence with that change of mood within our profession—that change which came to push the polishing of silver to the position of central importance it still by and large maintains today. The shift was, I believe, like some many other major shifts around this period, a generational matter; it was during during these years that our generation of butlers 'came of age', and figures like Mr Marshall, in particular, played a crucial part in making silver-polishing so central.

1. The reference to Mr Marshall in line 10 primarily serves to

(A) discredit the results of an action
(B) defend an unpopular decision
(C) criticize a polemical individual
(D) highlight the consequences of an innovation
(E) draw attention to an influential figure

4. The grey fox, so called
actually the color of wet sand
here on the Cape, pads
daintily past the herb garden.

See, I murmur to her or him,
you still exist. I argued
with a park biologist
you hadn't died out here.

I've seen you eating wild
grapes near the dunes.
I watched your kits run
up pitch pines for safety.

Even with the coywolves
hunting you and the red
fox claiming your territory
you are at home where

you belong, stopping to
check out birdseed we
scattered on needles, left-
over cashews you gobble.

You move like the wind
through dead grasses snow
has not yet flattened and
vanish brush of tail last.

1. The third stanza (lines 9-12) primarily serves to

(A) bolster a rebuttal
(B) reflect on nature and engage the reader
(C) meditate on a fundamental need
(D) rectify a misunderstanding
(E) ponder the veracity of a belief

2. The primary purpose of the poem is to

(A) plead for a separation between the human and the natural worlds
(B) defend the right to observe wildlife in an unmediated way
(C) suggest that humans have much to learn from nature
(D) reflect on the resilience of a creature
(E) argue for the importance of preserving natural habitats

5. Karintha, at twelve, was a wild flash that told the other folks just what it was to live. At sunset, when there was no wind, and the pine-smoke from over by the sawmill hugged the earth, and you couldn't see more than a few feet in front, her sudden darting past you was a bit of vivid color, like a black bird that flashes in light. With the other children one could hear, some distance off, their feet flopping in the two-inch dust. Karintha's running was a whir. It had the sound of the red dust that sometimes makes a spiral in the road. At dusk, during the hush just after the sawmill had closed down, and before any of the women had started their supper-getting-ready songs, her voice, high-pitched, shrill, would put one's ears to itching. But no one ever thought to make her stop because of it.

1. The primary function of lines 9-11 ("Karintha's running . . . road") is to

(A) communicate the exhilaration of intense physical activity
(B) highlight the impulse to escape from the everday world
(C) emphasize the frenetic quality of a character's movement
(D) establish an informal tone and elicit the reader's interest
(E) reveal the narrator's admiration for a feat of athleticism

6. Love is not all: it is not meat nor drink
Nor slumber nor a roof against the rain;
Nor yet a floating spar to men that sink
And rise and sink and rise and sink again;
Love can not fill the thickened lung with breath,
Nor clean the blood, nor set the fractured bone;
Yet many a man is making friends with death
Even as I speak, for lack of love alone.
It well may be that in a difficult hour,
Pinned down by pain and moaning for release,
Or nagged by want past resolution's power,
I might be driven to sell your love for peace,
Or trade the memory of this night for food.
It well may be. I do not think I would.

1. One effect of the shift in line 7 is to

(A) reveal the speaker's fundamental hypocrisy about love
(B) argue that personal ideas about love should be accorded greater respect
(C) highlight the shortsightedness of an overly romantic perspective
(D) introduce the idea that individual conceptions of love can vary greatly
(E) imply that the intangible benefits of love outweigh its practical shortcomings

7. The train sped northward, under innumerable tunnels. It was only an hour's journey, but Mrs. Munt had to raise and lower the window again and again. She passed through the South Welwyn Tunnel, saw light for a moment, and entered the North Welwyn Tunnel, of tragic fame. She traversed the immense viaduct, whose arches span untroubled meadows and the dreamy flow of Tewin Water. She skirted the parks of politicians. At times the Great North Road accompanied her, more suggestive of infinity than any railway, awakening, after a nap of a hundred years, to such life as is conferred by the stench of motor-cars, and to such culture as is implied by the advertisements of antibilious pills*. To history, to tragedy, to the past, to the future, Mrs. Munt remained equally indifferent.

The station for Howards End was at Hilton, one of the large villages that are strung so frequently along the North Road, and that owe their size to the traffic of coaching and pre-coaching days. Being near London, it had not shared in the rural decay, and its long High Street had budded out right and left into residential estates. For about a mile a series of tiled and slated houses passed before Mrs. Munt's inattentive eyes, a series broken at one point by six Danish tumuli** that stood shoulder to shoulder along the highroad, tombs of soldiers. Beyond these tumuli, habitations thickened, and the train came to a standstill in a tangle that was almost a town.

The station, like the scenery struck an indeterminate note. Into which country will it lead, England or Suburbia? It was new, it had island platforms and a subway, and the superficial comfort exacted by business men. But it held hints of local life, personal intercourse, as even Mrs. Munt was to discover.

1. The primary function of the third paragraph (lines 30-36) is to

(A) allege that the quality of interpersonal relationships has diminished
(B) emphasize the tension between tradition and modernity
(C) reassure readers of the importance of social interaction
(D) convey the narrator's suspicion of modern forms of transportation
(E) lament the increasing homogenization of the landscape

*Pills to soothe an upset stomach

**Ancient hills or mounds

8. We could deny our winters, refuse to cut
Our hands mining the sharp ores of grief
Whenever the cold comes, we could follow

the arrowheads of geese shafting south
to an azure place where whales sing offshore
and otters frolic in the wanton surf.

We could grow soft as children in the arms
of leisure, but we might never learn in time
how to stoke the cold fire of the will

in that winter we cannot refuse, when we must glean
from the icy fields the last scattered grains
we once disdained, with only the luminous pallor

of the moon scarfed in clouds to light our way,
rising above the outstretched arms of the trees
in its long slow journey through the night.

1. The fourth and fifth stanzas (lines 10-15) primarily serve to

(A) indicate the speaker's regrets about a decision
(B) establish a personal tone and soothe the reader
(C) document a memorable scene from the speaker's past
(D) emphasize the devastating consequences of loneliness
(E) evoke a set of conditions requiring great fortitude

9. It stood upon a low hill, above the river—the river being the Thames at some forty miles from London. A long gabled front of red brick, with the complexion of which time and the weather had played all sorts of pictorial tricks, only, however, to improve and refine it, presented to the lawn its patches of ivy, its clustered chimneys, its windows smothered in creepers. The house had a name and a history; the old gentleman taking his tea would have been delighted to tell you these things: how it had been built under Edward the Sixth, had offered a night's hospitality to the great Elizabeth* (whose august person had extended itself upon a huge, magnificent and terribly angular bed which still formed the principal honour of the sleeping apartments), had been a good deal bruised and defaced in Cromwell's** wars, and then, under the Restoration, repaired and much enlarged; and how finally, after having been remodelled and disfigured in the eighteenth century, it had passed into the careful keeping of a shrewd American banker, who had bought it originally because (owing to circumstances too complicated to set forth) it was offered at a great bargain: bought it with much grumbling at its ugliness, its antiquity, its incommodity, and who now, at the end of twenty years, had become conscious of a real aesthetic passion for it, so that he knew all its points and would tell you just where to stand to see them in combination and just the hour when the shadows of its various protuberances—which fell so softly upon the warm, weary brickwork—were of the right measure.

1. The primary effect of the parenthetical statement in lines 12-16 ("whose . . . apartments") is to

(A) introduce a note of wryly humorous commentary
(B) emphasize the old gentleman's excessive pride in the house
(C) underscore the importance of maintaining accurate historical records
(D) defend the house's pedigree from potential detractors
(E) imply that the old gentleman has an exaggerated sense of his social rank

*Queen Elizabeth I (1533-1603)

** Seventeenth-century English general and politician

10. An embankment ten or fifteen feet high guards both banks of the Mississippi all the way down that lower end of the river, and this embankment is set back from the edge of the shore from ten to perhaps a hundred feet, according to circumstances; say thirty or forty feet, as a general thing. Fill that whole region with an impenetrable gloom of smoke from a hundred miles of burning bagasse piles, when the river is over the banks, and turn a steamboat loose along there at midnight and see how she will feel. And see how you will feel, too! You find yourself away out in the midst of a vague dim sea that is shoreless, that fades out and loses itself in the murky distances; for you cannot discern the thin rib of embankment, and you are always imagining you see a straggling tree when you don't. The plantations themselves are transformed by the smoke, and look like a part of the sea. All through your watch you are tortured with the exquisite misery of uncertainty. You hope you are keeping in the river, but you do not know. All that you are sure about is that you are likely to be within six feet of the bank and destruction, when you think you are a good half-mile from shore. And you are sure, also, that if you chance suddenly to fetch up against the embankment plantation one night, at such a time, and had to stay there a week. But there was no novelty about it; it had often been done before.

1. The primary function of lines 11-28 ("And see . . . to do") is to

(A) defend a viewpoint and qualify an assertion
(B) dramatize an experience and draw in the reader
(C) explicate a viewpoint and explore an alternative
(D) highlight the subjective nature of experience
(E) refute skeptics and defend a point of view

Explanations: Reading for Function

1.1 D

Lines 5-8 emphasize the profound sense of foreignness and disconnection one feels while driving through the Green Mountains. In fact, the writer insists on the otherworldly quality of the journey (*you have the continual sensation of being upon some terrace in the moon*). That corresponds to "a sense of alienation," making the answer (D). (B), (C), and (E) are all off-topic, but be careful with (A): the word *beauty* does appear in line 14, but the question asks only about lines 5-8.

2.1 D

Lines 1-6 are devoted to listing some of the things that love cannot do (feed or house people, save them from drowning, heal the sick...). In other words, they emphasize "the limits of love's power." How is this accomplished linguistically? Through the repeated use of negations (*not, nor*). That corresponds directly to (D).

3.1 E

The last sentence states that *Mr. Marshall, in particular, played a crucial role in making silver-polishing so central*. In other words, he was "an influential figure," making (E) correct. Playing process of elimination, the reference is clearly positive, whereas (A)-(C) all have negative components, and (D) does not fit because the focus of the last sentence is on Mr. Marshall and not on the consequences of the introduction of silver polish (i.e., "an innovation").

4.1 A

Although this question asks about the third stanza, it can only be answered in context of the second stanza. There the poem refers to an encounter with a park biologist in which the speaker *argued you* (the grey fox) *hadn't died out here*. The unstated implication is that the park biologist asserted that the grey fox had died—otherwise, the speaker would not have needed to refute. Given that information, the description of the fox and her kits' activities in lines 9-12 serves to support, i.e., "bolster," the speaker's "rebuttal." That makes the answer (A).

4.2 D

The poem focuses on the fact that the fox is a survivor—the speaker states that they "argued" to the park biologist that the fox is still alive (presumably because the park biologist claimed the contrary), then goes on to point out that the fox is still *at home where/you belong, stopping to/check out birdseed* despite being hunted by coywolves and having her territory "claimed" by the red fox (fourth stanza). None of the other options is directly supported by the passage.

5.1 C

Lines 9-11 state that *Karintha's running was a whir. It had the sound of the red dust that sometimes makes a spiral in the road.* In other words, the character's movement has a non-stop, whirlwind quality—i.e., it is "frenetic." The passage says nothing about how running made Karintha (or anyone else) feel, eliminating (A). The narrator gives no indication that Karintha wanted to "escape from the everyday world," eliminating (B). (D) does not fit because the tone in lines 9-11 is not particularly informal. (E) is incorrect because the description is relatively neutral—the narrator does not use the sort of strongly positive language that would indicate "admiration."

6.1 E

The question asks you to identify the effect of the shift in line 7, so start by determining what the poem is shifting *from*. Lines 1-6 focus on the many things that love cannot do, whereas the word *Yet* in line 7 signals that the speaker will be introducing an opposing idea. That statement that *many a man is making friends with death/Even as I speak, for lack of love alone* indicates that although love cannot accomplish many things (i.e., it has many "practical shortcomings"), it is nevertheless so important in a more abstract sense (i.e., it has "intangible benefits") that in some cases it is impossible to live without. That corresponds directly to (E). (A) is wildly off topic. For (B), don't get distracted by the word *I* in line 8—the focus here is not on the speaker's personal opinion, but rather on the ill effects other people suffer for lack of love. (C) does not fit because the speaker's goal is not to point out how love narrows people's vision, but rather how its absence can be destructive. (D) is overly broad and off-topic.

7.1 B

The passage as a whole is laced with indications that the world Mrs. Munt is traveling through is undergoing a shift. Her train, for example, moves alternately and uneasily through *untroubled meadows* to *the Great North Road…awakening, after a nap of a hundred years, to such life as is conferred by the stench of motor-cars* (lines 11-13). In that context, the third paragraph highlights the opposition between old (*England*) and new (*suburbia*), with the narrator pointing out that the station has elements of modernity (*island platforms and a subway*) and tradition (*it held hints of local life, personal intercourse*). That description corresponds directly to (B).

8.1 E

The last two stanzas of the poem serve to describe the type of landscape that people who *grow soft as children in the arms/of leisure* are unprepared to cope with. The speaker emphasizes its isolated, barren quality (*icy fields* with *only the luminous pallor/of the moon scarfed in clouds to light our way*)—essentially, this is a place that requires great strength, i.e., "fortitude," to survive in. (E) is thus correct. (A) and (C) are entirely unsupported by the passage; (B) is incorrect because there is no shift in tone—the speaker uses *we* from the beginning. Although the landscape described in the fourth and fifth stanzas may be lonely, (D) is incorrect because the speaker is not talking about the consequences of loneliness but rather the lack of preparation for living in difficult conditions.

9.1 A

Although this question is phrased in terms of function, it could also be considered a tone question. Essentially, you must recognize that the deliberately exaggerated language in lines 13-15 (*august person; huge, magnificent, and terribly angular bed; principal honour*) is designed to drily poke fun at the house's illustrious heritage. (B) might seem tempting, but the passage only indicates that the old gentleman *would have been delighted* to recount the house's history, not that he was "excessively proud" of it. Likewise, (E) is incorrect because the information in the parentheses does not at all imply that the old gentleman had developed an outsized sense of his own social importance based on the fact that the house has hosted royalty. (C) is completely off-topic, and (D) does not fit because the passage does not mention, or even allude to, anyone who might dispute the house's pedigree.

10.1 B

The use of the second-person narration is key here: in this passage, the narrator shifts from an objective, third-person perspective to addressing the reader as *you* in order to help them imagine what it is like to be navigating a steamboat in the middle of a foggy, gloomy river, unable to perceive where the water ends and the shore begins. In other words, lines 11-28 serve to heighten the sense of drama ("dramatize an experience") and give the reader the sense of being in the middle of the action ("draw in the reader"). (A), (C), and (E) are all inconsistent with the focus of the passage: the narrator is providing a detailed description intended to evoke a particular experience, not arguing for a particular viewpoint. (D) is contradicted by the passage: the narrator's point is not that reactions to the experience of being on the river are subjective, varying according to the individual, but rather that anyone who happens to be reading will presumably react in a particular way.

Glossary of Function Words

Account for – Explain

Acknowledge (a point) – Recognize the merit or validity of an idea

Advocate – Promote or encourage

Bolster – Support, provide additional evidence for an idea

Concede (a point) – Recognize the merit or validity of an opposing idea (additional explanation on p. 100)

Condemn – Harshly attack on moral grounds

Convey – Indicate

Defend – Stand up for

Discredit – Disprove (literally, demonstrate a lack of credibility); typically too extreme and inconsistent with the literary focus of the exam to be correct

Dismiss – Deny the importance or validity of an idea

Downplay – Deliberately understate, imply that something is unimportant

Evoke – To summon, call up (a memory, impression, etc.), recreate through description

Explicate – Explain in great detail

Highlight – Emphasize, call attention to

Jeer at – Make fun of in a cruel or harsh manner; more extreme synonym for *mock* and *scoff at*, and typically too extreme to be correct

Minimize – Deliberately understate the importance of an idea; synonym for *downplay* and *trivialize*

Mock – Make fun of

Qualify – Provide more information about a statement in order to make it seem less extreme, or indicate the conditions under which it would be true (additional explanation on p. 100)

Satirize – Make fun of by using irony, sarcasm, or parody

Scoff at – Make fun of, suggest that something is unworthy of serious consideration

Simulate – Recreate an experience

Substantiate – Give evidence or support for, back up

Trivialize – Downplay, treat as unimportant; synonym for *downplay* and *minimize* but more extreme and thus unlikely to appear as a correct answer

Undermine – Weaken or attack the foundation of; subvert secretly; unlikely to appear as a correct answer because it is typically associated with argumentative rather than literary writing

Underscore – Emphasize

Chapter Six

Rhetorical Strategies and Points of View

In the past, the reading portion of the AP Literature Exam directly tested the ability to recognize advanced rhetorical figures such as antithesis, metonymy, and apostrophe, but that is no longer the case. You should be particularly aware of this change if you are studying or teaching from exams administered before 2019, or if you are using practice material created by a commercial test-prep publisher; the latter may not reflect the updated version of the exam.

That said, some rhetorical terminology does still appear in multiple-choice answers, often in terms of function (as discussed in Chapter 5) but sometimes in other contexts as well. Even when rhetorical devices are included as "distractor" elements in incorrect answers, it is useful to know what they actually mean so that you do not fall into the trap of picking options merely because they sound complex and sophisticated. **You should therefore make sure to know the following high-frequency terms**.

- **Allusion** - reference
- **Analogy** - Comparison made to illustrate or clarify an idea
- **Assertion** - Claim or argument
- **Descriptive Language** - language using strong and evocative adjectives
- **Diction** - word choice (note that this is an exceedingly broad category—all texts contain "diction"—and can be specified in many different ways)
- **Imagery** - visually descriptive language, often containing metaphors
- **Juxtaposition** - side-by-side placement of two opposing or contradictory elements
- **Metaphor** - comparison in the form of *x is y*. (A **simile** is a comparison that uses *like* or *as*.)
- **Parallel Structure** - repeated use of the same construction to emphasize that two elements are of equal importance
- **Repetition** - use of the same word, phrase, or construction multiple times, usually within a small section of text
- **Syntax** - word order

You may also encounter the following devices, although they are somewhat less likely to appear.

• **Anecdote** - brief story • **Aside** - brief, direct address to the reader • **Concession** - admission that an opposing viewpoint has merit • **Digression** - off-topic discussion • **Euphemism** - replacement of a harsh or offensive term with a more pleasant one • **Hyperbole** - exaggeration • **Irony** - language signifying the opposite of a literal meaning, for humor or mockery	• **Paradox** - apparent contradiction • **Passive voice** - construction in which the subject and verb are flipped: *x did y* becomes *y was done by x* • **Qualification** - specification of a statement with additional information; often used to "soften" harsh or absolute language • **Understatement** - deliberate down-playment of a situation

As discussed in Chapter 5, rhetorical devices are most often invoked in the context of function questions. In such cases, it is generally possible to determine the answer without knowing the exact definition of the rhetorical term, as long as you understand the gist of the relevant lines.

To reiterate, in the question below, notice how the reference to the rhetorical figure is embedded in the question itself.

Love is not all: it is not meat nor drink
Nor slumber nor a roof against the rain;
Nor yet a floating spar to men that sink
And rise and sink and rise and sink again;
Love can not fill the thickened lung with breath,
Nor clean the blood, nor set the fractured bone;
Yet many a man is making friends with death
Even as I speak, for lack of love alone.
It well may be that in a difficult hour,
Pinned down by pain and moaning for release,
Or nagged by want past resolution's power,
I might be driven to sell your love for peace,
Or trade the memory of this night for food.
It well may be. I do not think I would.

The poet uses parallel structure in lines 3-4 in order to...

OR:

The effect of the parallel structure in lines 3-4 is to...

Explanation: If you can simply rephrase the question as "What is the purpose of lines 3-4?," you most likely do not need to worry about the term "parallell structure" at all. You must simply consider the purpose of the lines in question, the way you would for any other function question.

Now take a look at this example. It's less likely that you'll encounter a question in this format, but just in case, we're going to see how one works.

Love is not all: it is not meat nor drink
Nor slumber nor a roof against the rain;
Nor yet a floating spar to men that sink
And rise and sink and rise and sink again;
Love can not fill the thickened lung with breath,
Nor clean the blood, nor set the fractured bone;
Yet many a man is making friends with death
Even as I speak, for lack of love alone.
It well may be that in a difficult hour,
Pinned down by pain and moaning for release,
Or nagged by want past resolution's power,
I might be driven to sell your love for peace,
Or trade the memory of this night for food.
It well may be. I do not think I would.

1. The author's writing in lines 1-6 ("It is . . . bone") is characterized by the use of

(A) understatements that downplay an emotion
(B) descriptive language that reveals the speaker's sorrow
(C) active verbs that create a mood of tension
(D) repetition that reinforces a negation
(E) asides that create a sense of pettiness

Explanation: Don't be fooled by the seeming complexity of these answer choices—they're basically word salad designed to confuse you. If you're not sure where to begin, a good rule of thumb is to start with the options that are easiest to recognize. Correct answers frequently include terms that are both general and relatively straightforward to identify, so working this way can save you considerable time and energy.

In this case, "descriptive language" and "repetition" are the most generic terms, with "repetition" being easiest to identify: all you have to do is scan the lines in question and look for repeated words. Sure enough, *nor* appears three times, and the phrase *rise and sink* appears twice. Although the reference to a "negation" in (D) might seem confusing, this term simply refers to a negative statement like the one at the very beginning of the poem: *Love is* <u>*not*</u> *all.* And in fact, the repeated use of *nor* serves to emphasize, i.e., "reinforce," that idea. So (D) is correct. It is not even necessary to consider the other options.

Let's look at one more example of how rhetorical terms can be used as distractors to make questions seem artificially difficult. For example, consider the following:

Love is not all: it is not meat nor drink
Nor slumber nor a roof against the rain;
Nor yet a floating spar to men that sink
And rise and sink and rise and sink again;
Love can not fill the thickened lung with breath,
Nor clean the blood, nor set the fractured bone;
Yet many a man is making friends with death
Even as I speak, for lack of love alone.
It well may be that in a difficult hour,
Pinned down by pain and moaning for release,
Or nagged by want past resolution's power,
I might be driven to sell your love for peace,
Or trade the memory of this night for food.
It well may be. I do not think I would.

1. In context, the sentence "I do not think I would" (line14) serves as

(A) a dismissal of a possibility
(B) a gentle admonition
(C) a paradoxical claim
(D) a euphemistic understatement
(E) a satirical concession

Explanation: The primary danger presented by a set of answers such as this is that you will become so distracted by complex terminology that you lose sight of what you do know and overlook key information that you understand perfectly well.

Like the other questions we've looked at, and perhaps even more so, this question is far simpler than it appears. What is the speaker literally saying in the last line? That s/he would *not* do something (i.e., trade away love for something else of value). Literally, the speaker is "dismissing a possibility." That makes the answer (A). Note, incidentally, that this option is less cluttered with rhetorical terminology than the others.

Finally, in rare cases, a common rhetorical figure may be referred to in a question itself, as in the case below. Although it is possible to answer the question based only on a general understanding of the passage, knowing the definition of a "paradox" (apparent contradiction) will help you approach the choices in a more focused way, or even predict the answer before you look at them.

April this year, not otherwise
Than April of a year ago,
Is full of whispers, full of sighs,
Of dazzling mud and dingy snow;
Hepaticas that pleased you so
Are here again, and butterflies.
There rings a hammering all day,
And shingles lie about the doors;
In orchards near and far away
The grey wood-pecker taps and bores;
The men are merry at their chores,
And children earnest at their play.
The larger streams run still and deep,
Noisy and swift the small brooks run
Among the mullein stalks the sheep
Go up the hillside in the sun,
Pensively,—only you are gone,
You that alone I cared to keep.

1. Which of the following best characterizes a central paradox of the poem?

(A) The speaker relishes country life, yet many people around her take it for granted.
(B) The speaker is lives in the middle of nature but is unable to appreciate it.
(C) The speaker reminisces about a happy period but grows increasingly dejected.
(D) The speaker is surrounded by a joyful scene yet does not experience pleasure.
(E) The speaker is surrounded by enjoyable activities but has no desire to participate.

Explanation: As mentioned above, a paradox is a statement or situation that appears to be self-contradictory, although you don't have to worry about the "appears" part in this question. In addition, each answer choice describes a paradox, so answering the question is simply a matter of selecting the correct one. Essentially, the right answer will restate the main idea of the passage.

If you were to answer this question on your own, you might say something like "This April = last April BUT you're missing": the poem focuses on a happy springtime scene, emphasizing its similarities to that of the previous spring, in order to emphasize a loved one is no longer present (*only you are gone/You alone that I cared to keep*). In other words, the speaker is "surrounded by a joyful scene yet does not experience pleasure." That makes (D) correct.

Qualification and Concession

These strategies are common sources of confusion, so we're going to look at them closely here. Although they are generally associated with the types of arguments made in non-fiction writing, they can also appear in poetry and novels, and you should be able to recognize them.

Qualification involves providing specifying information about a broad statement in order to make it less extreme or harsh. For example, consider the following excerpt from George Eliot's novel *Middlemarch*:

These peculiarities of Dorothea's character caused Mr. Brooke to be all the more blamed in neighboring families for not securing some middle-aged lady as guide and companion to his nieces. But he himself dreaded so much the sort of superior woman likely to be available for such a position, that he allowed himself to be dissuaded by Dorothea's objections, and was in this case brave enough to **defy the world—that is to say, Mrs. Cadwallader the Rector's wife, and the small group of gentry with whom he visited in the northeast corner of Loamshire**.

1. The statement following the dash in lines 9-12 (that is . . . Loamshire) can best be characterized as

(A) a concession
(B) a command
(C) a qualification
(D) an apology
(E) a justification

Explanation: The statement that appears after the dash serves to specify, i.e., **qualify**, what the narrator means by *the world* (very broad). That is important information because far from being meant literally, the term refers to a very small group of people. (C) is thus correct.

A **concession** is an acknowledgment that an opposing perspective is valid or that part of one's argument is incorrect. The excerpt below, from Mark Twain's *Personal Recollections of Joan of Arc*, provides a clear example of this strategy:

Joan fell on her knees before the majesty of France, and the other frivolous animal in his lap—a sight which it pained me to see. What had that man done for his country or for anybody in it, that she or any other person should kneel to him?...

However, to be fair, one must grant that Charles acquitted himself very well for the most part, on that occasion—very much better than he was in the habit of doing. He passed his pup to a courtier, and took off his cap to Joan as if she had been a queen. Then he stepped from his throne and raised her, and showed quite a spirited and manly joy and gratitude in welcoming her and thanking her for her extraordinary achievement in his service.

1. The sentence in lines 6-9 can best be characterized as

(A) a concession
(B) a command
(C) a qualification
(D) an apology
(E) a justification

Explanation: The statements *to be fair* and *one must grant that Charles acquitted himself very well* clearly indicate that the narrator recognizes the king behaved very graciously, despite the fact that he did not deserve to be kneeled down to. (A) is thus correct.

Types of Perspectives

Although reading questions are unlikely to ask you to identify different narrative points of view, or perspectives, by name, the ability to recognize various perspectives and spot changes involving them is an important skill for answering questions dealing with passage type and organization. This holds true for both poetry and prose.

A **first-person** narration is written from the perspective of the narrator and includes the word *I* and/or *my*. All personal anecdotes are, by definition, written in the first person. For example:

> A fool **I** was to sleep at noon,
> And wake when night is chilly
> Beneath the comfortless cold moon;
> A fool to pluck **my** rose too soon,
> A fool to snap **my** lily.

A **third-person** narration, on the other hand, is written from an objective perspective and describes other people rather than the narrator him- or herself. For example:

> In nothing—as the expert on whose advice families moved to new neighborhoods to live there for a generation—was Babbitt more splendidly innocent than in the science of sanitation. He did not know a malaria-bearing mosquito from a bat; he knew nothing about tests of drinking water; and in the matters of plumbing and sewage he was as unlearned as he was voluble.

Second-person narrations are written to *you*—they address the reader directly and, like first-person narratives, tend to be more personal than third-person ones. While this type of narration is found only rarely in prose works, it is much more common in poetry, which frequently includes addresses to people who are not literally present. For example:

> I am a little world made cunningly
> Of elements, and an angelic spright,
> But black sin hath betrayed to endless night
> My worlds both parts, and oh! both parts must die.
> **You, which beyond that heaven which is most high**
> **Have found new spheres and of new lands can write,**
> **Pour new seas in mine eyes, that so I might**
> **Drown my world with my weeping earnestly,**
> **Or wash it, if it must be drowned no more:**

Here, the speaker uses the second person to directly address God (who lives *beyond that heaven which is most high*), asking him to cleanse him of sin.

Important: whenever you encounter a perspective change in a passage, mark that spot in your test booklet with an arrow or a star—there is a good chance that you will be asked a question involving it.

How Much Does the Narrator Know?

In some cases, questions that involve perspective may ask you to identify whether a passage is told from **a single character's perspective or from multiple characters' perspectives**.

You should also be able to recognize how much the narrator knows about the characters:

- An **omniscient narrator** has full access to all the characters' subjective thoughts and feelings and is able to relay their various perspectives fully.
- A **limited, or semi-omniscient, narrator** has full access to only one character's mind.
- A **detached narrator** is an outside observer who can describe actions and events objectively but does not have access to any of the characters' minds.

Note that the AP Literature exam may or may not use the above terms when testing these concepts, e.g., an omniscient narrator may be referred to as such or as "a narrator who gives the reader access to all the characters' thoughts."

For example, consider the following excerpt from George's Eliot's novel *Middlemarch*:

Dorothea checked herself suddenly with self-rebuke for the presumptuous way in which she was reckoning on uncertain events, but she was spared any inward effort to change the direction of her thoughts by the appearance of a cantering horseman round a turning of the road. The well-groomed chestnut horse and two beautiful setters could leave no doubt that the rider was Sir James Chettam. He discerned Dorothea, jumped off his horse at once, and, having delivered it to his groom, advanced towards her with something white on his arm, at which the two setters were barking in an excited manner.

"How delightful to meet you, Miss Brooke," he said, raising his hat and showing his sleekly waving blond hair. "It has hastened the pleasure I was looking forward to."

Miss Brooke was annoyed at the interruption. This amiable baronet, really a suitable husband for Celia, exaggerated the necessity of making himself agreeable to the elder sister. Even a prospective brother-in-law may be an oppression if he will always be presupposing too good an understanding with you, and agreeing with you even when you contradict him. The thought that he had made the mistake of paying his addresses to herself could not take shape: all her mental activity was used up in persuasions of another kind. But he was positively obtrusive at this moment, and his dimpled hands were quite disagreeable. Her roused temper made her color deeply, as she returned his greeting with some haughtiness.

1. Which of the following best describes the way the passage is narrated?

(A) The reader is limited to Dorothea's perspective.
(B) The point of view shifts from one character to another.
(C) The narrator maintains a detached distance from both characters.
(D) The reader views the scene the way Sir James Chettam does.
(E) The narrator comments on Sir James Chettam's attitude toward Miss Brooke.

Explanation: Essentially, this question requires you to distinguish between the characters present in the passage (two) and the number of perspectives offered by the narrator (one). In fact, the reader is made privy to the perspective of Dorothea (i.e., Miss Brooke) only. Although the narrator describes the interaction between her and Sir James, as well as the actions of Sir James, the reader is allowed access to Dorothea's thoughts alone. We learn that Dorothea is annoyed at being interrupted by Sir James, and that she finds him irritating. In contrast, we are told only what Sir James *does*—we do not know what he thinks or feels. Because the passage is narrated from a single perspective, the answer is (A).

Now look at this example, also from *Middlemarch.* (Note: Celia is Dorothea's sister, and Mr. Causabon is Dorothea's suitor.)

Celia was really startled at the suspicion which had darted into her mind. She was seldom taken by surprise in this way, her marvellous quickness in observing a certain order of signs generally preparing her to expect such outward events as she had an interest in. Not that **she now imagined** Mr. Casaubon to be already an accepted lover: she had **only begun to feel** disgust at the possibility that anything in Dorothea's mind could tend towards such an issue. Here was something really to vex her about Dodo: it was all very well not to accept Sir James Chettam, but the idea of marrying Mr. Casaubon! Celia **felt a sort of shame** mingled with a sense of the ludicrous. But perhaps Dodo, if she were really bordering on such an extravagance, might be turned away from it: experience had often shown that her impressibility might be calculated on.

Dorothea was in fact thinking that it was desirable for Celia to know of the momentous change in Mr. Casaubon's position since he had last been in the house: **it did not seem fair** to leave her in ignorance of what would necessarily affect her attitude towards him; but it was impossible not to shrink from telling her.

1. Which of the following best describes the way the passage is narrated?

(A) The reader is limited to Dorothea's perspective.
(B) The point of view shifts from one character to another.
(C) The narrator maintains a detached distance from both characters.
(D) The reader experiences the scene only from Celia's point of view.
(E) The narrator reproaches Celia for her dislike of Mr. Casaubon.

Explanation: In contrast to the previous example, here the narrator allows the reader insight into the minds of both Celia and Dorothea, describing each girl's thought process and feelings in turn. In other words, the perspective "shifts from one character to another." That makes the answer (B).

You may also be asked to identify the narrator's relationship to the story—whether they are outside the action (usually the case for a third-person narrator) or participate directly (possible for a first-person narrator), and what sort of interest they have in recounting it.

As an example, let's work with the following passage:

One evening of late summer, before the nineteenth century had reached one-third of its span, a young man and woman, the latter carrying a child, were approaching the large village of Weydon-Priors, in Upper Wessex, on foot. They were plainly but not ill clad, though the thick hoar of dust which had accumulated on their shoes and garments from an obviously long journey lent a disadvantageous shabbiness to their appearance just now.

The man was of fine figure, swarthy, and stern in aspect; and he showed in profile a facial angle so slightly inclined as to be almost perpendicular. He wore a short jacket of brown corduroy, newer than the remainder of his suit, which was a fustian waistcoat with white horn buttons, breeches of the same, tanned leggings, and a straw hat overlaid with black glazed canvas. At his back he carried by a looped strap a rush basket, from which protruded at one end the crutch of a hay-knife, a wimble* for hay-bonds being also visible in the aperture. His measured, springless walk was the walk of the skilled countryman as distinct from the desultory shamble of the general labourer; while in the turn and plant of each foot there was, further, a dogged and cynical indifference personal to himself, showing its presence even in the regularly interchanging fustian folds, now in the left leg, now in the right, as he paced along.

What was really peculiar, however, in this couple's progress, and would have attracted the attention of any casual observer otherwise disposed to overlook them, was the perfect silence they preserved. They walked side by side in such a way as to suggest afar off the low, easy, confidential chat of people full of reciprocity; but on closer view it could be discerned that the man was reading, or pretending to read, a ballad sheet which he kept before his eyes with some difficulty by the hand that was passed through the basket strap. Whether this apparent cause were the real cause, or whether it were an assumed one to escape an intercourse that would have been irksome to him, nobody but himself could have said precisely; but his taciturnity was unbroken, and the woman enjoyed no society whatever from his presence. Virtually she walked the highway alone, save for the child she bore.

*Marbleworker's brace for drilling

1. The narrator's perspective throughout the passage might best be described as that of a

(A) a current inhabitant
(B) a fiery moralizer
(C) an interested observer
(D) a biting satirist
(E) a pretentious scholar

Explanation: Strictly speaking, recognizing that the passage contains a third-person narration does not provide a significant amount of help—in principle, any of the individuals mentioned in the answer choices could narrate the passage in the third person. If you think in terms of how test questions are typically constructed, however, it does provide some direction.

Generally speaking, third-person narratives are used to convey an objective perspective. At the same time, extreme and specific wording (e.g. "fiery moralizer," "biting satirist," "pretentious scholar") is most often used for distractors. (A) and (C) are thus the most probable answers. Nothing indicates that the narrator lives in Weydon-Priors, so only (C) is left. In fact, it is correct: the absence of strong language combined with detailed observations of the family's behavior indicates that the narrator is in fact an "interested observer."

Note that you do not need to read the entire passage for this information—like most big-picture questions, it can be answered with information from the first few paragraphs.

Passage Types

We already looked at this question type from a big-picture perspective in Chapter 2, but now we're going to consider it in terms of narrative point of view.

Love is not all: it is not meat nor drink
Nor slumber nor a roof against the rain;
Nor yet a floating spar to men that sink
And rise and sink and rise and sink again;
Love can not fill the thickened lung with breath,
Nor clean the blood, nor set the fractured bone;
Yet many a man is making friends with death
Even as **I** speak, for lack of love alone.
It well may be that in a difficult hour,
Pinned down by pain and moaning for release,
Or nagged by want past resolution's power,
I might be driven to sell your love for peace,
Or trade the memory of this night for food.
It well may be. **I** do not think I would.

1. The poem as a whole is best understood as

(A) a wistful lament for a lost love
(B) an uplifting tribute to a former love
(C) a personal meditation on the value of love
(D) a theoretical treatise on the power of love
(E) an ironic commentary on the fickleness of love

Explanation: As we saw earlier, you can answer this question by focusing on the content of the passage; however, in this version you can also use point of view to quickly zero in on the answer. Here, the repeated appearance of the word *I* indicates that the passage is in part written from a first-person perspective—that is, it is *personal.* Using that information combined with the beginning of each answer, you can immediately jump to (C) as the most likely option.

On the other hand, consider this example:

In the oval flower bed the snail, whose shell had been stained red, blue, and yellow for the space of two minutes or so, now appeared to be moving very slightly in its shell, and next began to labour over the crumbs of loose earth which broke away and rolled down as it passed over them. It appeared to have a definite goal in front of it, differing in this respect from the singular high stepping angular green insect who attempted to cross in front of it, and waited for a second with its antenna trembling as if in deliberation, and then stepped off as rapidly and strangely in the opposite direction.

1. The passage is best understood as

(A) a fantastical account
(B) a lighthearted reminiscence
(C) a personal meditation
(D) a detailed treatise
(E) a detached description

Explanation: Unlike the previous passage, this one is written entirely in the third person, so (C) can be eliminated immediately. (B) is also likely incorrect because a "reminiscence" is a memory, something typically associated with a first-person narrator.

Otherwise, (D) does not fit because a treatise is a formal, often theoretical exposition of a topic—this type of writing does not normally appear on the AP Literature exam, and it certainly does not describe this passage. (A) is incorrect because something "fantastical" is wild and outlandish, whereas this passage is specific and concrete. The objective, third-person narration is consistent with the idea of detachment, making (E) the answer.

Paragraph/Stanza and Passage Organization

Questions that ask about the organization of ideas in a paragraph or entire passage test rhetorical strategies on a larger scale. They are typically phrased in the following ways:

- Which statement best describes the organization of this passage/paragraph?
- The statement in line x signals a shift from…

Note that some organization questions may also include individual answer choices that allude to changes in narrative point of view. Answers involving point of view may also appear in questions that do not directly ask about that concept.

To answer organization questions correctly and quickly, you must be able to identify places in the passage where key ideas, relationships, or descriptions appear, or where there is a shift in perspective. You must also pay attention to transition words that indicate relationships between these elements.

If a question asks about the **organization of a paragraph or stanza**, you should begin by skimming for important transitions within that paragraph. Then, once you have identified those transitions, consider how the information before and after them is connected.

If a question asks about the overall **organization of a passage**, you should focus on the introduction and the first (topic) sentence of each subsequent paragraph/stanza. Note that if a poem is not clearly divided into stanzas, you will need to do the work of identifying major shifts that signal new sections on your own.

Other questions will ask you to identify **where a change or shift occurs in the passage**. As a general rule, you must back up and read the information preceding the line cited in the question. That line will only tell you what the passage is shifting *to*—to determine what it is shifting *from*, you must start reading before the line reference. You must also be able to recognize key places in the development of the passage, particularly where new or contradictory information is introduced and where important ideas are emphasized.

You should therefore **pay attention to—and preferably mark—changes in point of view**. For example, if a poem moves from a first-person to a second- or third-person narration, or vice-versa, the spot where the change occurs is a prime target for questions testing changes in perspective.

On the next page, we're going to look at some examples. Notice that although the questions may be phrased in different ways, they are all fundamentally targeting the same set of concepts; the wording only varies to give the impression of variety.

Love is not all: it is not meat nor drink
Nor slumber nor a roof against the rain;
Nor yet a floating spar to men that sink
And rise and sink and rise and sink again;
Love can not fill the thickened lung with breath,
Nor clean the blood, nor set the fractured bone;
Yet many a man is making friends with death
Even as I speak, for lack of love alone.
It well may be that in a difficult hour,
Pinned down by pain and moaning for release,
Or nagged by want past resolution's power,
I might be driven to sell your love for peace,
Or trade the memory of this night for food.
It well may be. I do not think I would.

1. Which of the following best describes the organization of this poem?

(A) A formal presentation is made, followed by a more colloquial discussion.
(B) A general claim is made, followed by supporting evidence.
(C) A general reflection is offered, followed by a personal consideration.
(D) A belief is stated, followed by a concession.
(E) An observation is described, followed by a justification.

2. In relation to lines 1-7, lines 8-14 represent a shift to

(A) a more colloquial style
(B) a more detached perspective
(C) a more personal tone
(D) a less ironic stance
(E) a less convivial attitude

Explanation: In line 8, *I* signals a shift to a personal perspective, so (C) is correct in both cases.

Passages with separate paragraphs/stanzas may also have questions phrased this way:

I heard the trailing garments of the Night
Sweep through her marble halls!
I saw her sable skirts all fringed with light
From the celestial walls!

I felt her presence, by its spell of might,
Stoop o'er me from above;
The calm, majestic presence of the Night,
As of the one I love.

I heard the sounds of sorrow and delight,
The manifold, soft chimes,
That fill the haunted chambers of the Night,
Like some old poet's rhymes.

From the cool cisterns of the midnight air
My spirit drank repose;
The fountain of perpetual peace flows there, —
From those deep cisterns flows.

O holy Night! from thee I learn to bear
What man has borne before!
Thou layest thy finger on the lips of Care,
And they complain no more.

Peace! Peace! Orestes*-like I breathe this prayer!
Descend with broad-winged flight,
The welcome, the thrice-prayed for, the most fair,
The best-beloved Night!

*Character in Greek mythology

1. The relationship between the fourth stanza and the fifth is best characterized as

(A) abstract to concrete
(B) objective to personal
(C) action to consequence
(D) criticism to defense
(E) description to direct address

Explanation: Focus on the pronouns used in each stanza. In the fourth stanza, the word *my* indicates a first-person perspective, whereas in the fifth stanza, *thee* and *thou* indicates that the speaker is addressing night directly. (E) is consistent with that change, making it correct.

Exercises: Rhetorical Strategies

1. A noiseless patient spider,
I mark'd where on a little promontory it stood isolated,
Mark'd how to explore the vacant vast surrounding,
It launch'd forth filament, filament, filament, out of itself,
Ever unreeling them, ever tirelessly speeding them.

And you O my soul where you stand,
Surrounded, detached, in measureless oceans of space,
Ceaselessly musing, venturing, throwing, seeking the spheres to connect them,
Till the bridge you will need be form'd, till the ductile anchor hold,
Till the gossamer thread you fling catch somewhere, O my soul.

1. The statements in the first stanza are best described as

(A) obscure allusions
(B) grudging concessions
(C) startling revelations
(D) elaborate justifications
(E) personal observations

2. Which of the following best describes the relationship between the first stanza and the second?

(A) A paradox that is introduced in the first paragraph is resolved in the second.
(B) The first paragraph has an external focus; the second focuses on an aspect of the speaker's self.
(C) The diction is more formal in the first paragraph and more conversational in the second.
(D) The confident tone in the first stanza becomes somewhat less certain in the second.
(E) The first paragraph is concerned with mundane events, the second with moral questions.

2. Samuel Michael had never been a talkative man, but his calm, steady habits had brought a sense of security and consistency to their home. Mattie had been the only child of his autumn years, and so for as long as she could remember, he had been an old man with set and exacting ways. Unlike her mother he never raised his voice, and when the two had a difference of opinion, her mother would charge around the house, mumbling and banging pans, while he would just sit on the porch rocker and read his Bible.

Once Mattie had wanted a pair of patent-leather pumps like the girls in town, and her mother had said they were too expensive and impractical for their dusty country roads. Sam refused to take sides in the battle over the shoes, but he went and hired himself out in the sweet potato fields for a month of Saturdays, brought home the shoes, and dropped them in her lap—"Wear 'em only on Sundays" were his first and last words on the matter.

1. In relationship to the first paragraph, the second paragraph represents a shift from

(A) a family history to a particular character
(B) an omniscient perspective to a character's perspective
(C) an earnest discussion to an ironic commentary
(D) a general description to a specific ancedote
(E) an objective account to an exaggerated depiction

3. Slow, slow, fresh fount, keep time with my salt tears;
Yet slower, yet, O faintly, gentle springs!
List to the heavy part the music bears,
Woe weeps out her division, when she sings.
Droop herbs and flowers;
Fall grief in showers;
Our beauties are not ours.
O, I could still,
Like melting snow upon some craggy hill,
Drop, drop, drop, drop,
Since nature's pride is now a withered daffodil.

1. The narrator's perspective throughout the passage might best be described as that of

(A) a detached observer
(B) a spurned suitor
(C) an ironic commentator
(D) a woebegone mourner
(E) a fantastical storyteller

2. The statements in lines 1-2 can best be described as

(A) commands
(B) rationalizations
(C) apologies
(D) explanations
(E) descriptions

4. The train sped northward, under innumerable tunnels. It was only an hour's journey, but Mrs. Munt had to raise and lower the window again and again. She passed through the South Welwyn Tunnel, saw light for a moment, and entered the North Welwyn Tunnel, of tragic fame. She traversed the immense viaduct, whose arches span untroubled meadows and the dreamy flow of Tewin Water. She skirted the parks of politicians. At times the Great North Road accompanied her, more suggestive of infinity than any railway, awakening, after a nap of a hundred years, to such life as is conferred by the stench of motor-cars, and to such culture as is implied by the advertisements of antibilious pills*. To history, to tragedy, to the past, to the future, Mrs. Munt remained equally indifferent.

The station for Howards End was at Hilton, one of the large villages that are strung so frequently along the North Road, and that owe their size to the traffic of coaching and pre-coaching days. Being near London, it had not shared in the rural decay, and its long High Street had budded out right and left into residential estates. For about a mile a series of tiled and slated houses passed before Mrs. Munt's inattentive eyes, a series broken at one point by six Danish tumuli** that stood shoulder to shoulder along the highroad, tombs of soldiers. Beyond these tumuli, habitations thickened, and the train came to a standstill in a tangle that was almost a town.

1. In relation to the first paragraph (lines 1-16), the second paragraph (lines 17-29) represents a shift from

(A) a discussion of a place to a discussion of a character
(B) an omniscient narration to a personal account
(C) a description of a voyage to a description of a destination
(D) a satirical account to a sincere reflection
(E) a historical perspective to a modern perspective

2. Lines 9-16 are characterized by

(A) abstract language that creates a sense of detachment
(B) repetition that emphasizes a description
(C) active verbs that create a sense of movement
(D) direct address that engages the reader
(E) digressions that detract from the passage's focus

*Pills to soothe an upset stomach

**Ancient hills or mounds

5. We could deny our winters, refuse to cut
Our hands mining the sharp ores of grief
Whenever the cold comes, we could follow

the arrowheads of geese shafting south
to an azure place where whales sing offshore
and otters frolic in the wanton surf.

We could grow soft as children in the arms
of leisure, but we might never learn in time
how to stoke the cold fire of the will

in that winter we cannot refuse, when we must glean
from the icy fields the last scattered grains
we once disdained, with only the luminous pallor

of the moon scarfed in clouds to light our way,
rising above the outstretched arms of the trees
in its long slow journey through the night.

1. Which of the following best describes the organization of this poem?

(A) A claim is presented and is followed by a justification.
(B) A meditation on nature is followed by a critique of human interference.
(C) A theoretical discussion is followed by a reflection on a particular place.
(D) A subjective reflection is followed by an objective commentary.
(E) A delineation of a choice is followed by a description of its repercussions.

6. The grey fox, so called
actually the color of wet sand
here on the Cape, pads
daintily past the herb garden.

See, I murmur to her or him,
you still exist. I argued
with a park biologist
you hadn't died out here.

I've seen you eating wild
grapes near the dunes.
I watched your kits run
up pitch pines for safety.

Even with the coywolves
hunting you and the red
fox claiming your territory
you are at home where

you belong, stopping to
check out birdseed we
scattered on needles, left-
over cashews you gobble.

1. The second stanza (lines 5-8) marks a shift to

(A) a more neutral stance
(B) a more dismissive tone
(C) a more personal perspective
(D) a less ironic point of view
(E) a less reflective attitude

7. From the oval-shaped flower-bed there rose perhaps a hundred stalks spreading into heart-shaped or tongue-shaped leaves half way up and unfurling at the tip red or blue or yellow petals marked with spots of colour raised upon the surface; and from the red, blue or yellow gloom of the throat emerged a straight bar, rough with gold dust and slightly clubbed at the end. The petals were voluminous enough to be stirred by the summer breeze, and when they moved, the red, blue and yellow lights passed one over the other, staining an inch of the brown earth beneath with a spot of the most intricate colour. The light fell either upon the smooth, grey back of a pebble, or, the shell of a snail with its brown, circular veins, or falling into a raindrop, it expanded with such intensity of red, blue and yellow the thin walls of water that one expected them to burst and disappear. Instead, the drop was left in a second silver grey once more, and the light now settled upon the flesh of a leaf, revealing the branching thread of fibre beneath the surface, and again it moved on and spread its illumination in the vast green spaces beneath the dome of the heart-shaped and tongue-shaped leaves. Then the breeze stirred rather more briskly overhead and the colour was flashed into the air above, into the eyes of the men and women who walk in Kew Gardens in July.

The figures of these men and women straggled past the flower-bed with a curiously irregular movement not unlike that of the white and blue butterflies who crossed the turf in zig-zag flights from bed to bed. The man was about six inches in front of the woman, strolling carelessly, while she bore on with greater purpose, only turning her head now and then to see that the children were not too far behind. The man kept this distance in front of the woman purposely, though perhaps unconsciously, for he wished to go on with his thoughts.

"Fifteen years ago I came here with Lily," he thought. "We sat somewhere over there by a lake and I begged her to marry me all through the hot afternoon. How the dragonfly kept circling round us: how clearly I see the dragonfly and her shoe with the square silver buckle at the toe. All the time I spoke I saw her shoe and when it moved impatiently I knew without looking up what she was going to say: the whole of her seemed to be in her shoe. And my love, my desire, were in the dragonfly; for some reason I thought that if it settled there, on that leaf, the broad one with the red flower in the middle of it, if the dragonfly settled on the leaf she would say 'Yes' at once. But the dragonfly went round and round: it never settled anywhere, of course not, happily not, or I shouldn't be walking here with Eleanor and the children."

1. The relation between the second paragraph (lines 28-38) and the third (lines 39-55) is best described as

(A) exposition and critique
(B) description and reminiscence
(C) assertion and qualification
(D) claim and concession
(E) summary and specific focus

2. The final sentence of the first paragraph (lines 24-27) differs from the rest of the paragraph in that it

(A) relies less on impressionistic language
(B) introduces a new perspective
(C) has a more conversational style
(D) makes a novel claim
(E) draws a conclusion from previously presented information

8. The bridesmaids were here, and yet the bridegroom had not come. Ursula wondered if something was amiss, and if the wedding would yet all go wrong. She felt troubled, as if it rested upon her. The chief bridesmaids had arrived. Ursula watched them come up the steps. One of them she knew, a tall, slow, reluctant woman with a weight of fair hair and a pale, long face. This was Hermione Roddice, a friend of the Criches. Now she came along, with her head held up, balancing an enormous flat hat of pale yellow velvet, on which were streaks of ostrich feathers, natural and grey. She drifted forward as if scarcely conscious, her long blanched face lifted up, not to see the world. She was rich. She wore a dress of silky, frail velvet, of pale yellow colour, and she carried a lot of small rose-coloured cyclamens. Her shoes and stockings were of brownish grey, like the feathers on her hat, her hair was heavy, she drifted along with a peculiar fixity of the hips, a strange unwilling motion. She was impressive, in her lovely pale-yellow and brownish-rose, yet macabre, something repulsive. People were silent when she passed, impressed, roused, wanting to jeer, yet for some reason silenced. Her long, pale face, that she carried lifted up, somewhat in the Rossetti fashion, seemed almost drugged, as if a strange mass of thoughts coiled in the darkness within her, and she was never allowed to escape.

Ursula watched her with fascination. She knew her a little. She was the most remarkable woman in the Midlands. Her father was a Derbyshire Baronet of the old school, she was a woman of the new school, full of intellectuality, and heavy, nerve-worn with consciousness. She was passionately interested in reform, her soul was given up to the public cause. But she was a man's woman, it was the manly world that held her.

Hermione knew herself to be well-dressed; she knew herself to be the social equal, if not far the superior, of anyone she was likely to meet in Willey Green. She knew she was accepted in the world of culture and of intellect. She was a Kulturtrager, a medium for the culture of ideas. With all that was highest, whether in society or in thought or in public action, or even in art, she was at one, she moved among the foremost, at home with them. No one could put her down, no one could make mock of her, because she stood among the first, and those that were against her were below her, either in rank, or in wealth, or in high association of thought and progress and understanding. So, she was invulnerable. All her life, she had sought to make herself invulnerable, unassailable, beyond reach of the world's judgment.

1. Which of the following best describes the way the passage is narrated?

(A) The reader is limited to a fully detached perspective.
(B) The narrator shifts the perspective from character to character.
(C) The narrator chasistes Hermione for her peculiar appearance.
(D) The reader experiences the scene from Hermione's point of view.
(E) The narrator provides a series of subjective impressions.

Explanations: Rhetorical Strategies

1.1 E

Don't overthink this question: the presence of the word *I* in line 2 indicates a first-person, i.e., "personal," perspective, which corresponds to (E). And in fact, the detailed description of the spider's actions can be best described as a series of "observations." All the other answers essentially serve as nonsense distractors.

1.2 B

What is the focus of the first stanza? The spider—that is, something "external" to the speaker. What is the focus of the second stanza? The speaker's soul—that is, "an aspect of the speaker's self." That corresponds directly to (B). The poem does not mention a "paradox," eliminating (A); there is no change in register (level of formality) or style between the stanzas, eliminating (C) and (D), and (E) is entirely off-topic.

2.1 D

As is true for many "shift" questions, it is easier to work from the shift "from" than the "shift to"—the beginning of the second paragraph or stanza in question will often provide key information that can be quickly used to answer the whole question. Here, the answer effectively hinges on the second paragraph's first sentence: *<u>Once</u> Mattie had wanted a pair of patent-leather pumps like the girls in town, and her mother had said they were too expensive and impractical for their dusty country roads.* The use of *once* at the beginning of the sentence indicates that the narrator is about to recount a story about a particular incident ("a specific anecdote"), something that corresponds directly to (D). If that isn't enough information to select that answer comfortably, you can at least assume that "ironic commentary" and "exaggerated depiction" are inconsistent with the moderate, straightforward tone and eliminate (C) and (E) accordingly. If you then look at the first paragraph, you will find that although it describes the family, it is not a "family history," so (A) can be crossed out as well. Finally, (B) can be eliminated because there is no change in perspective between the two paragraphs—both involve the same, seemingly detached third-person narrator.

3.1 D

The most striking feature of this poem is its sadness: the phrases *salt tears*, *Woe weeps out her division*, and *Droop herbs and flowers* make the overall mood clear. The narrator is not "detached," "ironic," or "fantastical," so (A), (C), and (E) can be eliminated. (B) is a bit too specific: the poem gives no indication that the speaker is sad because he was in love with someone who rejected him, and inferring as much would go well beyond the bounds of the poem. On the other hand, the speaker is obviously in mourning, a fact that corresponds to (D).

3.2 A

In the first two lines, the speaker addresses the fount (fountain) and orders it to match its rhythm to the person's weeping. Although these statements are not worded harshly, the fact that the speaker is telling the fount what to do means that they can be characterized as "commands." That makes (A) correct.

4.1 C

Although the question asks about two full paragraphs, the beginning of the first paragraph provides nearly enough information to identify the answer. The second sentence indicates that Mrs. Munt is taking a journey (i.e., "a voyage"), then proceeds to describe her train trip. Once you've established this focus, you can skim through the rest of the paragraph, or even skip it entirely and jump to the beginning of the second paragraph, which the narrator begins with a reference to the Howards End *station*. Why mention the station? Logically, because Mrs. Munt is arriving there—i.e., it is her destination. That corresponds directly to (C).

4.2 B

As a general rule, you should work through this type of rhetorical strategy question by checking the options in order of most to least concrete—or rather, easiest to hardest to observe. More often than not, the answer will be one of the more straightforward options. That is the case here: "repetition" and "direct address" are the easiest answers to check, so you can simply look for them in order. If you work this way and make sure to read the line reference through to the end, you'll find the answer right away. The phrase *to such* appears twice, in lines 12 and 13, and *to* appears four times, in successive parallel phrases, in the final sentence. (B) is thus correct.

5.1 E

In the first part of the poem, the speaker lays out what would seem to be an appealing option (i.e. a "choice") for many people, namely turning away from life's difficulties in favor of a more pleasurable existence. In the second part, however, the speaker details the unpleasant consequences (i.e, "repercussions") of that choice—the inability to cope with serious challenges. Only (E) captures this structure.

6.1 C

The introduction of the pronoun *I*, which appears for the first time in line 5, signals a shift to a first-person, i.e., a "personal," perspective.

7.1 B

The simplest—if not necessarily the most obvious—way to approach this question is to focus on the third paragraph because it is somewhat more concrete and focused than the second. In particular the first sentence, *"Fifteen years ago I came here with Lily," he thought*, indicates that the man is looking back on, i.e., reminiscing about, an event in the past. Based on that piece of information, (A), (C), and (D) can be eliminated because a "critique," "qualification," and "concession" are all inconsistent with the idea of a memory. If you're not comfortable choosing (B), look at the second paragraph. It's a general description of a scene, whereas a summary is really a reduction of an argument into a more condensed form. So (E) doesn't quite fit, whereas (B) is much more consistent with the passage.

7.2 A

Lines 1-23 are characterized by highly descriptive language—long, evocative sentences that are intended to vividly depict the movement of light and its effects on the colors of a range of different objects. In fact, there is no action otherwise; the language serves to convey a series of impressions. In contrast, the final sentence of the paragraph is more straightforward and less overtly literary, functioning as a transition to the more pedestrian description of the people in the second paragraph. The actual perspective (third-person), however, is the same as in the rest of the paragraph, eliminating (B). Although the style is more direct, it is not more conversational (it remains moderately formal), eliminating (C). (D) and (E) do not fit because the final sentence does not make a claim or draw a conclusion—these answers are entirely off-topic. Only (A) is consistent with the fact that the language in the final sentence is less "impressionistic" than the language of the previous sentences.

8.1 B

Although this question asks about the passage as a whole, it can actually be answered very quickly with information from the beginning of each paragraph. Although the passage contains a third-person narration, the second sentence of the first paragraph establishes that the reader is seeing the scene from Ursula's perspective (as indicated by the statement, *Ursula wondered if something was amiss, and if the wedding would yet all go wrong*). The second paragraph continues from Ursula's perspective, as indicated in the first two sentences; however, the third paragraph shifts to Hermione's point of view (*Hermione knew herself to be well dressed...*) In other words, the narrator "shifts the perspective from character to character," making (B) correct.

Chapter Seven

Tone and Attitude

Tone and attitude questions ask about a narrator or character's emotions toward a particular person, event, or situation. While relatively few questions directly target these concepts, answer choices to other question types may reference them, and **you should be able discuss them in your essays as well**. If tone/attitude questions do appear, they will likely be phrased in the following ways:

- In line x, the author's tone/style can best be described/characterized as…
- The author would most likely view the events described in lines x-y as…
- In lines x-y, the narrator's attitude toward z can best be described as…

As is true for the test in general, **answers to these can often be approached in terms of positive, negative, and neutral**. You should also pay careful attention to the level of intensity in the answer choices relative to that in the passage. **While literary texts do often involve high levels of joy, sadness, etc., that is not always the case, and you should be careful not to ascribe more intense emotions to a narrator or character than the ones directly conveyed in the passage.**

For example, consider the question below. We're going to look at it in the abstract, without a passage, in order to focus on the language used in the answer choices.

1. Which of the following is true of Character X's attitude toward Character Y throughout the passage?

   (A) It shifts from mild acceptance to intense abhorrence.
   (B) It grows increasingly scornful.
   (C) It alternates between appreciation and irritation.
   (D) It oscillates between affection and apathy.
   (E) It abruptly swings from disdain to sympathy.

Looking only at the level of extremity in the phrasing, (A) can be eliminated because the word "intense" is, well, probably too intense. In (B), "scorn" (extreme disdain) also comes off as questionable, as is "apathy" (total lack of interest) in (D). Between the two remaining options, (C) is overall more neutral, with "abruptly" acting as a slight danger signal in (E). Furthermore, "disdain" is stronger than "irritation," lending additional weight to (C).

Tone and Attitude Vocabulary

While there are theoretically thousands of possible answers to tone/attitude questions, in reality a relatively small number of words—both correct and incorrect—tend to recur fairly frequently. The chart below lists some common answer choices.

To reiterate: The presence of "moderate" words does not necessarily indicate a correct answer, nor does the presence of "extreme" words indicate an incorrect answer. You should simply keep in mind that the language used in the correct answer choice **may in some cases** be more neutral than that used in the passage, and that if you are stuck between two options, you should check whether one answer contains more neutral language than the other.

In addition, remember that challenging, less common words (e.g., "polemical," "irreverent," "laudatory") are often used as distractors, so never choose an answer just because it sounds sophisticated! In contrast, correct answers may be as simple as "disliking" or "admiring."

	Positive	**Negative**	**Neutral**
Moderate	Admiring Amused Appreciative Approving Conversational Humorous Informal Nostalgic Optimistic Proud Sympathetic Wistful	Apologetic Argumentative Critical Disapproving Disbelieving Disdainful Dismissive Disparaging Dubious Ironic Lamenting Perplexed Skeptical Wary	Analytical Contemplative Detached Dispassionate Evenhanded Impartial Informative Measured Neutral Objective Restrained Tempered Understated
Extreme	Awed Ecstatic Irreverent Laudatory Reverent Whimsical Witty	Angry Apprehensive Contemptuous Envious Facetious Flippant Hostile Incredulous Irate Mocking Polemical Resentful Scornful	Aloof Apathetic Indifferent Philosophical Resigned

Tone vs. Attitude

Although the terms "tone" and "attitude" are often used more or less interchangeably, they are not precisely the same thing, and it is important to understand the distinction between them.

A narrator or speaker can present information about a topic in a relatively neutral tone but still have a distinct point of view, so it is important not to confuse lack of strong language with a neutral attitude. While much of the time tone and attitude will go together (e.g., a positive attitude will be expressed using clearly positive words), it is entirely possible for a character to express a clear like or dislike without over-the-top diction. For example, compare the following two passages:

Passage 1

I wonder by my troth, what thou and I
Did, till we loved? Were we not wean'd till then?
But suck'd on country pleasures, childishly?
Or snorted we in the Seven Sleepers' den*?
'Twas so; but this, all pleasures fancies be;
If ever any beauty I did see,
Which I desired, and got, 'twas but a dream of thee.

*Cave in which a group of ancient youths hid to escape persecution.

Passage 2

The chief—almost the only—**attraction** of the young woman's face was its mobility. When she looked down sideways to the girl she became **pretty**, and **even handsome**, particularly that in the action her features caught slantwise the rays of the strongly coloured sun, which made transparencies of her eyelids and nostrils and set fire on her lips.

Even though these passages both convey a positive attitude and address the same basic theme of beauty, they approach it very differently from a tone standpoint.

In the first passage, the speaker uses lofty language, asserting that *any* beauty he saw before meeting the beloved was only a dream. The language is exaggerated and typically poetic.

In the second passage, in contrast, the narrator describes the woman's attractiveness in less flowery, more down-to-earth terms, although still generally positive ones. He explains what aspect of the woman's face is attractive (*its mobility*) and precisely under what circumstances she appears pretty (*When she looked down sideways* and *her features caught slantwise the rays of the strongly coloured sun*). Unlike in the previous example, the language is concrete and specific.

Reading Closely to Identify Tone and Attitude

While a familiarity with common answer choice patterns will certainly help you identify likely answers to tone questions faster, that approach does have its limits. Unless you want to treat the test like a glorified guessing game, you must know how to distinguish between choices when things aren't so clear cut and to recognize how particular types of words/phrases correspond to particular types of answers.

Important: Because hearing how a passage sounds is a key element in identifying tone, it can help to read the lines in question aloud (very quietly). Recognizing which words are emphasized and which ones are less important can be very useful, especially when the tone isn't clearly positive or negative.

Like and Dislike

At the simplest level, positive and negative tones may be identified by the presence of exclusively positive or negative words and phrases.

Like (admiration, appreciation, approval):

I shall never forget my first sight of Mary Cavendish. Her tall, slender form, outlined against the bright light; the vivid sense of slumbering fire that seemed to find expression only in those **wonderful** tawny eyes of hers, **remarkable** eyes, different from any other woman's that I have ever known; the **intense power** of stillness she possessed, which nevertheless conveyed the impression of a wild untamed spirit in an **exquisitely civilised** body—all these things are burnt into my memory.

Dislike (disapproval, wariness):

With the presence of Mr. Inglethorp, a sense of **constraint** and **veiled hostility** seemed to settle down upon the company. Miss Howard, in particular, took no pains to conceal her feelings. Mrs. Inglethorp, however, seemed to notice nothing unusual. Her volubility, which I remembered of old, had lost nothing in the intervening years, and she poured out a steady flood of conversation… Occasionally she referred to her husband over a question of days or dates. His watchful and attentive manner never varied. From the very first I took a **firm and rooted dislike** to him, and I flatter myself that my first judgments are usually fairly shrewd.

Although narrators of the above passages use moderate language to convey their relative like and dislike, their attitudes are clear and uncomplicated by additional or conflicting emotions.

A **celebratory** or **laudatory** tone offers up a high level of praise. Because this type of language is by definition extreme, it is more likely to appear in poetry, as in the example below:

O useful element and clear!
My sacred wash and cleanser here,
My first consigner unto those
Fountains of life where the Lamb goes!
What sublime truths and wholesome themes
Lodge in thy mystical deep streams!
Such as dull man can never find
Unless that Spirit lead his mind
Which first upon thy face did move,
And hatch'd all with his quick'ning love.
As this loud brook's incessant fall
In streaming rings restagnates all,
Which reach by course the bank, and then
Are no more seen, just so pass men.
O my invisible estate,
My glorious liberty, still late!

Because of the poem's clear religious orientation, the speaker's tone and attitude could also be described as **reverent** (worshipful).

A slightly more specific type of positive tone/attitude is **sympathy**, characterized by compassion for someone who has encountered a difficult situation. In the following excerpt from Mark Twain's *The Tragedy of Pudd'nhead Wilson*, for instance, the narrator describes the trouble that Wilson has inadvertently brought upon himself with an poorly thought-out remark, and is clearly sensitive toward the fact that Wilson will need to work very hard to remedy the situation:

> [His] deadly remark had ruined his chance—at least in the law. No clients came. He took down his sign, after a while, and put it up on his own house with the law features knocked out of it. It offered his services now in the humble capacities of land surveyor and expert accountant. Now and then he got a job of surveying to do, and now and then a merchant got him to straighten out his books. With **patience and pluck** he resolved to live down his reputation and work his way into the legal field yet. **Poor fellow,** he could foresee that it was going to take him such a weary long time to do it.

A somewhat more complex positive emotion involves **nostalgia** or **wistfulness**. This type of tone involves looking back on a particularly enjoyable time in one's life, sometimes in ways that romanticize it or exaggerate its greatness. For example, consider this excerpt from Alfred, Lord Tennyson's poem "Ulysses," in which the hero looks back on his exploits during the Trojan War:

> Much have I seen and known; cities of men
> And manners, climates, councils, governments,
> Myself not least, but **honoured of them all**;
> And **drunk delight** of battle with my peers;
> Far on the ringing plains of windy Troy.
> I am a part of all that I have met;
> Yet all experience is an arch wherethrough
> Gleams that untravelled world, whose margin fades
> For ever and for ever when I move.
> **How dull it is to pause, to make an end,**
> **To rust unburnished, not to shine in use!**

Here, Ulysses contrasts the present dullness of his life with the excitement and camaraderie he experienced on the battlefield and in his travels. It's clear that he misses those experiences deeply.

Like positive tones/attitudes, negative ones come in many varieties, some subtler than others.

In the passage below from Jane Austen's novel *Emma*, the tone and attitude are negative, but they're a more extreme and specific kind of negative than in the example we looked at initially:

> At first it was **downright dullness** to Emma. She had never seen Frank Churchill so **silent and stupid**. He said **nothing worth hearing—looked without seeing—admired without intelligence—listened without knowing what she said.** While he was **so dull**, it was no wonder that Harriet should be **dull** likewise; and they were both **insufferable**.

The insistence on Frank's dullness and inability to exhibit any sort of intelligence or interest clearly indicates that Emma looks down on Frank. Her attitude could be described as **disdainful** or **scornful**. Her willingness to criticize Frank in such strong terms (is he truly as dull as she makes him out to be?) also suggests a bit of **arrogance** on her part.

Although these kinds of adjectives are more exaggerated than mere like or dislike, in a passage like this they are entirely justified.

A speaker who employs a **lamenting** tone is bemoaning—that is, strongly regretting—an action or decision. For instance, in the poem by Christina Rossetti below, the speaker repeatedly **admonishes** or **chastises** (scolds) themselves for their irresponsible behavior:

> **A fool I was** to sleep at noon,
> And wake when night is chilly
> Beneath the comfortless cold moon;
> **A fool** to pluck my rose too soon,
> **A fool** to snap my lily.

A **resentful** tone or attitude includes elements of bitterness and jealousy, and is expressed by someone who feels that they have not received the recognition they deserve. In the excerpt below, for example, a character who works as a professional ghostwriter (someone who discreetly writes books for well-known people) expresses her frustration at having the difficulty of her work go continually unrecognized:

> By and large, the books she helped write were interesting, she often reminded herself, and if not, it was her job to make them interesting. And though she might pooh-pooh her own work just to be modest, **it irked her when others did not take her seriously. Even Art did not seem to recognize how difficult her job was.** But that was her fault. She preferred to make it look easy. She would rather others discern themselves what an incredible job she did in spinning gold out of dross. **They never did, of course.**

Another unhappy tone in this general grouping is defensiveness: a **defensive** speaker or character feels that they must protect themselves against accusations that are false/unjustified, or that they must explain why they behaved the way they did:

> I record no crimes; my faults may easily be pardoned; for **they proceeded not from evil motive but from want of judgement**; and I believe **few would say that they could, by a different conduct and superior wisdom, have avoided the misfortunes to which I am the victim**. My fate has been governed by necessity, a hideous necessity.

On the other hand, a character who employs an **apologetic** tone is expressing remorse or guilt:

> [W]hen he asked where Mrs. Lydgate was, he was told that she was in her bedroom. He went up and found her stretched on the bed pale and silent, without an answer even in her face to any word or look of his. He sat down by the bed and leaning over her said with almost a cry of prayer
>
> **–"Forgive me for this misery, my poor Rosamond! Let us only love one another."**

Finally, the thoughts or words of a character who experiences conflicting positive and negative emotions will convey **ambivalence** (*ambi* - both; *val* – value), as in the passage below:

> In those days, returning to the Nakagawa district still provoked in me **mixed emotions of sadness and pleasure**. It is a hilly area, and climbing again those steep narrow streets between the clusters of houses **never failed to fill me with a deep sense of loss.** Though not a place I visited on casual impulse, **I was unable to stay away for long.**

Certainty and Uncertainty

Strong vs. hesitant language can also be referred to not in terms of positive and negative but in terms of certainty and uncertainty.

Writing that is **emphatic**, **decisive**, **vehement**, **resolute**, or full of **conviction** (the state of being convinced) has some pronounced characteristics:

- It contains short, blunt, declarative statements, e.g., *It is most definitely true.*
- It contains extreme words and phrases, e.g., *always*, *only*, and *most*.
- It lacks **qualifying** words or phrases, e.g., *sometimes*, *could*, or *might*, to soften its meaning.

For example, consider the famous opening sentence of Jane Austen's novel *Pride and Prejudice*:

> It is a truth **universally acknowledged**, that a single man in possession of a good fortune must be in want of a wife. However little known the feelings or views of such a man may be on his first entering a neighbourhood, **this truth is so well fixed** in the minds of the surrounding families, that he is considered as the rightful property of some one or other of their daughters.

Here, the narrator speaks in terms of absolutes, like a deity coming down from the heavens to describe an eternal rule of reality for mere mortals. It is nothing if not certain.

In contrast, a **speculative** tone is characterized by an avoidance of overly strong statements and the use of **hypothetical** words such as *may*, *might*, and *could*—words that indicate **hesitancy** and **tentativeness**, and **caution**. The second half of Edna St. Vincent Millay's sonnet "Love Is Not All" offers a stellar example:

> It **well may be** that in a difficult hour,
> Pinned down by pain and moaning for release,
> Or nagged by want past resolution's power,
> I **might** be driven to sell your love for peace,
> Or trade the memory of this night for food.
> It **well may** be. **I do not think I would.**

Formal vs. Informal

Register refers to how **formal** or **informal** a text is. For example, compare the following:

Informal	When Mike **showed up** at the hotel, the **first thing he asked** was if his sister was **there yet**. When it **turned out** that she wasn't, Mike didn't think it was a **big deal**, and he decided to **hang out** in the lobby.
Moderate	When Michael **reached** the hotel, he **immediately asked** whether his sister had **arrived**. **Told** that she hadn't, Michael was **unconcerned**, and he decided to **wait** in the lobby.
Formal	When Michael had **disembarked** from the taxi and **made his way** into the hotel, he did not **hesitate to inquire after** his sister's presence. **Apprised** that her **arrival remained forthcoming**, Michael was not in the least **disconcerted**, and he **contrived** to await her in the lobby.

Although passages typically range from moderately to extremely formal, they may sometimes contain more casual, or **colloquial**, language, which you should be prepared to identify.

As discussed in Chapter 6, **objectivity**, **impartiality**, **neutrality**, and **detachment** are generally associated with a third-person perspective, although it is also possible for a first-person narrator to employ an **objective tone** (or **style**). While this type of writing can in some cases be very descriptive, it is also characterized by plain, straightforward language and a lack of strong emotional involvement on the part of the narrator or speaker—that is, its tone is often **restrained** or **tempered**. At the same time, it is typically associated with a **moderately formal style**, or **register**.

For example, in the following passage from Henry James' novel *The Ambassadors*, the idea of detachment operates at the level of both the tone/style and of the attitude of the character on whom the passage focuses: a man named Strethers, who has recently traveled to England from the United States. The narrator not only relays the events in a clear, decidedly unpoetic manner, but also describes Strethers's notably detached, unengaged behavior:

> There were people on the ship with whom [Strethers] had easily consorted—so far as ease could up to now be imputed to him—and who for the most part plunged straight into the current that set from the landing-stage to London; there were others who had invited him to a tryst at the inn and had even invoked his aid for a "look round" at the beauties of Liverpool; but he had **stolen away from everyone alike**, had **kept no appointment** and **renewed no acquaintance**, **had been indifferently aware** of the number of persons who esteemed themselves fortunate in being, unlike himself, "met," and had even **independently, unsociably, alone,** without encounter or relapse and by **mere quiet evasion**, given his afternoon and evening to the immediate and the sensible.

A **didactic** tone is associated with the **second person** point of view, in which the narrator addresses the reader or another character directly in order to instruct them. It typically makes use of straightforward and moderately formal language as well. This book, for instance, is written in a didactic tone. For another example, consider this snippet from a Sherlock Holmes novel:

> "Really, Hopkins," said he, "I have high hopes for your career, but **you must learn patience** before rushing off to pursue the first conclusion which occurs to you. **Examine every fact**, **test every link** in your chain and only then **take action**."

On the other hand, a passage whose tone is **lofty** or **elevated** is full of poetic flights of fancy and **exaggeratedly formal** language. In the poem below, note the use of a second-person narration (the speaker is addressing humanity in general) and the references to various heavenly beings:

> If man alone engross not **Heav'n's high care**,
> Alone made perfect here, immortal there:
> Snatch from his hand the balance and the rod,
> Rejudge his justice, be the **God of God**.
> In pride, in reas'ning pride, our error lies;
> All quit their sphere, and rush into the skies.
> Pride still is aiming at the **blest abodes**,
> Men would be **angels, angels would be gods**.

At the other extreme, a first- or second-person narrative can be used to create a more **informal** or **conversational** tone, as in the example below:

> It was big—and Babbitt respected bigness in anything; in mountains, jewels, muscles, wealth, or words. He was, for a spring-enchanted moment, the lyric and almost unselfish lover of Zenith. He thought of the outlying factory suburbs; of the Chaloosa River with its strangely eroded banks; of the orchard-dappled Tonawanda Hills to the North, and all the fat dairy land and big barns and comfortable herds. As he dropped his passenger he cried, **"Gosh, I feel pretty good this morning!"**

Whereas the third-person narration includes language that is fairly sophisticated, even poetic (*spring-enchanted, orchard-dappled*), the last line contains far more casual, or **colloquial**, everyday language (*Gosh, pretty good*). In other words, it passes from a register that is moderately formal to one that is extremely informal.

Note that multiple-choice questions may target this type of register shift, so if you encounter one as you read a passage, you should mark it in your test booklet.

A first-person narration is not necessarily informal, however, particularly in poetry. That said, it is by definition more **personal**, and it may be more **confessional** as well.

Love is not all: it is not meat nor drink
Nor slumber nor a roof against the rain;
Nor yet a floating spar to men that sink
And rise and sink and rise and sink again;
Love can not fill the thickened lung with breath,
Nor clean the blood, nor set the fractured bone;
Yet many a man is making friends with death
Even as I speak, for lack of love alone.
It well may be that in a difficult hour,
Pinned down by pain and moaning for release,
Or nagged by want past resolution's power,
I might be driven to sell your love for peace,
Or trade the memory of this night for food.
It well may be. I do not think I would.

Here, the use of the first person also adds to the poem's **contemplative** or **meditative** (although not quite **philosophical**) tone. The speaker is not merely thinking through a subject in a dry and dispassionate manner but is rather deeply engaged with it on an individual level.

Humor, Sarcasm, and Irony

If AP Literature passages do include occasional flashes of humor, is unlikely to be the obvious, laugh-out-loud type. Rather, **humorous** or **irreverent** tones will be subtle and based on **wordplay** that either involves punning on alternate meanings of words; using words to mean the **opposite** of what they normally mean; or otherwise **violating the reader's expectations**. For example, consider the following quotations from George Eliot's novel *Middlemarch*:

Example #1

> The business was felt to be so important that it required dinner to feed it.

The humor here derives from the fact that the "business" is not a person and does not need to be fed—indeed cannot eat—at all. Obviously, it is the people who need to eat in order to continue discussing the business, but Eliot deliberately avoids stating this fact literally, creating an element of surprise. The reader's expectations are also violated because the second half of the sentence does not logically follow from the first half.

Example #2

> The weavers and tanners of Middlemarch...had never thought of Mr. Brooke as a neighbour, and were **not more attached to him than if he had been sent in a box from London**.

As in the previous example, Eliot plays with the reader's expectations by creating a gap, or incongruity, between the two halves of the sentence; it ends in a way that the beginning does not suggest at all. Mr. Brooke is quite human, and so the image of him being sent *in a box from London*, as if he were a new suit or a packet of sweets, is a wholly ridiculous one.

Example #3

> Miss Brooke had that kind of beauty which seems to be thrown into relief by poor dress. Her hand and wrist were so finely formed that she could wear sleeves not less bare of style than those in which the Blessed Virgin appeared to Italian painters; and her profile as well as her stature and bearing seemed to gain the more dignity from her plain garments, which by the side of provincial fashion **gave her the impressiveness of a fine quotation from the Bible—or from one of our elder poets—in a paragraph of to-day's newspaper**.

Here, the humor results from the juxtaposition of formal and informal elements. The lofty references to how *the Blessed Virgin appeared to Italian painters* and *a fine quotation from the Bible* stand in sharp contrast to the dullness of *a paragraph of to-day's newspaper*. Again, the ending is entirely unexpected.

Now, to make matters somewhat more complicated, **literary humor often blurs the line between positive and negative** and often involves **irony**—that is, saying one thing while meaning the opposite (like a kid who rolls his eyes and groans "great!" when asked to take out the trash).

Wry or **dry humor** often appears in passages when a speaker has a **negative attitude** and wants to criticize someone or something without being overly heavy-handed about it. (Often these situations involve hypocrisy, or presenting oneself as one thing while behaving in the opposite way.) In such cases, the tone can typically be described as **mocking**, **ironic**, **satirical**, **sardonic**, **sarcastic**, **flippant** or **facetious**. Although some of these terms are stronger than others, for the purposes of the AP English Literature Exam they can be considered interchangeable.

Unfortunately, there are no specific types of words that invariably signal these types of tones; rather, you must use the general context of the passage. That said, some types of rhetorical strategies and punctuation do provide clues. **Quotation marks**, for example, can indicate that an author does not intend for a particular word or phrase to be understood literally. Likewise, **exclamation points** (typically associated with informal writing), **repetition**, unnecessary **capitalization** and either **exaggeration** (**hyperbole**) or **understatement** can be used to emphasize the distance between what is being stated and what is actually happening.

As an example, we're going to return to *The Tragedy of Pudd'nhead Wilson*, which, like many of Twain's novels, is a satire. Consider the following excerpt:

> Pembroke Howard, lawyer and bachelor, aged almost forty, was another old Virginian grandee with proved descent from the First Families. He was a fine, majestic creature, a gentleman according to the nicest requirements of the Virginia rule, a devoted Presbyterian, an authority on the "code", and a man always courteously ready to stand up before you in the field if any act or word of his had seemed doubtful or suspicious to you, and explain it with any weapon you might prefer from bradawls to artillery.

In this passage, the irony results from the gap between the characterization of Pembroke Howard as a *gentleman according to the nicest requirement of the Virginia rule*—that is, an eminently civilized person—and his willingness to resort to exceedingly violent means (*any weapon you might prefer from bradawls to artillery*). Obviously, that is not a particularly "courteous" act, nor does one literally "explain" one's speech or actions with weapons: that is what words are for.

Note that the quotation marks around "code" highlight the divergence between the meaning that would normally be understood in a legal context (Howard is a lawyer) and the implied meaning (code of honor). One is designed to provide a framework for solving problems through non-violent means, the other for exactly the opposite.

Now let's work through a few sample questions:

Slow, slow, fresh fount, keep time with my salt tears;
Yet slower, yet, O faintly, gentle springs!
List to the heavy part the music bears,
Woe weeps out her division, when she sings.
Droop herbs and flowers;
Fall grief in showers;
Our beauties are not ours.
O, I could still,
Like melting snow upon some craggy hill,
Drop, drop, drop, drop,
Since nature's pride is now a withered daffodil.

1. Throughout the poem, the speaker's tone can best be characterized as

(A) condescending
(B) laudatory
(C) philosophical
(D) bemused
(E) lamenting

Explanation: As mentioned in previous discussions of this poem, the predominant mood is one of intense sadness. As a result, it is an ideal example of a question that can be approached by playing positive/negative/neutral. Although correct answers to tone questions are sometimes phrased more neutrally than the passages themselves, the speaker's dejection here is so strong that you can assume the correct answer will be negative.

"Laudatory" (strongly praising) is positive, and "philosophical" is neutral, so (B) and (C) can be eliminated easily. "Bemused" (puzzled) is slightly negative but is entirely inconsistent with the passage, eliminating (D) as well. "Condescending" (arrogant, disdainful) is strongly negative but is also off-topic. The speaker is merely very sad, not looking down on anyone. Only (E), "lamenting," appropriately captures the speaker's sorrow.

Next, let's try a prose passage:

Mr. Ralph Nickleby sat in his private office one morning, ready dressed to walk abroad. He wore a bottle-green spencer over a blue coat; a white waistcoat, grey mixture pantaloons, and Wellington boots drawn over them. The corner of a small-plaited shirt-frill struggled out, as if insisting to show itself, from between his chin and the top button of his spencer; and the latter garment was not made low enough to conceal a long gold watch-chain, composed of a series of plain rings, which had its beginning at the handle of a gold repeater in Mr. Nickleby's pocket, and its termination in two little keys: one belonging to the watch itself, and the other to some patent padlock. He wore a sprinkling of powder upon his head, as if to make himself look benevolent; but if that were his purpose, he would perhaps have done better to powder his countenance also, for there was something in its very wrinkles, and in his cold restless eye, which seemed to tell of cunning that would announce itself in spite of him. However this might be, there he was; and as he was all alone, neither the powder, nor the wrinkles, nor the eyes, had the smallest effect, good or bad, upon anybody just then, and are consequently no business of ours just now.

1. Compared with the narrator's attitude in lines 14-20 (" He wore…him"), the narrator's attitude in the final sentence (lines 21-25) can best be characterized as

(A) more critical and suspicious
(B) more restrained and detached
(C) more appreciative and optimistic
(D) less hostile and irate
(E) less cynical and contemptuous

Explanation: What is the focus of lines 14-20? Mr. Nickleby's futile attempt to make himself appear kindly, and the slightly menacing impression he gives despite this. The narrator's attitude is moderately negative and could be described as "suspicious" or "wary."

Now, what is the focus of lines 21-25? The fact that Mr. Nickleby is alone, and that his off-putting air is therefore not bothering anyone. How does that information relate to the previous set of lines? It's somewhat **less negative** or, stated the other way, somewhat **more positive**.

(A): "More critical and suspicious" = more negative. Eliminate it.

(B): "More restrained and detached" = neutral/very slightly positive. Keep it.

(C): "More appreciative and optimistic" = more positive, but it's too positive. Eliminate it.

(D): "Less hostile and irate" = less negative, but still too negative. The narrator doesn't display anger in the first set of lines. Eliminate it.

(E): "Less cynical and contemptous" = less negative, but like (D), this option is too negative.

That leaves (B) as the answer.

Shortcut: The statement that no aspect of Mr. Nickleby's appearance *had the smallest effect, good or bad, upon anybody just then, and are consequently* <u>*no businesss of ours just now*</u> (lines 23-25) conveys the narrator's "detachment" (lack of emotional engagement). That corresponds to (B).

One more example:

The automobile and bridge-whist had not only made more evident the social divisions in Gopher Prairie but they had also enfeebled the love of activity. It was so rich-looking to sit and drive—and so easy. Skiing and sliding were "stupid" and "old-fashioned." In fact, the village longed for the elegance of city recreations almost as much as the cities longed for village sports; and Gopher Prairie took as much pride in neglecting coasting as St. Paul—or New York—in going coasting. Carol did inspire a successful skating-party in mid-November. Plover Lake glistened in clear sweeps of gray-green ice, ringing to the skates. On shore the ice-tipped reeds clattered in the wind, and oak twigs with stubborn last leaves hung against a milky sky. Harry Haydock did figure-eights, and Carol was certain that she had found the perfect life. But when snow had ended the skating and she tried to get up a moonlight sliding party, the matrons hesitated to stir away from their radiators and their daily bridge-whist imitations of the city. She had to nag them. They scooted down a long hill on a bob-sled, they upset and got snow down their necks they shrieked that they would do it again immediately—and they did not do it again at all. She badgered another group into going skiing. They shouted and threw snowballs, and informed her that it was SUCH fun, and they'd have another skiing expedition right away, and they jollily returned home and never thereafter left their manuals of bridge.

1. The capitalization of "SUCH" in line 27 indicates that this word

(A) holds particular significance for the skiers
(B) is meant to emphasize the skiers' enjoyment
(C) is intended to be read ironically
(D) would normally be used in a different context
(E) indicates the speakers' conviction in their assertion

Explanation: Consider what the skiers say they'll do (go skiing again right away) vs. what they actually do (show no interest in ever skiing again). In that context, the capitalization is used to signal irony—the gap between what is stated and what is really meant.

Exercises: Tone and Attitude

1. As late I rambled in the happy fields,
What time the sky-lark shakes the tremulous dew
From his lush clover covert;—when anew
Adventurous knights take up their dinted shields:
I saw the sweetest flower wild nature yields,
A fresh-blown musk-rose; 'twas the first that threw
Its sweets upon the summer: graceful it grew
As is the wand that queen Titania wields.
And, as I feasted on its fragrancy,
I thought the garden-rose it far excell'd:
But when, O Wells! thy roses came to me
My sense with their deliciousness was spell'd:
Soft voices had they, that with tender plea
Whisper'd of peace, and truth, and friendliness
unquell'd.

1. The tone of the statement in lines 11-15 is best characterized as

(A) sarcastic
(B) appreciative
(C) disdainful
(D) philosophical
(E) admonishing

2. The whole of the Glen Oriole project was a suggestion that Babbitt, though he really did hate men recognized as swindlers, was not too unreasonably honest. Operators and buyers prefer that brokers should not be in competition with them as operators and buyers themselves, but attend to their clients' interests only. It was supposed that the Babbitt-Thompson Company were merely agents for Glen Oriole, serving the real owner, Jake Offutt, but the fact was that Babbitt and Thompson owned sixty-two per cent. of the Glen, the president and purchasing agent of the Zenith Street Traction Company owned twenty-eight per cent., and Jake Offutt (a gang-politician, a small manufacturer, a tobacco-chewing old farceur who enjoyed dirty politics, business diplomacy, and cheating at poker) had only ten per cent., which Babbitt and the Traction officials had given to him for "fixing" health inspectors and fire inspectors and a member of the State Transportation Commission. But Babbitt was virtuous. He advocated, though he did not practise, the prohibition of alcohol; he praised, though he did not obey, the laws against motor-speeding; he paid his debts; he contributed to the church, the Red Cross, and the Y. M. C. A.; he followed the custom of his clan and cheated only as it was sanctified by precedent; and he never descended to trickery.

1. The tone of the sentence in lines 21-22 ("But…virtuous") is best characterized as

(A) celebratory
(B) philosophical
(C) regretful
(D) ironic
(E) restrained

3. I heard the trailing garments of the Night
Sweep through her marble halls!
I saw her sable skirts all fringed with light
From the celestial walls!

I felt her presence, by its spell of might,
Stoop o'er me from above;
The calm, majestic presence of the Night,
As of the one I love.

I heard the sounds of sorrow and delight,
The manifold, soft chimes,
That fill the haunted chambers of the Night,
Like some old poet's rhymes.

From the cool cisterns of the midnight air
My spirit drank repose;
The fountain of perpetual peace flows there, —
From those deep cisterns flows.

O holy Night! from thee I learn to bear
What man has borne before!
Thou layest thy finger on the lips of Care,
And they complain no more.

Peace! Peace! Orestes*-like I breathe this prayer!
Descend with broad-winged flight,
The welcome, the thrice-prayed for, the most fair,
The best-beloved Night!

*Character in Greek mythology

1. Throughout the poem, the speaker's attitude toward the night can best be characterized as

(A) didactic
(B) nostalgic
(C) contemplative
(D) apologetic
(E) laudatory

4. A shadow blurred the sunlight in Nancy's face—there was uneasiness in it, and disappointment. A procession of disturbing thoughts began to troop through her mind. Saying nothing aloud, she sat with her hands in her lap; now and then she clasped them, then unclasped them, then tapped the ends of the fingers together; sighed, nodded, smiled—occasionally paused, shook her head. This pantomime was the elocutionary expression of an unspoken soliloquy which had something of this shape:

"I was afraid of it—was afraid of it. Trying to make our fortune in Virginia, Beriah Sellers nearly ruined us and we had to settle in Kentucky and start over again. Trying to make our fortune in Kentucky he crippled us again and we had to move here. Trying to make our fortune here, he brought us clear down to the ground, nearly. He's an honest soul, and means the very best in the world, but I'm afraid, I'm afraid he's too flighty."

1. Compared with the style of lines 8-11, the style of the second paragraph is best described as

(A) more conversational and relaxed
(B) more detached and objective
(C) more scholarly and pedantic
(D) less wary and skeptical
(E) less expressive and contemplative

5. There is a change—and I am poor;
Your love hath been, nor long ago,
A fountain at my fond heart's door,
Whose only business was to flow;
And flow it did; not taking heed
Of its own bounty, or my need.

What happy moments did I count!
Blest was I then all bliss above!
Now, for that consecrated fount
Of murmuring, sparkling, living love,
What have I? shall I dare to tell?

A comfortless and hidden well.
A well of love—it may be deep—
I trust it is,—and never dry:
What matter? if the waters sleep
In silence and obscurity.
—Such change, and at the very door
Of my fond heart, hath made me poor.

1. In the second stanza, the narrator's attitude can best be characterized as

(A) defensive
(B) bemused
(C) philosophical
(D) anxious
(E) nostalgic

6. Thomas Gradgrind, sir. A man of realities. A man of facts and calculations. A man who proceeds upon the principle that two and two are four, and nothing over, and who is not to be talked into allowing for anything over. Thomas Gradgrind, sir, peremptorily Thomas, Thomas Gradgrind. With a rule and a pair of scales, and the multiplication table always in his pocket, sir, ready to weigh and measure any parcel of human nature, and tell you exactly what it comes to. It is a mere question of figures, a case of simple arithmetic. You might hope to get some other nonsensical belief into the head of George Gradgrind, or Augustus Gradgrind, or John Gradgrind, or Joseph Gradgrind (all supposititious, non-existent persons), but into the head of Thomas Gradgrind—no, sir!

In such terms Mr Gradgrind always mentally introduced himself, whether to his private circle of acquaintance, or to the public in general. In such terms, no doubt, substituting the words "boys" and "girls," for "sir," Thomas Gradgrind now presented Thomas Gradgrind to the little pitchers before him, who were to be filled so full of facts.

Indeed, as he eagerly sparkled at them from the cellarage before mentioned, he seemed a kind of cannon loaded to the muzzle with facts, and prepared to blow them clean out of the regions of childhood at one discharge. He seemed a galvanizing apparatus, too, charged with a grim mechanical substitute for the tender young imaginations that were to be stormed away.

1. The author's tone in the first paragraph can best be characterized as

(A) fantastical, with descriptive language creating a sense of whimsy
(B) emphatic, with repetition conveying a sense of militancy
(C) celebratory, with strong imagery establishing a sense of pride
(D) restrained, with parallel constructions indicating judiciousness
(E) apprehensive, with tentative verbs emphasizing a cautious approach

7. The bridesmaids were here, and yet the bridegroom had not come. Ursula wondered if something was amiss, and if the wedding would yet all go wrong. She felt troubled, as if it rested upon her. The chief bridesmaids had arrived. Ursula watched them come up the steps. One of them she knew, a tall, slow, reluctant woman with a weight of fair hair and a pale, long face. This was Hermione Roddice, a friend of the Criches. Now she came along, with her head held up, balancing an enormous flat hat of pale yellow velvet, on which were streaks of ostrich feathers, natural and grey. She drifted forward as if scarcely conscious, her long blanched face lifted up, not to see the world. She was rich. She wore a dress of silky, frail velvet, of pale yellow colour, and she carried a lot of small rose-coloured cyclamens. Her shoes and stockings were of brownish grey, like the feathers on her hat, her hair was heavy, she drifted along with a peculiar fixity of the hips, a strange unwilling motion. She was impressive, in her lovely pale-yellow and brownish-rose, yet macabre, something repulsive. People were silent when she passed, impressed, roused, wanting to jeer, yet for some reason silenced. Her long, pale face, that she carried lifted up, somewhat in the Rossetti fashion, seemed almost drugged, as if a strange mass of thoughts coiled in the darkness within her, and she was never allowed to escape.

Ursula watched her with fascination. She knew her a little. She was the most remarkable woman in the Midlands. Her father was a Derbyshire Baronet of the old school, she was a woman of the new school, full of intellectuality, and heavy, nerve-worn with consciousness. She was passionately interested in reform, her soul was given up to the public cause. But she was a man's woman, it was the manly world that held her.

Hermione knew herself to be well-dressed; she knew herself to be the social equal, if not far the superior, of anyone she was likely to meet in Willey Green. She knew she was accepted in the world of culture and of intellect. She was a Kulturtrager, a medium for the culture of ideas. With all that was highest, whether in society or in thought or in public action, or even in art, she was at one, she moved among the foremost, at home with them. No one could put her down, no one could make mock of her, because she stood among the first, and those that were against her were below her, either in rank, or in wealth, or in high association of thought and progress and understanding. So, she was invulnerable. All her life, she had sought to make herself invulnerable, unassailable, beyond reach of the world's judgment.

1. Which of the following is true of the people's attitude toward Hermione in lines 20-28?

(A) It becomes progressively more defensive.
(B) It changes from bemusement to awe.
(C) It alternates between admiration and antipathy.
(D) It shifts abruptly from pity to dislike.
(E) It is generally laudatory.

Explanations: Tone and Attitude

1.1 B

In lines 11-15, the speaker offers glowing praise for the roses that Wells sent, interpreting them as a symbol of *peace, and truth, and friendliness/unquell'd.* The correct answer must reflect this positive tone. "Sarcastic," "disdainful," and "admonishing" (scolding) are all negative, so (A), (C), and (E) can all be eliminated. "Philosophical" is neutral and is inconsistent with the focus of the passage. Although "appreciative" is less strong than the language used in the poem, it is the only clearly positive option and is consistent with the speaker's expression of gratitude.

2.1 D

The section of the passage that follows the sentence in lines 21-22 is dedicated to listing the ways in which Babbitt makes a public pretense of behaving morally, or of supporting various laws, but then does not hesitate to cheat when it suits him, or when he knows he will not be punished. Someone who acts so hypocritically is the opposite of virtuous, so the sentence in question is intended to be read ironically. (D) is thus correct.

3.1 E

The poem is essentially devoted to praising the night, so it can be reasonably assumed that the correct answer will be strongly positive. "Laudatory" (full of praise) is the only option that fits. "Didactic" (instructive, intended to teach), "nostalgic" (longing for the past), "contemplative" (thoughtful), and "apologetic" all do not make sense.

4.1 A

Lines 8-11 are notable for their extremely formal style, as indicated by phrases such as *elocutionary expression* and *unspoken soliloquy.* The paragraph that follows—Nancy's interior monologue—stands in sharp contrast to the previous sentence, featuring a type of language typical of everyday speech. It employs a much simpler, less abstract level of vocabulary (*trying to make our fortune; had to settle; he brought us clear down to the ground, nearly*) and could therefore be characterized as "more conversational and relaxed." (A) is thus correct.

5.1 E

The exclamation *What happy moments did I count!/Blest was I then all bliss above* in lines 7-8 reveals that the speaker is looking back on, and experiencing a longing for, a happier time. That is the definition of "nostalgic," so (E) is correct.

6.1 B

Although this passage is extremely satirical, with a tone that could easily be described as "ironic" or "facetious," this question approaches it from a slightly different angle and phrases the answer in much more neutral terms. The short, barked-out phrases, the repetition of the name *Thomas Gradgrind* and the word *sir* create a mock-military (i.e. "militant") tone that can literally be characterized as "emphatic." There is nothing "fantastical" (bizarre and outlandish) about the tone—in fact, the faux-military rhythm creates just the opposite impression, eliminating (A). (C), (D), and (E) are also inconsistent with the tone the passage: there is nothing "celebratory" or "restrained" about it, and the short, declarative sentences are the exact opposite of "apprehensive" (anxious).

7.1 C

In lines 20-24, Hermione is described as provoking strongly conflicting emotions, both extremely positive (she is *impressive;* the people are *roused*) and extremely negative (*macabre, repulsive,* the people *[want] to jeer*). In other words, the people's attitude toward her "alternates between admiration and antipathy" (dislike, aversion), so (C) is correct. Playing process of elimination, "defensive" does not make sense—the people do not feel as if Hermione is accusing them of something, so (A) can be eliminated. Although Hermione is described as *impressive,* "awe" is too strong, and there is nothing to directly suggest that the people feel "bemused" (puzzled) by Hermione. Likewise, (D) is incorrect because there is no indication that the people "pity" Hermione. "Laudatory" (strongly praising) is directly contradicted by the passage, again leaving (C).

Part II: The Essays

Chapter Eight

Introduction to the Essays

The AP English Literature and Composition Exam includes three essays. They are always presented in the same order, but **you can answer them in any order you choose**. You are allotted a total of two hours, with the suggested breakdown as follows:

1) Poetry Analysis - 40 minutes
2) Prose Analysis - 40 minutes
3) Free-Response - 40 minutes

For each essay, you should take about 10 minutes to **read and outline** before you start to write.

Poetry Analysis

The first essay is an analysis based on a full-length classic or contemporary poem. While the specific prompt depends on the particular text, it typically involves instructions to address some aspect of a "complex" relationship or portrayal. Note that recent works are increasingly favored for this assignment. The course framework allots 25% of the test to 21st century works, and because contemporary poetry is often more loosely structured and ambiguous than classic works, it lends itself less well to multiple-choice questions and is used for the essay instead.

Prose Analysis

For the second essay, you will be given a passage of around 65-85 lines from a contemporary or a classic novel and asked to craft a thesis-driven essay analyzing a particular aspect of the text and supporting it with specific details. Although the passage is frequently drawn from an older work and may contain very challenging language, there is one major advantage: all the information you need is provided, so you do not need to spend time thinking of examples.

Free-Response

The third essay is the most open-ended of the three assignments, and the only one that requires outside knowledge. You are given a very general question concerning a common literary theme (idealism, the nature of a gift, mysterious origins) and asked to consider how it informs the meaning of the work as a whole. Although a list of sample works is provided, you are free to discuss any "complex" novel that you know well. While you are probably best off writing about a work you have studied in class, you are technically free to choose any work, even one that you have read independently.

Scoring

Essays are scored by trained readers (primarily high school English teachers and college English professors). **The rubric awards points in three main categories, with possible scores ranging from 0 (lowest) to 6 (highest).**

Thesis: 0-1 point

This is the most straightforward and objective of the three main criteria: having a clear thesis earns you one point; not having a clear thesis gets you no points.

Note, however, that it is almost impossible to earn a zero on the thesis while obtaining the maximum number of points in the other categories. By definition, an essay that lacks a clear thesis will be very difficult to support or argue in a sophisticated way.

1 - There is a clear, defensible thesis that takes a **specific position** on the prompt.

0 - The thesis is either absent, restates/rewords the prompt without taking a specific position, or is extremely vague (e.g., it states that a topic or theme is important to a work but does not make an argument about its role in the text).

The thesis can appear anywhere in your essay—it does not need to be placed at the end of the first paragraph in order to earn the point. **In most cases, however, placing it in the introduction will help to keep your essay focused and on-topic.**

The thesis may also consist of more than one sentence, provided that the sentences are placed near each other and convey a coherent argument.

Evidence and Commentary: 0-4 points

These points are awarded based on how effectively you support your argument, and on the depth of your analyses and explanations.

4 - Essays that earn a top score provide specific evidence or explanations for each claim; they also make clear how evidence/explanations support the various claims so that the reader is able to follow the logic of the argument. They also explain how specific words and phrases support your argument. **Note that essays with serious grammatical errors cannot earn a 4.**

3 - Essays that earn a 3 demonstrate many of the same qualities as "4" essays but do not provide specific evidence or explanations for all claims and/or do not make (fully) clear how evidence supports arguments or claims.

2 - Essays that earn a 2 fail to provide specific evidence or explain reasoning inconsistently. They may also include information that is off-topic or that does not support claims.

1 - Essays that earn a 1 make general claims rather than provide specific evidence and summarize evidence rather than explaining how it supports a claim.

0 - Essays that earn a 0 restate the thesis/information from the sources, or are off-topic.

Sophistication: 0-1 point

This is the most "open" of the three categories, and there are multiple ways to earn the point.

- **1 -** This point can be earned for either the strength of the writing (e.g., precise and colorful vocabulary, varied sentence structure and punctuation, clear transitions) or the analysis (providing broader context for an argument, discussing irony or contradictions in a nuanced way).
- **0 -** Essays that earn a 0 in this category do not contain the features necessary for a 1.

The point for sophistication is awarded based on an overall impression of engagement with the prompt and is thus more difficult to achieve than the "Thesis" point.

If you are concerned about essay scoring, keep in mind that the readers do take effort into account and are encouraged to give you the benefit of the doubt. They are not looking for excuses to mark you down but rather want you to do well. Moreover, they are explicitly instructed to take into account that the essays are first drafts written under intense time pressure, and to score them accordingly.

Although you may be most comfortable with the five-paragraph format, this structure is not required; it is, however, usually the most straightforward option. That said, if you believe that an alternate format is better suited to your argument, you are certainly free to use it.

Understanding the Essays

As an AP Literature student, you are probably accustomed to writing literary analysis essays for English class, but there are nevertheless a few test-specific points to keep in mind.

First, genre aside, **the Poetry and Prose Analysis Essays are essentially the same assignment and are therefore discussed in conjunction here**. While you can of course address rhetorical elements specific to the relevant genre, for example rhyme and meter in poetry or dialogue in prose, you are by no means required to do so. In fact, you can earn very high scores focusing exclusively on more general rhetorical strategies such as diction and imagery.

If you have written papers on individual poems, you will probably find little that is new about the AP Poetry Analysis essay. However, if you have not done timed, in-class assignments, you should keep in mind that 40 minutes go by very quickly—you will not have a chance to stop and ponder the meaning of an image or a turn of phrase. Instead, you must quickly seize on the most striking aspects of the text and consider how they inform the poem as a whole.

The Prose Analysis Essay differs from a typical English paper in the sense that it asks you to focus on the "micro" aspect of a text. Rather than consider a particular aspect of a narrative or character across a full-length novel, you must instead focus on how these elements are depicted in only about 65-85 lines. Because you will almost certainly have never seen the passage before, or be familiar with the novel or short story from which it is excerpted—passages tend to be taken from lesser-known works that are rarely studied in English classes—you will not be able to bring in outside knowledge about the work. **Essentially, you should approach it exactly as you would a poem.**

Although the question will impose some limits on your analysis, it will be sufficiently broad to allow you a good deal of leeway to focus on the aspects of the passage you find most interesting. **Your goal is to act as a "tour guide" to the text**: to indicate points of particular significance and explain how the author uses language to create specific effects or convey particular information about a character, event, or relationship. You should not feel obligated to cover the entire passage; rather, you should selectively focus on a few key places and discuss their importance to the passage as a whole.

While the AP English Literature and Composition Course Description now emphasizes skills over knowledge, the reality is that it is very difficult to write a strong literary analysis without a reasonable knowledge of rhetorical devices. Indeed, rhetoric *is* the language of literary analysis. For this reason, I have included an extended glossary of rhetorical figures at the end of this guide. It is certainly possible to score well on the Poetry and Prose Analysis Essays with a discussion of only basic rhetorical techniques; however, the more tools you have in your toolbox, so to speak, the easier it will be for you to identify places of interest in the passage and analyze them effectively. **As much as possible, the specific features of the text should drive your thesis. Formulating an argument based on a general impression and then going back and trying to find evidence to support it typically results in a much weaker analysis.** And given that you have only around 40 minutes to analyze the passage and write your essay, the faster you can comfortably work, the less stressful the exam will be.

The difficulty of the Free-Response Essay is exactly the opposite of what it is for the passage-based questions, namely that you are given exceedingly few limitations and must narrow down your options and stay focused regardless. It is very easy to go off-topic or to start making overly general statements! Furthermore, **writing a nuanced well-supported essay about a book you do not have physical access to means that you must know at least two or three works well enough to discuss their plots and characters in detail, from memory**. I recommend choosing a few books you've particularly enjoyed or understood well and making a study sheet that lists major themes, characters, and events. Spending even a moderate amount of time brainstorming beforehand will make the information much easier to access when you are under pressure.

Finally, two general points to keep in mind:

1) Score Correlates with Length

Generally speaking, longer essays tend to receive higher scores. More writing = more in-depth analysis. That said, **correlation is not causation**: An essay that is poorly structured, repetitive, and vague will not receive a high score, regardless of how long it is; nor will a perceptive, well-argued essay receive a lower score simply because it is on the shorter side.

2) Aim for Clarity and Coherence, Not Brilliance

Your readers will understand that you wrote your essay about an unfamiliar text, under extreme time pressure. As a result, they do not expect your writing to be spectacularly brilliant. Rather, they are looking to see whether you can cobble together a coherent, well-supported argument that demonstrates a moderately insightful interpretation. Focus on conveying your thoughts clearly, not weighing them down with flowery language.

Chapter Nine

Constructing an Essay

How to Write a Thesis

Simply put, **a thesis is an argument**, i.e., the main point: the central claim or assertion that your essay will be devoted to supporting.

To determine your thesis, you can use the following formula: **Who + So What + How?**

In other words:

- Who is the poem, passage, or novel about?
- What does the author convey about that person or idea?
- How does the author go about conveying it?

To be effective, a thesis must be both **specific** and **debatable**. It is **NOT** a factual statement or a description of the plot/theme(s).

- Nathaniel Hawthorne was one of the most important American writers of the nineteenth century.
- The passage describes how the governess sees ghosts that no one else can see.
- *The Awakening* by Kate Chopin deals with women's role in society.

It should **NOT** stretch beyond the **scope** of the passage or work—that is, it **should not consist of a grand, sweeping generalization about society or human nature**.

- The passage reveals the universal human tendency to be manipulated by flattery.
- Throughout history, people have always attempted to achieve a higher social status.
- Some individuals will always feel compelled to rebel against society's conventions.

This type of overly broad language can easily make an essay seem unfocused and cost you the "Sophistication" point as well as the "Thesis" point. And because it is very difficult to support such an overly broad statement effectively, you will almost certainly lose points in the "Evidence and Commentary" category as well.

Theses that are less sweeping but still overgeneralized should also be avoided, as should theses that consist of too many parts. **If you make two claims in your thesis, for example, you will be expected to support both claims and will be penalized for not doing so.**

Although you may eke out a point for the kinds of statements that appear below, they are difficult to develop in a focused way.

- The author shows how the characters have both similarities and differences.
- The author uses several techniques to reveal certain things about the characters.
- The author uses dialogue and diction to show that as members of society, people must take others' needs into consideration, and also to warn of the dangers of relying excessively on the approval of others.

In a literary analysis essay, **a strong thesis should address the specific literary techniques or devices** that the author uses to create a particular impression or convey an idea.

In addition to giving your essay clear focus, this information can also provide the essential structure of your essay: each main section (typically a paragraph, but more if necessary) can correspond to a particular technique.

In the examples below, notice how each of the "effective" options provides a clear and precise argument that limits the scope of the discussion. While the specifics vary, these examples are based on the essential formula ***the author uses x to convey y***.

Ineffective: Through his diction, the poet conveys the reality of war.

Effective: The poet uses a combination of metaphor, irony, and pathos to create an almost grotesque parody of the reality of war.

Ineffective: The passage from Kate Chopin's short story "The Storm" contains a lot of imagery and symbolism.

Effective: In the passage from the short story "The Storm," Kate Chopin uses short, choppy sentences and images of violent weather to symbolize the protagonist's rebellion against her conventional female role.

Ineffective: In Henry James' *The Turn of the Screw*, the governess clearly suffers from delusions.

Effective: In Henry James' *The Turn of the Screw*, the author employs rhetorical questions and fragmented statements to indicate the governess's increasingly delusional state.

Quick Check: Does It Get the Point?

Decide whether each of the statements below would receive the "Thesis" point. **(Answers are at the end of the guide, on p. 212.)**

1. Throughout the poem, the author uses diction to expose the truth while also being creative.

1 ________ 0 ___X___

2. Amy Tan's *The Joy Luck Club* has many descriptions of how Waverly Jong is both similar and different from her mother, Lindo.

1 ________ 0 ___X___

3. In the passage from the short story "The Birthmark," Hawthorne articulates the obsession with perfection through symbols, characters, and narrative voice.

1 ___X___ 0 ________

4. In "Landscape with the Fall of Icarus," Williams uses every grammatical trick in the book to represent a painting in the form of a poem.

1 ________ 0 ___X___

5. In the excerpt from the short story "Bartleby the Scrivener," Melville utilizes contrasting series of long and short words, as well as a vocabulary of illness and destruction, to convey the narrator's tortured relationship to Bartleby.

1 ___X___ 0 ________

What to Look for in a Passage

Unlike the non-fiction passages that appear on the SAT, ACT, and AP English Language Exam, poetry and fiction passages do not contain arguments, nor are they intended to persuade readers or inspire them to take a particular action. Instead, these excerpts are chosen because they illustrate particular themes, character traits/relationships, and types of language. Note that they may also be chosen because they are *not* entirely straightforward—that is, they may be open to multiple interpretations. As a result, there is no single "correct" answer, only responses that are more and less supported by the text.

You should therefore plan to read the poem or passage with one central goal in mind: identify a major theme, relationship, or character attribute that the author conveys, and note the specific places in the text where it is emphasized. In general, **key information is typically presented at the beginning and (re)emphasized at the end**, so you should make sure to pay particular attention to the first and last paragraphs. In addition, **make sure to read the blurb before the passage**—it may offer information necessary to keeping track of the characters or understanding the action.

The most effective way to approach this type of analysis is to have a list of specific textual features to look out for as you read. Although the assignment may suggest that you look for "style, tone, and selection of detail," responses that address only these elements in a general way are unlikely to achieve a high score in either the "Evidence and Commentary" or "Sophistication" category.

Five Key Questions:

1) Is the prevailing mood positive or negative? Why, and how do you know?

2) Does the passage contain any clear stylistic changes or shifts in focus? If so, where?

3) Is there any repetition of words/phrases? If so, what idea or trait does it emphasize?

4) Is there any "interesting" punctuation, e.g., question marks, dashes, or italics?

5) Diction: every passage contains diction, i.e., words. As a result, you should avoid merely stating that the author uses "diction." Rather, you should explain what **type of diction** is used. In particular, there are two simple things to consider:

    - Does the author use extreme language, e.g., *always, never, exceedingly, everywhere*, or vocabulary that is strongly positive or negative?

    - Does the author use language associated with a specific field, e.g., economics, medicine, war?

If you keep these questions in mind and mark down places of particular stylistic interest as you read, you will essentially have both your thesis and your primary points set right from the start.

Note that if you want to consider more complex literary devices, the glossary at the end of this guide provides a detailed list.

Tone and Attitude

Some essay questions may explicitly direct you to focus on the narrator's attitude, but even if this aspect of the text is not mentioned, both tone and attitude are often key to understanding what the poet or author wants to convey about a character or event.

As discussed in Chapter 7, tone and attitude are often aligned: the author will use extremely positive or negative words (i.e., tone) to indicate a strongly (dis)approving attitude on the part of the narrator or a character. In the two excerpts below, for instance, the tone and the attitude are strongly correlated.

Positive: The young woman was tall, with a figure of **perfect elegance** on a large scale. She had dark and abundant hair, **so glossy that it threw off the sunshine with a gleam**; and a face which, besides being **beautiful** from **regularity** of feature and **richness** of complexion, had the **impressiveness** belonging to a marked brow and deep black eyes. She was ladylike, too…characterised by a certain **state and dignity**…

Negative: [H]is passion had less **terror** for her than his **coldness**. The increasing frequency of the latter mood told her the **sad news** that he **disliked** her with a **growing dislike**. The more interesting that her appearance and manners became under the softening influences which she could now command, and in her wisdom did command, the more she seemed to **estrange** him.

On the other hand, an author can also convey a distinctly approving or disapproving view by using a much more **moderate** tone—that is, by using less extreme language. In such cases, you must be able to pick up on the necessary cues to understand what the author is implying; indeed, **places in the text where there is a gap between tone and attitude are particularly strong candidates for analysis because of what they indirectly reveal**.

For example, consider this example from Louise Erdrich's novel *The Round House*.

Positive: Whenever I s**ucceeded** in working loose a tiny tree, I placed it like a **trophy** beside me on the narrow sidewalk that surrounded the house…I thought it was a **wonder** the treelets had **persisted** through a North Dakota winter.

In the above excerpt, the text is devoid of the kind of strong language that characterizes the earlier example, but the narrator nevertheless conveys a distinctly positive attitude through the use of words such as *succeeded*, *trophy*, *wonder*, and *persisted*. The description conveys a small-scale triumph of life over the harshness of nature, and the narrator's appreciation of that fact. In this case, the narrator happens to be a 13-year-old boy, and so this type of description suggests that he is unusually mature and perceptive for his age.

Next, consider this example from Howells' "Editha," which operates at a similar level of tone but in the opposite direction.

Negative: [Editha] ran **impatiently** out on the veranda, to the edge of the steps, and **imperatively demanded greater haste of him with her will** before she called aloud to him: "George!"

Although the sentence is distinctly negative, Howells does not use over-the-top language to convey disapproval toward the title character. In fact, the first word with a negative connotation, *impatiently*, does not necessarily indicate that attitude; it is only the follow-up with the word *imperatively* (literally "commanding," but with a connotation of "demanding") here that the reader begins to develop a picture of Editha as someone stubborn and entitled. The narrator's attitude is revealed gradually, as the sentence progresses.

In many cases, the tone and attitude will not be exclusively positive or negative, nor will they remain consistent throughout a passage. More often, the text will convey shifting impressions, and you must be prepared to discuss emotions in a nuanced way. A character may be presented positively in one paragraph and then negatively in the next, or vice versa. The ability to identify and analyze these complexities is key to earning the "Sophistication" point. **To identify these shifts, focus on transitional words and phrases indicating contrast, e.g., *but*, *yet*, and *however*,** as well as changes in narrative point of view (discussed in Chapter 6).

For example, consider this passage from Nathaniel Hawthorne's novel *The Blithedale Romance*, on which the 2018 Prose Analysis Essay was based.

Shifting: In the gorgeousness with which [Zenobia] had surrounded herself—in the redundance of personal ornament, which the largeness of her physical nature and the rich type of her beauty caused to seem so suitable—I **malevolently beheld the true character of the woman, passionate, luxurious, lacking simplicity, not deeply refined, incapable of pure and perfect taste**.

But, the next instant, she was too powerful for all my opposing struggles. **I saw how fit it was that she should make herself as gorgeous as she pleased, and should do a thousand things that would have been ridiculous in the poor, thin, weakly characters of other women.** To this day, **however**, I hardly know whether I then beheld Zenobia in her truest attitude, or whether that were the truer one in which she had presented herself at Blithedale. In both, there was something like the illusion which a great actress flings around her.

Although the narrator spends the entire first paragraph castigating Zenobia for her excessive indulgence, he then pivots and asserts that she should be allowed to do as she wishes (*I saw how fit it was that she should make herself as gorgeous as she pleased…*). After that, he shifts direction yet again, insisting that he still does not fully understand who Zenobia was. By the end of the second paragraph, his attitude has evolved from bitter denunciation to utter perplexity at his own inability to grasp the situation.

Also to reiterate from Chapter 7, a common stumbling block involves recognizing humor, irony, and sarcasm. Remember that **literary humor often revolves around wordplay, the deliberate use of contrast (juxtaposition) between formal and informal, or the gap between what is said and what is actually true.**

If you are a strong reader and comfortable with old-fashioned language, you may find it helpful to try to "hear" the text internally as you read, but otherwise you will have to focus on the passage itself. Remember that **quotation marks** (to indicate skepticism, or non-literal usage) and **unusual capitalization** are both common techniques.

For example, consider the following sentence from Edith Wharton's *The Age of Innocence*, which is set among the members of New York's high society in the late nineteenth century.

> Sarcasm: Few things seemed to Newland Archer more awful than an offence against **"Taste,"** that far-off divinity of whom **"Form"** was the mere visible representative and vicegerent.

In the above sentence, Wharton employs both punctuation techniques, figuratively waving a red flag at the reader to signal that she is mocking the superficial ideals of the upper class.

Let's look at another example from the same novel.

> Sarcasm: There was no reason why the young man should not have come [to the opera] earlier, for he had dined at seven, alone with his mother and sister... But, in the first place, New York was a metropolis, and perfectly aware that in metropolises it was **"not the thing"** to arrive early at the opera; **and what was or was not "the thing" played a part as important in Newland Archer's New York as the inscrutable totem terrors that had ruled the destinies of his forefathers thousands of years ago**.

Here again, we have the use of quotation marks, this time around the phrase *(not) the thing* to indicate that Wharton is again poking fun at the seriousness with which certain arbitrary social conventions are treated. In this case, the casual register of the word *thing* also stands in contrast to the rather lofty reference to the opera (symbol of high culture).

Furthermore, the phrase *inscrutable totem terrors that had ruled the destinies of his forefathers thousands of years ago* also serves to make light of the conventions to which Newland is bound—by equating primitive superstitions (low, informal) with the strictures governing Newland's cultured, urbane New York (high, formal), Wharton suggests the absurd amount of weight placed on what are ultimately very low-stakes behaviors. Finally, the over-articulated alliteration in the phrase *totem terrors*, with its emphasis on the "t" sound, invokes a person stuttering in terror—a ridiculous image in this context.

For a list of common adjectives that describe tone and attitude, see the chart on p. 117.

Using Strong Language Effectively

Just as correct answers to multiple-choice tone questions must reflect the level of intensity in the text, the language you use to describe tones and attitudes should be proportionate to the level of extremity in the passage. **A common misconception is that a strong analysis is one that includes a lot of dramatic language; however, using overly forceful language to describe a part of the text that is not particularly extreme will actually *weaken* your analysis.**

What can make moderating your discussion in this way so challenging is that some passages, particularly poems, contain sections with very extreme language and emotions, as well as ones that are more measured in comparison. You must be able to adjust your discussion to account for these shifts; otherwise, not only do you risk losing the "Sophistication" point, but you may also misinterpret the work.

To illustrate, we're going to look the Keats poem "When I Have Fears That I May Cease to Be," which appeared on the 2008 exam.

When I have fears that I may cease to be
  Before my pen has gleaned my teeming brain,
Before high-pilèd books, in charactery,
  Hold like rich garners the full ripened grain;
When I behold, upon the night's starred face,
  Huge cloudy symbols of a high romance,
And think that I may never live to trace
  Their shadows with the magic hand of chance;
And when I feel, fair creature of an hour,
  That I shall never look upon thee more,
Never have relish in the faery power
  Of unreflecting love—then on the shore
Of the wide world I stand alone, and think
  Till love and fame to nothingness do sink.

This is an excellent example of a work that contains both very strong language and more restrained language, even if its overall subject—the poet's fear of dying and being unable to finish his work and see his beloved—is quite dramatic.

Some of the language directly conveys the magnitude of the speaker's feelings: the word *never*, for example, is repeated in lines 7, 10, and 11, suggesting the speaker is attempting to come to terms with the extent of his potential loss. In addition, the mention of *huge cloudy symbols of a high romance* in line 6 evokes the immense swirling passion of his writing.

However, the poem is also characterized by a quieter intensity in places: verbs such as *cease to be* (line 1), *stand* (line 13), and *sink* (line 14) are fairly moderate, for example, and the image of the poet tracing the clouds' *shadows with the magic hand of chance* brings the description down to a more intimate, thoughtful level. In fact, it is the tension between these two types of language that gives the poem so much of its power.

On the next page, we're going to look at two sample paragraphs: the first uses language that is disproportionately simplistic and extreme, whereas the second accurately discusses the type of language used in the poem and provides a far more sophisticated analysis.

Extreme: Keats ends the poem on an **extremely bleak** note. If he cannot have everlasting fame and love, then he feels **utter despair and isolation**. He sees his position in the universe and realizes how **minuscule** and insignificant our lives are compared to the **vastness** of the world and the **inexorable** passing of time. We cannot help but ponder our place within the **immenseness** of the universe, and when we do so, we must **inevitably** come to the conclusion that love and fame "to nothingness do sink."

Effective: Keats ends the poem on a **somewhat ambiguous** note. On one hand, we can interpret his decision to "stand alone" and watch as "love and fame" sink into "nothingness" as an admission of defeat: he has recognized that death is inevitable and, in his anguish, seeks only a state of numbness and oblivion. On the other hand, these lines also suggest a form of acceptance that is not despairing but rather serene: he perceives the ephemeral nature of the world and the superficiality of earthly goals and is thus able to achieve a state of transcendence.

Notice how the consistently strong language in the first example has a dulling effect on the analysis: essentially, the writer makes a point and then simply continues to make it. The argument is well supported, but it does not really go anywhere. In contrast, the second example focuses on an ambiguity in the text, discussing both sides and suggesting a less obvious interpretation. This is the type of discussion that would earn the second writer the "Sophistication" point.

Note that one way to discuss tone and attitude in a more sophisticated manner is to use **qualifiers** to indicate the level of intensity. To "qualify" a term means to provide more information about it, usually to soften it or make it less harsh with a word such as *slightly* or *somewhat* (used in the second example above), although qualification can also involve making language more extreme through the use of intensifiers (third column below). The following chart provides a range of options that you can use to adjust the intensity of your analysis.

Mild	**Moderate**	**Extreme**
Hardly	Considerably	Exceptionally
Marginally	Fairly	Extraordinarily
Mildly	Moderately	Extremely
Slightly	Rather	Highly
	Relatively	Intensely
	Somewhat	Wildly

The Narrator Is Not the Writer

One last and very important point to bear in mind as you analyze the texts provided is that **the narrator/speaker is not actually the poet or author and should not be treated as such**. Rather, **a narrator is a literary persona created for the purposes of a specific work**. The speaker in an Emily Dickinson poem, for example, is "the speaker" or "the narrator," not to be confused with Dickinson herself. There may be some overlap between the two, but they are not interchangeable.

Now, a narrator or speaker's situation or concerns may indeed be consistent with those in the writer's life, and if you do happen to have some biographical knowledge, you may wish to mention the connection should it be particularly relevant to your analysis. That said, **it is not—I repeat not—your job to speculate about the connection between a work of literature and its author's mental or emotional state**. Especially in the absence of any biographical knowledge, you should not suggest that a writer was depressed, unbalanced, or suffering from any form of psychiatric illness. That is a form of inference that goes far, far beyond what can be assumed from any text!

In other words, **do not** do anything like the following:

Avoid: "I felt a Funeral in my Brain" highlights the tragedies in Emily Dickinson's journey of life, which helps develop the poem's dark mood. Here, she questions not only herself, but the world around her. It seems that Dickinson wrote this poem during a difficult time in her life when she faced many issues, and she used poetry to cope and express herself. The poem demonstrates Dickinson's descent into insanity and uses a funeral as a metaphor for her depression.

Structuring Your Essay

You have two main options for structuring your Poetry and Prose Analysis Essays, and they depend on the organization of the passage itself.

1) By literary device

This is generally the more straightforward option and should be treated as the default.

When you have finished annotating the passage and making note of the various devices it contains, **choose no more than three prominent/significant ones, and devote a paragraph to each**. You should generally limit your discussion to three techniques because anything beyond that will leave you without enough time to develop each point sufficiently.

If there are two prominent techniques that appear throughout the passage, you also can focus on them alone and, if necessary, devote multiple paragraphs to a single one.

Focusing on only one device for the entire essay is risky, however, because you can easily run out of ideas and end up with an essay that is too repetitive. Only go with this choice if you are a very strong writer and certain that you have enough material to analyze.

2) Chronologically, in order of the passage

This is an option to consider if the author traces a clear change in a character or relationship over the course of the passage, as opposed to providing a description. Each point (paragraph) can correspond to a key step in the shift—try to choose one place from the beginning, one from the middle, and one from the end.

If you do use this structure, however, you must be careful not to simply narrate the events in the text; each step in your argument must make clear how the passage is moving the narrator/characters or action from point A to point B. You should also limit yourself to discussing two, or at most three, of the most important strategies in each section.

The Importance of Making an Outline

It is almost impossible to overstate the importance of spending a few minutes organizing your thoughts on paper before you begin writing, even if you know what your major points are. It is too easy to accidentally veer off course or forget a key point otherwise. Straying from your thesis is a guaranteed way to lose easy points in both the "Evidence and Commentary" and "Sophistication" categories, and having a clear outline will prevent you from falling into that trap.

In addition to your thesis, you should determine your major points/sections, as well as your examples, and have that information present to refer back to as you write. If you make sure in your outline that 1) your thesis clearly responds to the prompt; 2) each point clearly supports your thesis; and 3) each example clearly illustrates the relevant point, your argument will remain focused, and you are more or less guaranteed to score at least 4 out of 6. **Remember: your goal is to be clear and coherent, not brilliant.**

On the next page, we're going to start working with a sample Prose passage.

The following passage is from Edith Wharton's 1905 novel, *The House of Mirth*, which follows the life of a young woman named Lily Bart. In a well-written essay, analyze how the author portrays Selden's attitude toward Lily Bart through the use of literary techniques.

Selden paused in surprise. In the afternoon rush of the Grand Central Station his eyes had been refreshed by the sight of Miss Lily Bart. He was returning to his work from a hurried dip into the country; but what was Miss Bart doing in town? She stood apart from the crowd, letting it drift by her, and wearing an air of irresolution which might, as he surmised, be the mask of a very definite purpose. There was nothing new about Lily Bart, yet **he could never see her without a faint movement of interest: it was characteristic of her that she always roused speculation, that her simplest acts seemed the result of far-reaching intentions.**

An impulse of curiosity made him turn out of his direct line to the door, and stroll past her.

"Mr. Selden—what good luck!"

She came forward smiling, eager almost, in her resolve to intercept him. One or two persons, in brushing past them, lingered to look; for Miss Bart was a figure to arrest even the suburban traveller rushing to his last train.

Selden had never seen her more **radiant**. Her **vivid** head relieved against the **dull** tints of the crowd, made her more conspicuous than in a ball-room, and under her **dark hat and veil** she regained the **girlish smoothness, the purity of tint,** that she was beginning to lose after eleven years of late hours and indefatigable dancing. **Had she indeed reached the nine-and-twentieth birthday with which her rivals credited her?**

"What luck!" she repeated. "How nice of you to come to my rescue!"

He responded joyfully that to do so was his mission in life, and asked what form the rescue was to take.

"Oh, almost any—even to sitting on a bench and talking to me. One sits out a cotillion—why not sit out a train? It isn't a bit hotter here than in Mrs. Van Osburgh's conservatory—and some of the women are not a bit uglier." She broke off, laughing, to explain that she had missed the train to Rhinebeck. "And there isn't another till half-past five." She consulted the little jeweled watch among her laces. "Just two hours to wait. And I don't know what to do with myself. My maid came up this morning, and my aunt's house is closed, and I don't know a soul in town." She glanced plaintively about the station. "If you can spare the time, do take me somewhere for a breath of air."

He declared himself entirely at her disposal: the adventure struck him as diverting. As a spectator, he had always enjoyed Lily Bart; and his course lay so far out of her orbit that it amused him to be drawn into the sudden intimacy which her proposal implied.

"The resources of New York are rather meagre," he said; "but I'll find a hansom first, and then we'll invent something." He led her through the throng of returning holiday-makers, past sallow-faced girls in preposterous hats, and flat-chested women struggling with paper bundles and palm-leaf fans. **Was it possible that she belonged to the same race?** The **dinginess, the crudity**, of this average section of womanhood made him feel how **highly specialized** she was.

They turned into Madison Avenue and began to stroll northward. As she moved beside him, Selden was conscious of taking a luxurious pleasure in her nearness: in the modelling of her little ear, the crisp upward wave of her hair—**was it ever so slightly brightened by art?**—and the thick planting of her straight black lashes. Everything about her was at once vigorous and exquisite, at once strong and fine. He had a **confused sense** that she must have cost a great deal to make, that a great many dull and ugly people must, in some mysterious way, have been sacrificed to produce her. He was aware that the qualities distinguishing her from the herd of her sex were chiefly external: as though a **fine glaze of beauty and fastidiousness** had been applied to **vulgar clay**. Yet the analogy left him unsatisfied, for a coarse texture will not take a high finish; and **was it not possible that the material was fine, but that circumstance had fashioned it into a futile shape?**

Let's start by just summarizing the passage. Luckily, the action is pretty straightforward: A man named Selden is at the train station when he spots Lily Bart, a woman he knows slightly, and whom he finds intriguing. Lily spots him and tells him that she has missed her train, then asks him to entertain her for a couple of hours while she waits for the next one. He agrees, and they walk together out of the station.

Next, what is the focus of the passage?

Essentially, it's Selden's fascination with the somewhat mysterious Lily. We know that because he indicates his interest both at the end of the first paragraph (*[H]e could never see her without a faint movement of interest: it was characteristic of her that she always roused speculation, that her simplest acts seemed the result of far-reaching intentions.*) and throughout the entire last paragraph. That attitude is also conveyed in a variety of ways throughout the passage.

So that's half the thesis: **the author does x to convey Selden's fascination with Lily.**

Now, we find *x*. In other words, we look at the specific words, punctuation, sentence structures, etc. that the author uses in order to reveal the narrator's attitude.

If you circled "interesting" punctuation as you read the passage, you might have noticed that there are four question marks, including one in the very last sentence. (You can also just do a quick, purely visual scan of the passage to see whether anything jumps out at you.)

- *Had she indeed reached the nine-and-twentieth birthday with which her rivals credited her?*
- *Was it possible that she belonged to the same race [as the other women Selden sees]?*
- *Selden was conscious of taking a luxurious pleasure in her nearness: in the modelling of her little ear, the crisp upward wave of her hair—was it ever so slightly brightened by art?*
- *[W]as it not possible that the material was fine, but that circumstance had fashioned it into a futile shape?*

The ability to home in on punctuation this way is very important because it offers a straightforward "entry" point into the analysis, one that requires less time and attention to notice than many other devices.

Now, why include all those questions? Well, think about Selden's attitude toward Lily: he is curious about her—there is something about her he cannot quite pin down. So the questions serve to emphasize that fact.

If we look at the information around the questions, we can actually find a second major technique. Consider, for instance, the paragraph before the first question:

> *Selden had never seen her more* ***radiant****. Her* ***vivid*** *head, relieved against the* ***dull*** *tints of the crowd, made her more conspicuous than in a ball-room, and under her* ***dark hat and veil*** *she regained the* ***girlish smoothness****,* ***the purity of tint****, that she was beginning to lose after eleven years of late hours and indefatigable dancing.*

And the paragraph in which the second question appears:

> *He led her through the throng of returning holiday-makers, past* ***sallow-faced*** *girls in* ***preposterous hats****, and* ***flat-chested women*** *struggling with paper bundles and palm-leaf fans…The* ***dinginess****, the* ***crudity****, of this average section of womanhood made him feel how* ***highly specialized*** *she was.*

Both these sections, as well as the extended description in the final paragraph, make extensive use of **descriptive language** (adjectives) to set up a **contrast** (or **juxtaposition**) between the remarkable Lily Bart and the far more ordinary women that surround her.

This is already a lot of material to work with, so we can move to the thesis.

Thesis: Wharton's repeated use of questions as well as a series of highly descriptive contrasts serve to convey Selden's fascination with Lily Bart and depict her as an enigmatic figure.

Note that this is only one possible focus for the essay—there are many other aspects that could be discussed, but given the time constraint, you must decide quickly and stick to your choice!

Having established the thesis, we can now make an outline.

I. Introduction

Present passage - text from HOM, describes encounter betw. Selden + Lily. Selden is intrigued by Lily, wants to know more about her. End w/thesis.

II. Questions

A. Found throughout the passage - convey consistent sense of curiosity

B. Appearance vs. reality: question in 28-30 (is she really 29?)

C. Add'l quotes, reiterate mysterious quality - *was it ever so slightly brightened by art?*

III. Contrast, descriptive language 1

A. Emphasize L.'s extraordinary qualities

B. Lines 22-26 - extremely positive adjectives (radiant, vivid) - Selden is more than a little intrigued.

C. Lines 57-62 - contrast w/other women → more extreme. Very negative.

IV. Contrast, descriptive language 2

A. Final paragraph - Lily is herself a contradiction = mysterious

B. Repetition of *at once*, lines 69-70, emphasizes contradiction

V. Conclusion

Reader absorbs Selden's confusion - no clear idea of who Lily is.

Now let's look at how each part of the essay gets constructed.

Introduction

Because you will have less than 40 minutes to actually write your essay after reading/annotating the passage and (ideally) jotting down a quick outline, you must be able to move through your introduction quickly so that you can focus on the real substance of your analysis in the body paragraphs.

Your primary goal in the introduction is to "set the scene" in order to frame your discussion and orient the reader. It should provide just enough context for your analysis without turning into an extended summary of the passage or a partial analysis. For that reason, you should **try to limit the introduction to around five sentences**.

Note also the use of transitional words and phrases (in bold) to introduce new ideas and keep the reader oriented within the argument.

Step 1: Introduce the situation (1-2 sentences)

In the excerpt from Edith Wharton's novel *The House of Mirth*, a young man named Selden is passing through Grand Central Station when he spots an acquaintance—an intriguing young woman named Lily Bart. The two strike up a conversation, and Lily, who has missed her train, persuades Selden to entertain her for a couple of hours.

Step 2: Transition to your topic (1-2 sentences)

As the passage develops, it becomes clear that Selden views Lily as much more than an ordinary woman. **Indeed**, his words indicate that he finds her utterly exceptional, as well as somewhat mysterious.

Step 3: State your thesis and (optional) introduce examples. (1-2 sentences)

Throughout the text, Wharton uses repeated questions as well as a series of highly descriptive contrasts to convey Selden's fascination with Lily and depict her as an enigmatic figure.

Note that the **narrow scope** of the essay is established right from the beginning—the first couple of sentences indicate that the analysis will focus on the specific events of the passage.

A **less effective** opening, on the other hand, might go something like this:

> Psychology has found that people are often fascinated by individuals that are different from them.

Or:

> Throughout history, some people have always been too mysterious to understand.

Both of these statements are **far too broad**—your essay is not about psychology or mysterious people throughout history, and these statements make your writing seem vague and generic. Remember that you cannot make large generalizations based on characters you are only just encountering for the first time!

Body Paragraphs

At bare minimum, you should **aim for at least five or six sentences** in your body paragraphs, and more if necessary; anything less will not allow for sufficient development, causing you to lose points in the "Evidence and Commentary" category.

As we established in the outline, the first body paragraph will focus on Wharton's use of punctuation, specifically question marks.

Step 1: Transition + topic sentence

From the beginning of the passage, the author takes care to present Lily as a puzzling figure to Selden (we are told in line 12 that she "always roused speculation"), and one of the most striking ways in which she emphasizes this quality is through the use of questions.

Step 2: Introduce quotation(s) evidence

For example, in lines 28-29 Selden wonders whether Lily "had indeed reached the nine-and-twentieth birthday with which her rivals credited her."

Step 3: Analyze examples and explain their significance

It is significant that the narrator does not state Lily's age outright **but instead** presents it more ambiguously. Like Selden, we do not know for certain that she is nearly 30 (an old maid by 1905 standards!). **Rather**, this aspect of her identity is merely hinted at. By introducing us to Lily in this manner, Wharton establishes the character herself as a sort of question mark, someone who perhaps is not entirely what she appears to be.

Do not forget the second step, underlined above—quotations do not explain themselves! You must **explicitly** state the implications of your evidence; do not assume that the reader can put the pieces together.

Step 4: If necessary, repeat steps 2 and 3

This impression is affirmed as Selden observes Lily while they are walking out of the station: observing the "upward wave of her hair," he asks himself, "was it ever so slightly brightened by art?" (lines 67-68). With these words, the narrator again subtly suggests that Lily's youthful appearance is something of a mirage. **Interestingly**, this ambiguity makes her no less alluring to Selden; **in fact**, he finds her all the more entrancing for it, taking "luxurious pleasure in her nearness."

Again, notice how the quotation is not simply left hanging. Both the second and third sentences comment on it, not by merely restating what it says in descriptive language (a very common trap) but rather by using it to push the analysis forward.

Now let's look at the rest of the sample essay in regular form. Notice how **quotations are never just dropped in without a discussion afterward**. Rather, specific aspects of the language are discussed and used to advance the analysis. Notice also the **consistent use of transitions** to orient the reader within the argument.

Rest of the essay:

Throughout the passage, the use of contrast to Lily Bart is striking **as well. If** the repeated questions emphasize her elusive quality, **then** the opposing pairs of adjectives serve to both reinforce this idea and emphasize her contradictory nature—**as well as** the extraordinary impression she makes in comparison to other, more ordinary individuals. **For example**, in lines 22-26, in which Selden observes Lily up close for the first time, she is described as "radiant" and "vivid," adjectives that contrast sharply with the "dull tints of the crowd." **Here**, Lily is established as a sort of beacon, shining above the faceless masses—in Selden's perception, at least.

As the paragraph progresses, however, the contradiction shifts onto Lily herself: her "dark hat and veil" (obvious symbols of ageing) are juxtaposed with her "girlish smoothness, [her] purity of tint." **Like** the question that follows, this image serves to suggest the distance between appearance and reality, and to imply that the face Lily presents to the world is perhaps no longer representative of who she truly is. That idea is presented only briefly here, **however**, and is not returned to until the end of the passage—almost as if to tease the reader. **In the meantime**, the narrator takes care to underline the gap between Lily and the women who surround her, most notably in lines 56-59. **As the narrator describes**, Selden "led [Lily] through the throng of returning holiday-makers, past sallow-faced girls in preposterous hats, and flat-chested women struggling with paper bundles and palm-leaf fans." The presentation of the other women in the station as exaggeratedly unattractive ("sallow-faced"), asexual ("flat-chested"), quasi-ridiculous figures (their hats are "preposterous"), presumably as Selden sees them, suggests the extent to which he idealizes (and idolizes) Lily.

It is in the final paragraph of the passage that Selden's attitude becomes less straightforwardly worshipful and more ambiguous—and ambivalent. **In particular**, the repetition of "at once" and the use of antithesis ("vigorous" vs. "exquisite"; "strong" vs. "fine") in lines 69-70, as well as the opposition between "fine glaze of beauty and fastidiousness" and "vulgar clay" in lines 76-77, create the impression of a woman composed of a mass of contradictions. **Indeed**, the reference to Selden's "confused sense" further emphasizes Lily's destabilizing effect on him. **As the paragraph moves on**, Selden's thoughts begin to reflect this confusion: in the last few lines, he is unable to even form a clear analogy to explain to himself the qualities that distinguish Lily from "the herd of her sex." The word "herd" is particularly crude and animalistic, suggesting that Selden is becoming increasingly carried away. Clearly, this is no simple infatuation.

Conclusion

Your conclusion does not need to be particularly long, and in fact, if your final body paragraph ends on a sufficiently strong note, you may not need a separate conclusion at all.

That said, if you do want to include one, you can aim for about three or four sentences—just enough to finish things off without seeming overly abrupt.

Step 1: Transition from the previous paragraph

It is unsurprising, then, that the passage should end with an uneasy question about which aspects of Lily are superficial and which are genuine. Is she merely a beautiful façade hiding something far less attractive, or does the exterior reflect the interior?

Step 2: Tie it back to the thesis

Through this final gesture, the author conveys the extent of Lily's sheer magnetism and enchanting quality, as well as her elusive and contradictory nature.

Step 3: Finish it off

Like Selden himself, the reader is left with a question: who, truly, is Lily Bart?

Chapter Ten

The Elements of Style

Now, having considered the big picture, we're going to look at some general stylistic issues. While you will not lose points for minor spelling or grammatical errors, repeated and flagrant mistakes will give your readers an impression of sloppiness and make it difficult for them to follow your argument. That will almost certainly cost you the "Sophistication" point.

Tense Consistency

As a general rule, **use the literary present when discussing works of literature**.

Incorrect: In Cormac McCarthy's The Road, the protagonists' commitment to each other **was** tested in dangerous and life-threatening situations, but they **found** a way to stick together. They **overlooked** each other's mistakes and **were** able to move forward because they **knew** that holding a grudge or going separate ways would lead to their demise.

Correct: In Cormac McCarthy's The Road, the protagonists' commitment to each other **is** tested in dangerous and life-threatening situations, but they **find** a way to stick together. They **overlook** each other's mistakes and **are** able to move forward because they **know** that holding a grudge or going separate ways will lead to their demise.

Only use the past tense to discuss events that clearly occurred prior to the action of the story.

Correct: McCarthy creates a world barren of life, except for the few who **managed** to survive the catastrophe that has left the earth devoid of natural resources.

Note that the past perfect (*had + verb*) indicates a finished action in the past that came **before** a second finished action. As a result, this tense should not generally be used.

Passive Voice

In an **active** construction, the subject of a sentence typically comes before the object. The emphasis is on the person or thing performing the action.

William Shakespeare	wrote	*Hamlet*.
subject	**verb**	**object**

In a **passive** construction, however, the subject and the object are flipped. The passive voice also includes a form of the verb *to be* + *past participle* and the preposition *by*. As a result, *x did y* becomes *y was done by x*. The emphasis is on the object as the receiver of the action.

Hamlet	was written	by	William Shakespeare.
subject	**verb**	**preposition**	**object**

Although the passive voice is commonly treated as something of a grammatical punching bag, there are times when it is perfectly appropriate for a given situation, e.g., to indicate that something is being done *to* a character.

Acceptable: In Kate Chopin's "The Story of an Hour," the protagonist **is confined** to the traditional role of wife and mother **by** both her husband and nineteenth-century American society as a whole.

In this case, the use of the passive voice makes sense because it serves to emphasize that the protagonist is on the receiving end of the action.

On the other hand, the repeated and indiscriminate use of the passive can create constructions that are unnecessarily wordy and awkward.

Awkward: In "The Story of an Hour," the emotions of a woman who is married and uncomfortably confined to her role of wife and mother **are described by Kate Chopin**. The customs of American society in the nineteenth century **are depicted by the author**, and a story that accurately reflects the experiences of many women of that time **is created by her**.

In the above example, the repeated use of the passive bogs the prose down. In contrast, the active verbs in the version below make the prose cleaner and easier to absorb.

Clear: In "The Story of an Hour," **Kate Chopin describes** the emotions of a woman who is married and uncomfortably confined to her role of wife and mother. **The author depicts** the customs of American society in the nineteenth century and **creates** a story that accurately reflects the experiences of many women of that time.

Use Verbs and Nouns, Not -ING Words (Gerunds)

Another way to strengthen your writing is to avoid the unnecessary use of -ING words (gerunds). Like the passive, this construction can easily become awkward and weigh down your writing.

Awkward: **Because of the narrator's believing** that no one could possibly thwart his attempt to find literary gold, he exhibits an excessive amount of confidence.

Clear: **Because the narrator believes** that no one could possibly thwart his attempt to find literary gold, he exhibits an excessive amount of confidence.

Clear: **Because of the narrator's belief** that no one could possibly thwart his attempt to find literary gold, he exhibits an excessive amount of confidence.

"Vague" Pronouns

Another common trap involves pronouns like *this*, *that*, and *what*.

Although it is fine to use these words without a noun or phrase afterward, you should be very careful to limit your reliance on this construction because it can easily make your writing seem vague and overly casual.

Vague: Conflict and human experience are necessary ingredients in a great novel. The passage from A Farewell to Arms contains both of **these**. **This** causes the reader to become intrigued about **what will happen**.

Specific: Conflict and human experience are necessary ingredients in a great novel. The passage from A Farewell to Arms contains both of **these elements, causing the reader to become intrigued about how the plot will develop**.

To reiterate, phrases beginning with *what* are particularly ambiguous.

Vague: In the novel Middlemarch, Dorothea Brooke becomes unhappy because of **what she does**.

Instead of just referring to "what she does," you need to **explicitly state** the action—do not force your reader to guess.

Specific: In the novel Middlemarch, Dorothea Brooke becomes unhappy because of **her decision to marry the dull and scholarly Mr. Casaubon.**

Using Transitions Effectively

Transitional words and phrases indicate whether you are presenting evidence, moving to a new example, or drawing a conclusion. They serve as "signposts" that help readers orient themselves in your argument, and their effective use is crucial to achieving a high score.

Example 1: **Initially**, Selden's attitude toward Lily is primarily one of curiosity, but as the passage progresses, he becomes increasingly entranced by her charms.

Example 2: Throughout the passage, the repetition of the word "forever" conveys the depth of the narrator's longing. **Moreover**, it creates a timeless quality, as if the action were occurring outside the constraints of the everyday world.

Example 3: The House of Mirth depicts the intricate art of keeping up appearances and maintaining one's status within the leisure class. **At the same time**, it subtly critiques this social order.

One simple way to make your writing sound more sophisticated is to place an occasional transition in the middle of a sentence rather than at the beginning.

Beginning: Throughout the passage, Melville includes images related to sailors and the sea; **however,** he also employs a variety of other techniques, including repetition and alliteration.

Middle: Throughout the passage, Melville includes images related to sailors and the sea. He also**, however,** employs a variety of other techniques, including repetition and alliteration.

In both sentences, the transition serves exactly the same purpose: to connect the second statement to the first. The second version simply moves the transition to a less-expected location, making the sentence more interesting stylistically.

For an extended list of transitional words and phrases, see the chart on p. 79.

Varying Your Sentence Structure

Using a variety of sentence structures and types of punctuation can help make your writing livelier and more interesting.

Boring: There are several themes present in the excerpt from Fielding's Tom Jones. One important theme involves the conflict between parental authority and individual choice in matters of love and marriage. In the passage, characters often express ideas about love to other characters. When they do this, they also raise questions about autonomy and self-determination.

The above paragraph is acceptable, but on a stylistic level, it's fairly dull. Compare it to this version, which flows much more effectively.

Interesting: Among the themes present in the excerpt from Fielding's Tom Jones, one of the most important ones involves the conflict between parental authority and individual choice in matters of love and marriage. When characters express their ideas about love—as occurs frequently in the passage—they also raise questions about autonomy and self-determination.

Avoiding Repetition

One common pitfall to avoid involves latching onto a particular word and using it repeatedly. In addition to making your writing seem simplistic stylistically, excessive repetition can also prevent you from developing your analysis and obtaining the "Sophistication" point.

Repetitive: In "Editha," William Dean Howells tells the story of an **idealistic** young girl who manipulates her fiancé, George, into going off to war. Throughout Editha's interactions with George, Howells demonstrates how **idealism** can lead a person to develop unethical **ideals**. Editha's **idealistic** view of war leads her to underestimate its dangers, and readers are taught the importance of loving someone for who they are.

There's nothing wrong with the word "idealistic," but using a version of it four times in three sentences is excessive. Compare it to this version, which rephrases it in a variety of ways:

Varied: In "Editha," William Dean Howells tells the story of an **idealistic** young girl who manipulates her fiancé, George, into going off to war. Throughout Editha's interactions with George, Howells demonstrates how **excessive romanticism** can lead a person to develop unethical **principles**. Editha's **naive** view of war leads her to underestimate its dangers—and readers are taught the importance of loving someone for who they are.

Now the paragraph contains a mix of sentence types and punctuation. Compared to the first version, the second version reads much more smoothly and is more engaging.

Another area in which it is particularly easy to become repetitive involves quotations. The verbs *say* and *states* are typically the default options for introducing direct citations from the text, but you should attempt to find more colorful, precise alternatives whenever possible.

Boring: In lines 31-32, Lily **says,** "How nice of you to come to my rescue!"

Interesting: In lines 31-32, Lily **exclaims,** "How nice of you to come to my rescue!"

The list below provides a range of options.

• asserts	• implies
• calls attention to	• indicates
• claims	• insinuates
• confirms	• insists
• contends	• points out
• describes	• reiterates
• emphasizes	• reveals
• exclaims	• suggests
• explains	• underlines
• illustrates	• underscores

It is important to avoid repetition at the paragraph level as well.

Once you have introduced a point, move on to another part of your argument (citing from the text, tying it back to your thesis, etc.)—while you may want to reiterate the point once, and ideally from a slightly different angle, after you have finished your analysis, **repeating your point throughout a paragraph is not a substitute for analyzing the text**.

Repetitive: Kate Chopin was a writer who **wrote to depict obstacles** and instances occurring **within her time period**. **Writing about personal obstacles**, as well as issues occurring **in the time period she lived**, Chopin proved to be an **ambitious individual**. Kate Chopin was a determined author, with **true ambition** and ability to produce writings that placed a higher value on women's experiences and **the obstacles they overcame**.

Notice that the argument here never progresses—the writer simply repeats the same point over and over. Compare it to the version below.

Stronger: Kate Chopin was a writer who wrote to depict obstacles and instances occurring within her time period. **As a woman in the nineteenth century, she was preoccupied with the restrictions imposed on her gender and ambitiously sought to depict the reality of women's lives.**

Register and Conventions

Register refers to how **formal** or **informal** a writer's language is. The Prose Analysis Essay must be written in the same **moderately formal style** as any paper you would write for English class and observe the same conventions of standard written English.

Avoid casual language.

Casual: Edna Pontellier, the novel's heroine, is a wife and mother of two **little kids**.

Correct: Edna Pontellier, the novel's heroine, is a wife and mother of two **young children**.

All words should be written out (with the exception of titles that are normally abbreviated, e.g., Dr. and Mr.). Do not use ampersands (& signs) or other abbreviations.

Incorrect: In Kate Chopin's novel The Awakening, Edna Pontellier demonstrates her newfound **passion & independence** through painting.

Correct: In Kate Chopin's novel The Awakening, Edna Pontellier demonstrates her newfound **passion and independence** through painting.

Write out numbers smaller than 10.

Incorrect: At the beginning of The Awakening, Edna Pontellier is a happy woman with a husband and **2 children**, vacationing at Grand Isle.

Correct: At the beginning of The Awakening, Edna Pontellier is a happy woman with a husband and **two children**, vacationing at Grand Isle.

Refer to authors by their last names.

Incorrect: In The Awakening, **Kate** depicts the liberation and subsequent downfall of Edna Pontellier, a wife and a mother who rebels against her socially prescribed role.

Correct: In The Awakening, **Chopin** depicts the liberation and subsequent downfall of Edna Pontellier, a wife and a mother who rebels against her socially prescribed role.

Titles of literary works should be capitalized.

Incorrect: In Kate Chopin's novel **the awakening**, Edna Pontellier, a wife and a mother, rebels against her socially prescribed role, with tragic results.

Correct: In Kate Chopin's novel **The Awakening**, Edna Pontellier, a wife and a mother, rebels against her socially prescribed role, with tragic results.

Titles of novels should be underlined.

Incorrect: In Kate Chopin's novel **The Awakening**, Edna Pontellier, a wife and a mother, rebels against her socially prescribed role, with tragic results.

Correct: In Kate Chopin's novel **<u>The Awakening</u>**, Edna Pontellier, a wife and a mother, rebels against her socially prescribed role, with tragic results.

Titles of poems should be placed in quotation marks.

Incorrect: **American Smooth**, which was written by the poet Rita Dove, describes an interaction between a pair of dance partners.

Correct: "**American Smooth**," which was written by the poet Rita Dove, describes an interaction between a pair of dance partners.

Diction

In addition to being able to analyze this aspect of the text effectively, you must also maintain control over your own vocabulary in order to convey your ideas clearly. In particular, make sure to know the differences between these commonly confused pairs of words.

Imply vs. Infer

Imply – Suggest; the writer implies something *to* the reader

Infer – Draw a conclusion based on unstated information; the reader infers the meaning *from* what the author has (not) written

Incorrect: In his short story "Editha," Howells **infers** that an excessively idealistic mindset can lead people to adopt unethical principles.

Correct: In his short story "Editha," Howells **implies** that an excessively idealistic mindset can lead people to adopt unethical principles.

Denote vs. Connote

Denotation – Literal definition of a word

Connotation – Literal or non-literal implication of a word or image

Incorrect: Throughout the passage, the image of smoke **denotes** confusion and uncertainty.

Correct: Throughout the passage, the image of smoke **connotes** confusion and uncertainty.

Beyond correct use of these pairs, one of the key differences between lower- and higher-scoring essays is the level of vocabulary they employ. Although it is unnecessary to flood your writing with "ten-dollar" words, a handful of moderately sophisticated terms will make your work seem more polished. In particular, the use of strong and specific verbs will make your analyses clearer and more engaging.

Weaker: The novel Silas Marner, written by George Eliot, contains two characters who **cross paths with one another**. Silas Marner, a **poor** old man, is framed for a crime **that wasn't his fault**. With no evidence **to back him up**, Silas **gets kicked out** of his hometown, forcing him to stay in Raveloe. However, his luck **gets better** when he adopts a young girl, Eppie, who helps him **learn to believe in others again**.

Stronger: The novel Silas Marner, written by George Eliot, contains two characters whose paths **become intertwined**. Silas Marner, a **destitute** old man, is framed for a crime **he did not commit**. With no evidence to **exonerate** him, Silas **is exiled from** his hometown, forcing him to stay in Raveloe. However, his luck **improves** when he adopts a young girl, Eppie, who helps him **regain his faith in others**.

At the same time, you should not get carried away. Although it might impress your English teacher, excessively flowery or verbose writing detracts from the reader's ability to follow your argument. **You are commenting on a piece of literature, not *writing* a piece of literature.** The second example below, for instance, combines sophisticated yet precise vocabulary with an effective use of transitions to keep the reader oriented and move them logically from point to point within the argument.

Excessive: In The Mayor of Casterbridge, the characters' duplicity, though well-intentioned, forms a tent-flap of emotional insurance around their lives, a flimsy fabric of fleeting tranquility threatening to cave in at the slightest whim of a rumorous wind.

Clear: In The Mayor of Casterbridge, the characters' duplicity, though well-intentioned, serves only to insulate them emotionally. **Ultimately, however**, that mask is flimsy and does nothing to protect them. **Indeed**, it reveals their fragility, **for** they become psychologically destabilized at the slightest hint of trouble.

A related issue involves the misconception that an easy way to score points is to offer effusive praise for the author. While the writer of the passage may very well have been renowned, brilliant, etc., pointing out this information in overblown language will weaken your essay.

Avoid: Kate Chopin was a **determined and brilliant writer, with exceptional ambition and an extraordinary ability** to produce novels that rescued women from the debased state into which nineteenth-century society placed them.

Working with Quotations

One of the factors taken into account for both your "Evidence and Commentary" and "Sophistication" scores is your ability to cite the passage effectively. Because both the Poetry and Prose Analysis Essays require you to quote extensively, you should be comfortable punctuating both direct and indirect quotations, and integrating them smoothly into your analyses.

- In **direct speech**, a person's words are presented directly. Quotation marks are used.
- In **indirect speech**, the writer restates a person's words. No quotation marks are used.

Direct: For example, Robert Cohn asks Jake, **"Don't you ever get the feeling that all your life is going by and you're not taking advantage of it?"**

Indirect: For example, Robert Cohn asks Jake **whether he ever gets the feeling that all his life is going by without him taking advantage of it.**

Notice that in the "indirect" version, no quotation marks are used because Robert Cohn's words have been **rephrased** by the writer.

When the word *that* is used to set off an indirect quotation, no comma is placed after it.

Incorrect: When Lana Lee is initially unable to persuade Jones to take his glasses off, she repeats **that, she** told him to remove his glasses.

Correct: When Lana Lee is initially unable to persuade Jones to take his glasses off, she repeats **that she** told him to remove his glasses.

Likewise, when a direct quotation is integrated directly into a sentence, no comma is used.

Incorrect: Physically hidden behind his glasses and metaphorically hidden behind his stereotype, Jones skillfully escapes any interpretation by Lana Lee, who sees him only **as, "the** cloud of smoke and the broom."

Correct: Physically hidden behind his glasses and metaphorically hidden behind his stereotype, Jones skillfully escapes any interpretation by Lana Lee, who sees him only **as "the** cloud of smoke and the broom."

To condense a quotation, use **ellipses** (three dots) to show that material has been left out.

Correct: The blinds of the King's Arms hotel are deliberately left open so that outsiders and passersby can view the "babble of voices **and...the** drawing of corks."

If you change a word or phrase in order to integrate a quotation into a sentence, the altered information should be placed in **brackets**.

Correct: Henry's devotion to Catherine is evident when he repeatedly says that "if **[she isn't] with [him], [he]** hasn't a thing in the world."

Make sure to introduce your quotations—do not just drop them into the text without warning!

No intro: Editha's fiancé, George, is a committed pacifist as a result of his upbringing. However, Editha believes that war is glorious and that George enlisting in the army would be a symbol of his love to her. **"[I]f he could do something worthy to have won her—be a hero, her hero…"**

The point of the quote is clear enough, but the writer does nothing to let the reader know it's coming. Compare it to this version, which integrates the quotation smoothly into the analysis.

Intro: Editha's fiancé, George, is a committed pacifist as a result of his upbringing. However, Editha believes that war is glorious and that George's enlisting in the army would be a symbol of his love to her. **Caught in her own fantasy, she muses, "if he could do something worthy to have won her—be a hero, her hero…"**

Here, the quote is integrated much more naturally into the surrounding text. It is no longer necessary for the reader to stop and reorient themselves within the argument.

Now let's look at what happens after the quotation.

Weaker: However, Editha believes that war is glorious and that George's enlisting in the army would be a symbol of his love to her. Caught in her own fantasy, she muses, "if he could do something worthy to have won her—be a hero, her hero…" **As the reader discovers, however, George is willing to do whatever it takes to please Editha, and she knows this too.**

The main thing to notice here is that once the quotation is finished, the writer does not engage with it further but rather moves on to the next idea—namely, that George compromises his ideals to please Editha. The essay does not suffer inordinately; however, the writer misses an excellent opportunity to explore some of the text's subtleties.

To reiterate: no matter how obvious their significance may seem to you, quotations do not explain themselves—and **to earn a high score in "Evidence and Commentary," you must make the relationship between your examples and your argument clear.** Even if your textual support is very strong and your analysis is otherwise on target, failure to comment on quotations will knock your score in this category from a 4 to a 3.

To move your argument to a more sophisticated level, you can use a quote as a sort of "springboard" that allows you to add more depth to your analysis. **Note that this does not mean *rephrasing* the quotation in fancier language. Rather, it involves considering its language, punctuation, etc., and using those specific features to support a larger point.**

For example, consider the repetition of the word *hero* as well as the use of ellipses afterward. An analysis that focused on these features might look like the following example.

Stronger: ...However, Editha believes that war is glorious and that George's enlisting in the army would be a symbol of his love to her. Caught in her own fantasy, she muses, "if he could do something worthy to have won her—be a hero, her hero..." **Here, the repetition of the word "hero" serves to underscore Editha's naively romantic tendencies; moreover, ellipses imply a sort of drifting off, emphasizing the daydreamy, almost cartoonish quality of her thoughts. The reader can very nearly imagine a thought-bubble appearing over Editha's head, filled with technicolor images of George returning triumphantly from the war to sweep her off her feet. But ridiculous as this image may be, its ultimate effect is to convey the tragic extent of Editha's self-involvement: she is willing to allow a man who genuinely loves her to sacrifice himself for her fantasy.**

The Text Must <u>Directly</u> Support Your Analysis

Although this is not technically a stylistic consideration, it bears reiterating here: One of the most common traps students fall into in their analyses involves extrapolating far beyond what the passage directly implies. Let's return to the *House of Mirth* passage. A typical example would go something like the excerpt below.

Too far: ...The narrator states that Lily "consulted the little jeweled watch among her laces" and that her "maid came up this morning." **This shows that Lily comes from a very wealthy background and has an haughty and condescending manner. Clearly, she looks down on Selden and perceives him as her social inferior.**

While these details certainly paint Lily as privileged—and the passage implies elsewhere that she is something of a party girl—the information cited simply does not support this interpretation, and you cannot project your own assumptions onto the text.

Now consider this version.

Stronger: ...The narrator states that Lily "consulted the little jeweled watch among her laces" and that her "maid came up this morning." **With this description, Wharton alludes to Lily's elevated social status without mentioning it directly, subtly explaining why Lily has managed to maintain such a frivolous lifestyle despite being at the limits of marriageable age. It also calls attention to the difference in class between Lily and Selden.**

In contrast to the previous example, the above paragraph keeps the analysis squarely within the bounds of the text.

In the next section, we're going to look at three original samples of each essay type (nine total) accompanied by detailed scoring analyses.

Although the passages are included, you may want to try reading the essays on their own first. The mark of a successful piece of analysis is that a reader can easily follow the argument even if they are unfamiliar with the passage or novel in question. See whether that is the case as you read.

Please note that essays are reprinted with original errors.

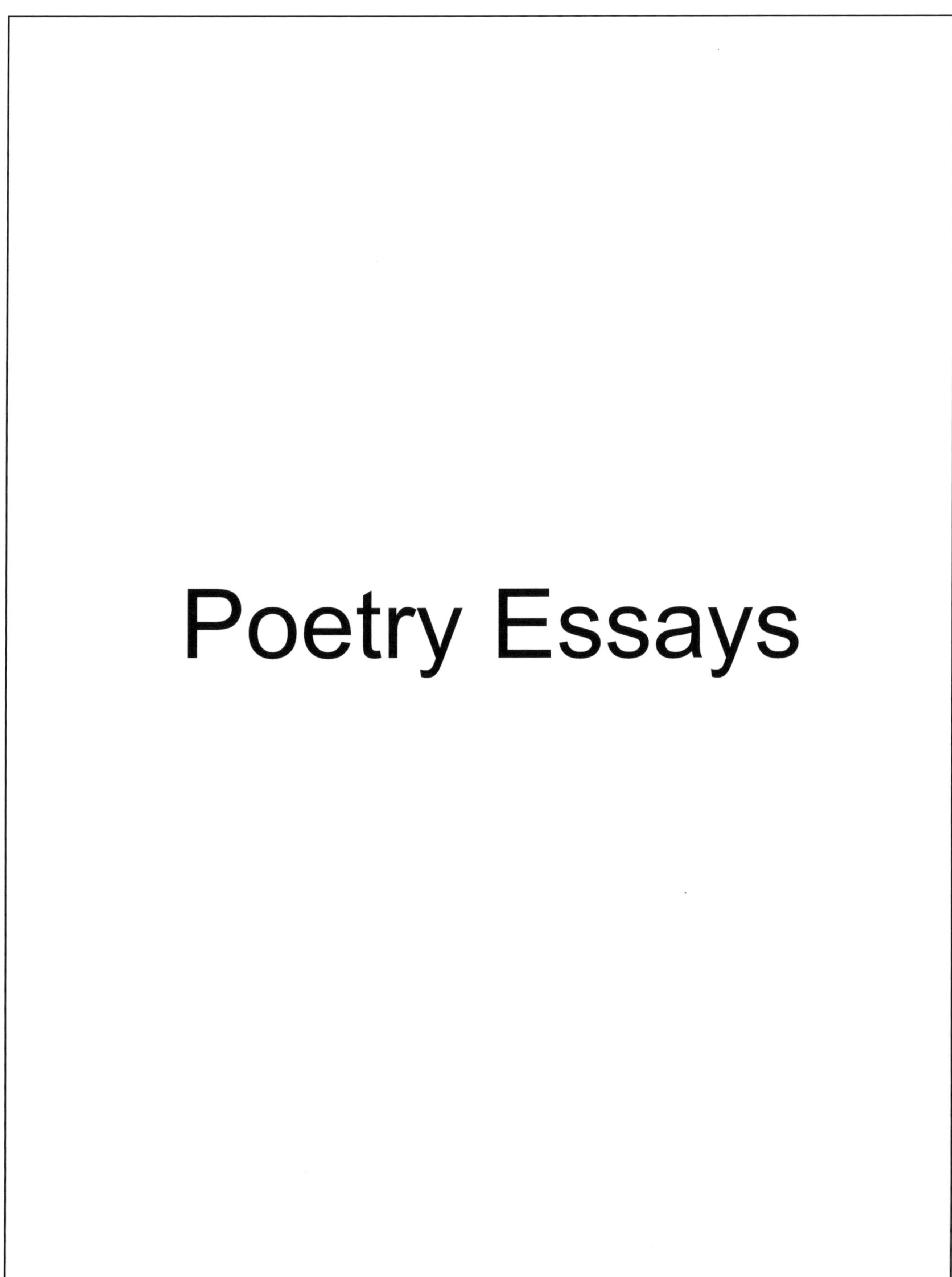

Poetry Essays

Poem 1: "To Autumn," John Keats (1819)

Season of mists and mellow fruitfulness,
  Close bosom-friend of the maturing sun;
Conspiring with him how to load and bless
  With fruit the vines that round the thatch-eves run;
To bend with apples the moss'd cottage-trees,
  And fill all fruit with ripeness to the core;
    To swell the gourd, and plump the hazel shells
  With a sweet kernel; to set budding more,
And still more, later flowers for the bees,
Until they think warm days will never cease,
    For summer has o'er-brimm'd their clammy cells.

Who hath not seen thee oft amid thy store?
  Sometimes whoever seeks abroad may find
Thee sitting careless on a granary floor,
  Thy hair soft-lifted by the winnowing wind;
Or on a half-reap'd furrow sound asleep,
  Drows'd with the fume of poppies, while thy hook
    Spares the next swath and all its twined flowers:
And sometimes like a gleaner thou dost keep
  Steady thy laden head across a brook;
  Or by a cyder-press, with patient look,
    Thou watchest the last oozings hours by hours.

Where are the songs of spring? Ay, Where are they?
  Think not of them, thou hast thy music too,—
While barred clouds bloom the soft-dying day,
  And touch the stubble-plains with rosy hue;
Then in a wailful choir the small gnats mourn
  Among the river sallows, borne aloft
    Or sinking as the light wind lives or dies;
And full-grown lambs loud bleat from hilly bourn;
  Hedge-crickets sing; and now with treble soft
  The red-breast whistles from a garden-croft;
    And gathering swallows twitter in the skies.

Poetry Essay #1

In "To Autumn," the poet John Keats evokes that season in rich detail, using imagery and personification to meditate upon the themes of transience and mortality. The poem is comprised of three stanzas that describe the progression of autumn from the twilight of summer to the harvest to the beginning of winter. Each stanza is 11 lines and can roughly be divided into two sections, the first following an ABAB rhyme scheme and the second a CDEDCCE or CDECDDE rhyme scheme. The first section outlines the theme of the stanza, and the second elaborates and muses upon that theme.

The first stanza describes autumn with sumptuous imagery that evokes autumn: mist, apples, "moss'd cottage-trees," gourds, and hazelnuts. Autumn is personified as someone who "conspires" with the sun to causes crops to grow and fruits to ripen. The picture Keats paints is one of early autumn. Phrases and words like "mellow fruitfulness," "maturing sun," "swell the gourd," and "plump the hazel shells" evoke an air of expectancy and growth. They foreshadow the harvest to come, which is depicted in the next stanza.

In contrast to the first stanza, which focuses on the general atmosphere of autumn in its early stages, the second stanza describes the actions associated with the harvest at the height of autumn. Autumn is again personified (the use of the second person in the first line refers to autumn), though here autumn is depicted as a passive observer who is seated and resting. Specifically, Keats probably intended to conjure up the image of a goddess of fertility and the harvest. The images here evoke both the harvest and the atmosphere of late afternoon and the end of a long day of labor: "hair soft-lifted by the winnowing wind," "half-reaped furrow sound asleep," "[d]rows'd with the fume of poppies." The word "hook" in the sixth line pierces the dreamy atmosphere created by the soft sounds in this stanza and hints at autumn's darker side. The scythe is, of course, associated with death/the Grim Reaper in many cultures.

Just as the harvest was equated with late afternoon in the previous stanza, the final stanza conjures up the image of evening. Following the progression set forth by the first two stanzas, it evokes the twilight of autumn and the world's descent into winter. The end of the day and the onset of winter are both associated with death, and the final stanza contains lots of imagery with morbid overtones: "soft-dying day," "wailful choir," "sinking as the light wind lives or dies." The mention of gathering swallows at the end is another allusion to the evening, since swallows gather in flocks at night.

The prevailing theme of this poem is the acceptance and finality of death. There is no protest or revolt against the progression of the seasons. Instead, it is presented as something perfectly natural, inevitable, and harmonious. Likening this transition to the course of a day emphasizes its cyclic nature and inevitability. The understated melancholy of this poem paints a picture of quiet desolation.

Score: 6/6

Thesis: 1/1

The essay easily earns a point in this category because the first sentence presents a clear and defensible thesis: *In "To Autumn," the poet John Keats evokes that season in rich detail, using imagery and personification to meditate upon the themes of transience and mortality.*

Evidence and Commentary: 4/4

The writer consistently cites Keats' poem to support the thesis, and the relationship between the material referenced and the writer's analysis is always clear. The essay follows a linear structure: each body paragraph corresponds to one of the three stanzas and discusses/comments on specific images and phrases that Keats uses to evoke the season's progression. The focus on the poem's chronological movement—from early to middle to late autumn—also allows the analysis to develop logically, with the discussion in each body paragraph following naturally from and building on the previous one. This structure also allows the reader to follow the writer's thoughts with ease.

The analysis is particularly well developed in the second paragraph, when the writer draws a parallel between late autumn and late afternoon. Notice how, in last three sentences, the writer not only cites multiple phrases from the poem to illustrate that relationship but then comments on how Keats' use of the word *hook* changes the atmosphere. In the last sentence, the comment about the scythe pushes the interpretation further and suggests a larger, more symbolic meaning that continues to be developed in the third body paragraph as well as in the conclusion.

In short, this is a compelling, well-structured essay that is solidly grounded in the specific language of the poem.

Sophistication: 1/1

As a result of the writer's thoughtful analysis and nuanced commentary, this essay easily earns the "Sophistication" point.

Poetry Essay #2

Poems written about seasons are generally easy to ascertain as most readers have experienced the qualities of such a feeling and time. John Keats' 1891 poem, "To Autumn," although written over a century ago, resonates with a modern audience because of its detailed depiction of senses that comprise the season's expectation. Yet Keats' complexity of description peeks into the memories of all readers who can relate to many, if not *all*, of his examples. Rather than list each Autumn component, he recreates an almost personalized version of fall, capitalizing "Autumn" by name. His poem is an homage to the season. Through imagery, selection of detail, and tone, "To Autumn" resonates as a love letter to the season and reflects the relationship to the brief joy that its months establish.

Keats effectively uses imagery to make the reader feel as if they are amidst a glorious Autumn, even if this season must come to an end. Keats' explores how Autumn ripens the flowers, gourds, and hazels to the point of never-ending life, confusing the bees so that they think "warm days will never cease, / For summer has o'er-brimmed their clammy cells," which reminds the reader of the transitional feeling of Autumn rounding out the summer and bringing on the winter. The imagery does not fall specifically to his own experience, but rather, a generalized-yet-specific-enough account of the feeling and expectation that Autumn brings, which draws in more readers. Furthermore, his imagery transforms from familiar sights of the season to the feeling, to the importance of its acknowledgment. He commands to "think not of the songs of spring," for they are futile compared to the beauty inherent in Autumn. Such beauty is detailed.

Keats' selection of detail creates a vivid picture in the reader's mind to make them feel as if they could look out their window to see the "gourd," "cyder-press" or "apples" typical of the day. Yet Keats does not rely merely upon the typical facets of Autumn alone, instead, expands to include a "patient look" and the "oozing" of time, a familiar feeling amidst days getting shorter, life-changing, and the knowing transition of seasons juxtaposed against the uncertain future ahead. Thus, Keats presents Autumn as a season necessary in its place amongst spring, summer, and winter, yet influential in what it brings to the earth and the people familiar with its grace.

Finally, Keats' honorary tone emphasizes the minutia that makes Autumn beautiful, the things that people may take for granted as they know when it *is* Autumn yet fail to stop and take a look around truly. Keats chooses to personify Autumn as a "close bosom-friend of the maturing sun" to signify its importance. Most importantly, Keats never disrespects the other seasons either for "thou has thy music too," rather, he emphasizes the frequently overlooked beauty that makes Autumn in a league all its own. His respect is mirrored by that of the "lambs," "red-breast(s)," and "hedge-crickets" who sing Autumn's praises, as well.

Therefore, Keats' uses imagery, selection of detail, and tone to create a poem that truly transports the reader into this beautiful time of year, respecting it as if he would a living-being. Keats shines a light on the life that fulfills the season and the life that the season creates, as part of the larger cycle of being, complete with all its beauty. By focusing on the expectation of Autumn, its complex components, and his feeling of the process, Keats not only becomes an avid supporter of the time, but also encourages the reader to do the same.

Score: 4/6

Thesis: 1/1

The essay earns the "Thesis" point because it contains a defensible argument: *Through imagery, selection of detail, and tone, "To Autumn" resonates as a love letter to the season and reflects the relationship to the brief joy that its months establish.* It also effectively introduces the main points of the argument and lays out the structure of the essay.

Evidence and Commentary: 3/4

Throughout the essay, the writer consistently quotes from the poem and discusses the material referenced. In the second paragraph, for example, the line *warm days will never cease/For summer has o'er brimmed their clammy cells* is used to support the idea that autumn is "glorious" but also a "transitional" time. The commentary does not develop these points beyond what is stated in the thesis, however, and becomes somewhat confused as the paragraph progresses (e.g., *The imagery does not fall specifically to his own experience, but rather, a generalized-yet-specific-enough account of the feeling and expectation that Autumn brings, which draws in more readers.*). Likewise, in the third and fourth paragraphs, a variety of words and phrases from the text are cited to illustrate Keats' depiction of autumn as a transitional time. The strongest commentary is offered in the third paragraph, where the writer describes the poem as evoking *a familiar feeling amidst days getting shorter, life-changing, and the knowing transition of seasons juxtaposed against the uncertain future ahead,* but the implications of this idea are not explored further.

Sophistication: 0/1

Despite ample use of quotations from the poem, the essay does not really move beyond a surface-level analysis in terms of examining the relationship between the language and the poem's larger themes. The argument remains overly generalized, underdeveloped, and sometimes unclearly expressed. While the level of vocabulary is acceptable, the writer's choice of words is not particularly advanced or precise. As a result, the essay does not earn the "Sophistication" point.

Poetry Essay #3

Autumn is the third season of the year. It's when fruits and crops are gathered by workers and leaves of all colors fall from trees. Lasting from September to December, it's a season of many faces and feelings. John Keats' in his 1819 poem "To Autumn" chooses to illustrate the season by utilizing imagery and figurative language which allows the reader to very efficiently visualize and interpret the setting in which Keats refers to. He writes, "To bend with apples the moss'd cottage-trees/And fill all fruit with ripeness to the core." With the diction the author chose, one could imagine the beauty of the apples and fruits in the autumn day he described. Full of ripe fruit from the trees leaves fallen everywhere with all sorts of greens, oranges, and reds. Keats chose to use this language because of the decadence that the rich colors of autumn bring to the air.

A stroll down the street on an autumn day is full of beauty and vivid colors, his use of imagery proves this. Keats knows it would be difficult to look around and not want to take it all in as the colors are all too deep and each plays a part in the tone they set for the season: Autumn is like a gloomy, yet a beautiful and cheery time of year with the tone set by the author of the poem. Keats was strategic in the way in which the chose his vocabulary for the poem, as it works in accordance with emotions felt during the season and it's changes of leaves falling and colors, temperature, and all things alike.

All to say that John Keats brought to this poem the physical and emotional aspects that the season brings in individuals and the environment forward with the use of his language, tones, and mood. Doing so added a wonderful touch to the poem because it gave it a sultry feeling while reading. Almost as if one needed a scarf to read along. These techniques are utmost important when referring to a specific setting or place. Keats borough autumn to readers, no matter where they are.

Score: 2/6

Thesis: 0/1

Although the essay contains an attempt at a thesis (*John Keats' in his 1819 poem "To Autumn" chooses to illustrate the season by utilizing imagery and figurative language which allows the reader to very efficiently visualize and interpret the setting in which Keats refers to*), this statement is more of an observation than a defensible argument. As a result, it does not earn this point.

Evidence and Commentary: 2/4

The use of specific textual support from the passage is limited to a single quotation in the second paragraph. Although the writer does tie this citation back to the thesis, explaining how Keats' evocation of *rich colors* helps the reader visualize the scene, the analysis is not substantially developed beyond this point. In the following paragraph, the writer makes unsupportable assertions (*Keats knows it would be difficult to look around and not want to take it all in as the colors are all too deep and each plays a part in the tone they set for the season*) and vague observations regarding Keats' goals (*Keats was strategic in the way he chose his vocabulary for the poem*) but does not discuss that statement in any detail or provide specific quotations from the poem to back it up. As a result the essay earns a low score for "Evidence and Commentary."

Sophistication: 0/1

Because the writer's analysis is superficial and lacking in complexity it does not earn the point for "Sophistication."

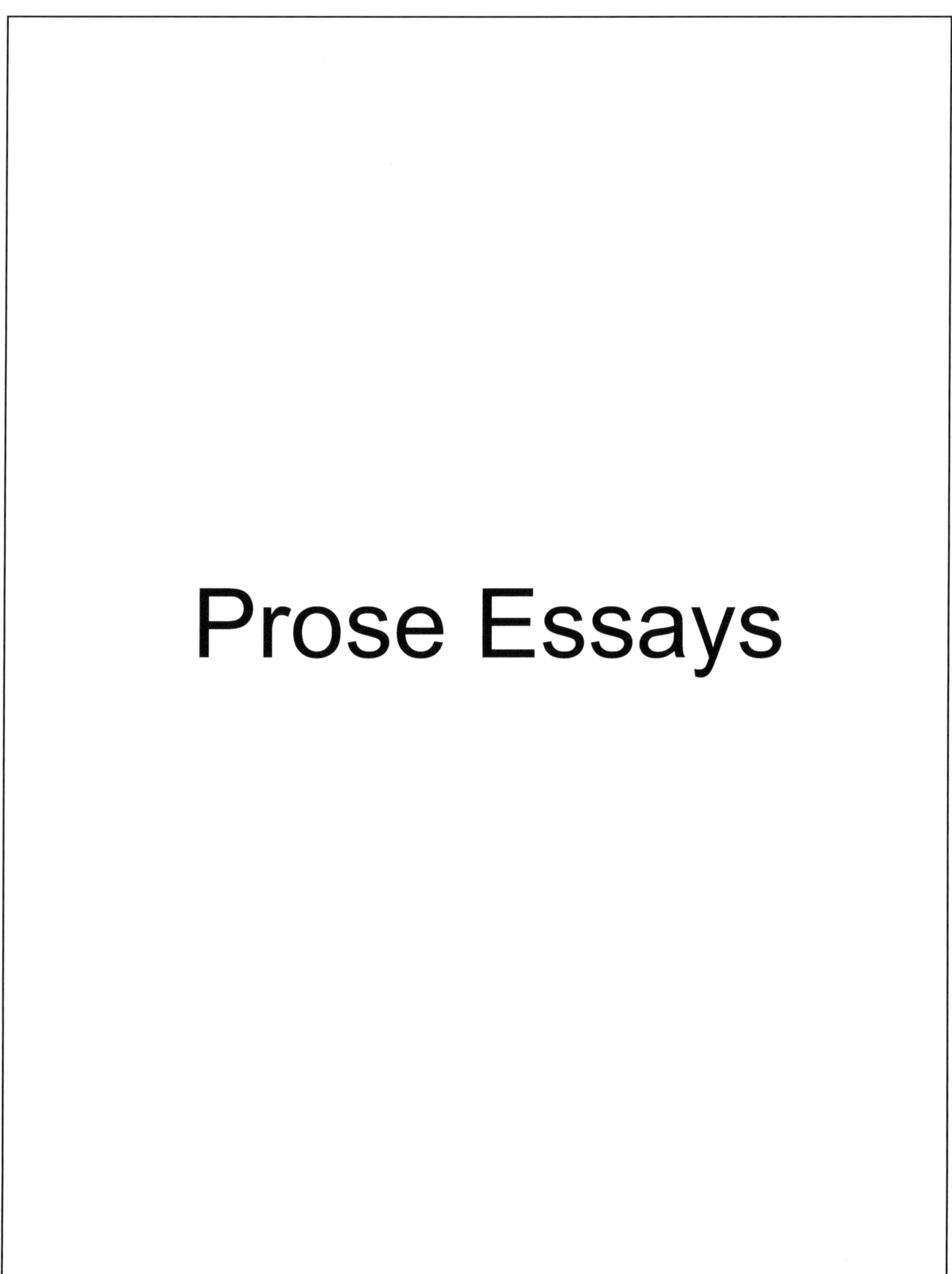

Prose Essays

Passage 1
(From *The Blithedale Romance* by Nathaniel Hawthorne, 1852; 2019 Exam)

Her manner bewildered me. Literally, moreover, I was dazzled by the brilliancy of the room. A chandelier hung down in the centre, glowing with I know not how many lights; there were separate lamps, also, on two or three tables, and on marble brackets, adding their white radiance to that of the chandelier. The furniture was exceedingly rich. Fresh from our old farm-house, with its homely board and benches in the dining-room, and a few wicker chairs in the best parlor, it struck me that here was the fulfillment of every fantasy of an imagination, revelling in various methods of costly self-indulgence and splendid ease. Pictures, marbles, vases; in brief, more shapes of luxury than there could be any object in enumerating, except for an auctioneer's advertisement—and the whole repeated and doubled by the reflection of a great mirror, which showed me Zenobia's proud figure, likewise, and my own. It cost me, I acknowledge, a bitter sense of shame, to perceive in myself a positive effort to bear up against the effect which Zenobia sought to impose on me. I reasoned against her, in my secret mind, and strove so to keep my footing. In the gorgeousness with which she had surrounded herself — in the redundance of personal ornament, which the largeness of her physical nature and the rich type of her beauty caused to seem so suitable — I malevolently beheld the true character of the woman, passionate, luxurious, lacking simplicity, not deeply refined, incapable of pure and perfect taste.

But, the next instant, she was too powerful for all my opposing struggles. I saw how fit it was that she should make herself as gorgeous as she pleased, and should do a thousand things that would have been ridiculous in the poor, thin, weakly characters of other women. To this day, however, I hardly know whether I then beheld Zenobia in her truest attitude, or whether that were the truer one in which she had presented herself at Blithedale. In both, there was something like the illusion which a great actress flings around her.

"Have you given up Blithedale forever?" I inquired.

"Why should you think so?" asked she.

"I cannot tell," answered I; "except that it appears all like a dream that we were ever there together."

"It is not so to me," said Zenobia. "I should think it a poor and meagre nature, that is capable of but one set of forms, and must convert all the past into a dream, merely because the present happens to be unlike it. Why should we be content with our homely life of a few months past, to the exclusion of all other modes? It was good; but there are other lives as good or better. Not, you will understand, that I condemn those who give themselves up to it more entirely than I, for myself, should deem it wise to do."

It irritated me, this self-complacent, condescending, qualified approval and criticism of a system to which many individuals — perhaps as highly endowed as our gorgeous Zenobia — had contributed their all of earthly endeavor, and their loftiest aspirations. I determined to make proof if there were any spell that would exorcise her out of the part which she seemed to be acting. She should be compelled to give me a glimpse of something true; some nature, some passion, no matter whether right or wrong, provided it were real.

"Your allusion to that class of circumscribed characters, who can live in only one mode of life," remarked I, coolly, "reminds me of our poor friend Hollingsworth. Possibly, he was in your thoughts, when you spoke thus. Poor fellow! It is a pity that, by the fault of a narrow education, he should have so completely immolated himself to that one idea of his; especially as the slightest modicum of common-sense would teach him its utter impracticability. Now that I have returned into the world, and can look at his project from a distance, it requires quite all my real regard for this respectable and well-intentioned man to prevent me laughing at him — as, I find, society at large does!"

Zenobia's eyes darted lightning; her cheeks flushed; the vividness of her expression was like the effect of a powerful light, flaming up suddenly within her. My experiment had fully succeeded. She had shown me the true flesh and blood of her heart, by thus involuntarily resenting my slight, pitying, half- kind, half-scornful mention of the man who was all in all with her. She herself, probably, felt this; for it was hardly a moment before she tranquillized her uneven breath, and seemed as proud and self-possessed as ever.

Prose Essay #1

In the "Blithedale" passage by Nathanial Hawthorne writes about the narrator's attitude towards Zenobia. **The passage is written from the first-person perspective, using imagery of opulence and analytical dialogue that indicates the narrator's first feeling of bewilderment which develops into contempt towards Zenobia.**

The first person perspective gives insight into the current events of the passage, the character awestruck by the abundance of wealth in the room, which is in contrast with the "farm-house, with its homely board and benches", that the narrator and Zenobia are coming from before. The imagery of the grand mirror, repeating and doubling this opulence shows Zenobia's figure that is basking in the wealth. The narrator observes how he is shameful of this wealth while Zenobia is prideful in her surroundings, describing to himself her switch of behavior. "I malevolently beheld the true character of the woman, passionate, luxurious, lacking simplicity, not deeply refined, incapable of pure and perfect taste". The narrator continues by describing Zenobia's prideful behavior "self-complacent, condescending, qualified approval and criticism" towards him, though they have both lived together in a rural commune. The internal thoughts and responses the narrator has towards Zenobia shift throughout the passage which the audience can understand where the feelings of disdain arise from. The first-person narration gives the central insight of the narrator's mind which exhibits the shift of attitude towards Zenobia.

Additionally, the visual of opulence is described throughout the passage strings along with the feelings of bewilderment to contempt. In the passage, Zenobia and the narrator come from the same humble living arrangements—a commune. This was a place that prompted the ideology of communalism, simple living, and sharing what little the community had. The room is the exact opposite of this, with "exceedingly rich furniture", "many lights", "three separate tables on marble brackets", "chandelier hanging down the center", and a glittering mirror. All these indicate the conflicting morals the narrator holds towards simple living, while Zenobia is absorbed into the room's gilded appearance. The narrator is taken aback by this apparent wealthy lifestyle Zenobia now lives, shifting his perspective on the women he used to know from the commune. This juxtaposes the life before to the life after the commune, showing the narrator he does not truly know Zenobia as he once did before.

Finally, the analytical dialogue that takes place between Zenobia and the narrator solidifies the narrator's feelings. The start of the passage explores the narrator's bewilderment of Zenobia's mannerism which then advances into his component for her pridefulness and vanity. The exchange between the characters displays their differences as the narrator rebuttals at Zenobia's comment about "commending those who give themselves up" to a more humble lifestyle. The narrator mentions their mutual friend, Hollingsworth, and how Zenobia must have been referencing him and others like him living in Blithedale. How they are laughed at by society at large, which would include Zenobia and her current position in society. Zenobia's physical reaction "eyes darted", "cheeks flushed", "flaming up", shows her true personality. The narrator is now solidified in Zenobia's prideful personality, her back turned on the people of her past community, and her superficial character. His attitude towards her is forever changed and he has lost all respect for her. The usage of first-person narration, imagery, and analytical dialogue, Hawthrone depicts the narrator's initial bewilderment and eventual contempt regarding Zenobia.

Score: 5/6

Thesis: 1/1

The essay earns a point in this category because it makes a defensible claim: *The passage is written from the first-person perspective, using imagery of opulence and analytical dialogue that indicates the narrator's first feeling of bewilderment which develops into contempt towards Zenobia.*

Evidence and Commentary: 3/4

On the whole, the writer effectively supports the argument with clear evidence from the passage. The body paragraphs are logically arranged in two parts, with the first part (paragraphs 2 and 3) corresponding to imagery of opulence and the second part (paragraph 4) corresponding to analytical dialogue. Within the body paragraphs, the writer offers extended commentary on the quotations, e.g., *The imagery of the grand mirror, repeating and doubling this opulence shows Zenobia's figure that is basking in the wealth. The narrator observes how he is shameful of this wealth while Zenobia is prideful in her surroundings, describing to himself her switch of behavior,* and *All these indicate the conflicting morals the narrator holds towards simple living, while Zenobia is absorbed into the room's gilded appearance.*

Despite the generally strong analysis, the third paragraph loses focus somewhat. Although it begins strongly, by reiterating the thesis (*Additionally, the visual of opulence is described throughout the passage strings along with the feelings of bewilderment to contempt*), the relationship between the discussion of communalism and "bewilderment" is not fully explained, nor is it reflected in the choice of quotations. In addition, the final paragraph is somewhat short on direct textual support: the writer alludes to the narrator's dialogue with Zenobia but does not cite from it directly, and reasons behind the shift from bewilderment to pride are insufficiently analyzed.

Certain statements are also awkward and do not clearly tie back to the point of the paragraph (e.g., *The narrator mentions their mutual friend, Hollingsworth, and how Zenobia must have been referencing him and others like him living in Blithedale. How they are laughed at by society at large, which would include Zenobia and her current position in society.*).

Sophistication: 1/1

Despite the minor shortcomings in "Evidence and Commentary," the writer nevertheless recognizes and discusses the complexities of the passage in an insightful way throughout the essay, commenting on the evolution of the narrator's feelings and making statements that analyze the conflicting emotions that drive the characters' relationship, e.g., *The imagery of the grand mirror, repeating and doubling this opulence shows Zenobia's figure that is basking in the wealth. The narrator observes how he is shameful of this wealth while Zenobia is prideful in her surroundings, describing to himself her switch of behavior.* The writer thus earns the "Sophistication" point.

Prose Essay #2

In this dialogue from an 1852 novel by Nathaniel Hawthorne between an unnamed narrator and Zenobia, the narrator's attitude towards Zenobia is exemplified through the narrator's personal thoughts and both direct and indirect characterization of Zenobia. The narrator begins by remarking on how Zenobia's ostentatious manner and self-image is reflected in her room's decor and excessive, even garish, splendor. The narrator's competitive attitude towards Zenobia and her domineering demeanor is evidenced by Hawthorne's use of diction and interrogative tone which is felt as soon as the exchange begins. **The overpowering contempt the narrator exhibits towards Zenobia in both personal, inward opinion and in the challenging questions directed at her show that upon leaving the communal rural lifestyle of Blithedale farm, these two characters see each other as anything but equal, both trying to one-up the other with every chance they get.**

The narrator's description of Zenobia's room is wordy and poetic, bordering on obsessive ranting, not trying to conceal the envy the narrator feels for her in the slightest. Nearly every line in the first paragraph is comparative: "The furniture was exceedingly rich," as compared to their, "old farm-house, with its homely board and benches in the dining-room, and a few wicker chairs in the best parlor," while Zenobia's quarters held "pictures, marbles, vases...more shapes of luxury than there could be any object of enumerating." After leaving a lifestyle where everything was impoverished and even those poor goods communally shared, the narrator feels awestruck at the splendor and luxury that Zenobia commands as her own, with such natural ease and dominance, no less. There is contempt for Zenobia's gaudy displays of wealth, as the narrator, "malevolently beheld the true character of the woman, passionate, luxurious, lacking simplicity, not deeply refined, incapable of pure and perfect taste." Here we are shown the narrator's own values, of the specific kind of modesty which is deemed acceptable, one of which Zenobia has no qualms of foregoing in place of her own self-expression. The narrator flat-out describes their feelings toward Zenobia as "malevolent", clearly they are competitors after having left the Blithedale farm.

However, the next paragraph reveals that while the narrator would not personally choose such a showy display of wealth and individuality, the narrator cannot deny that Zenobia, "gorgeous as she pleased," was able to pull it off herself, that she was able to, "do a thousand things that would have been ridiculous in the poor, thin, weakly characters of other women." Perhaps the narrator sees themselves as possessing such a weakly character. The narrator is hard-pressed to ascertain Zenobia's true nature, is she truly such a flamboyant and graceful creature or is masking something just as weakly, holding up, "the illusion which a great actress flings around her."

As the actual dialogue exchange begins we see that both the narrator and Zenobia are trading verbal jabs at each other, both are clearly aware of the game they are playing, as Zenobia seemingly mocks the narrator for taking the Blithedale farm as a thing of the past and only the past instead of simply another form of the continuous present. The narrator, desperate to find the kink in Zenobia's chain, mentions and disparages Hollingsworth, their mutual friend from the farm who was clearly a sore reminder for Zenobia. When the narrator bluntly insults him, highlighting the waste of his potential on the Blithedale farm,

"Zenobia's eyes darted lightening; her cheeks flushed; the vividness of her expression was like the effect of a powerful light, flaming up suddenly within her." The entire last paragraph continues in a triumphant tone, self-congratulatory as the narrator is proud of wounding the "proud and self-possessed" Zenobia.

From the beginning of the excerpt, the jealous, in-depth description of the Zenobia's room, full of both admiring and simultaneously negative adjectives, to the catty dialogue exchange, and finally the satisfaction of breaking Zenobia's stoicism, the narrator seems to really have it out for Zenobia, perhaps because of the majorly different ways the two characters are coping with the escape from the Blithedale farm. The fact that that narrator's prying question was seen as an, "experiment...finally succeeded," is the final clue that there was, indeed, a toxic competitive spirit between the narrator and Zenobia, with the narrator harboring feelings of envy for Zenobia's circumstances and her bewildering pride and self-possession.

Score: 5/6

Thesis: 1/1

The essay earns a point for the thesis because it presents a defensible, if somewhat convoluted, claim about the narrator's relationship with Zenobia (*The overpowering contempt the narrator exhibits towards Zenobia in both personal, inward opinion and in the challenging questions directed at her show that upon leaving the communal rural lifestyle of Blithedale farm, these two characters see each other as anything but equal, both trying to one-up the other with every chance they get*).

Evidence and Commentary: 3/4

Although the essay does include a number of quotations from the passage, they do not always support the points the writer intends to make. The second paragraph, for example, starts out on solid footing by citing the many comparisons between Zenobia's room and the old farmhouse as evidence for the idea that the narrator is driven by a need to compete with Zenobia; however, the discussion of the narrator's values and the description of Zenobia as "malevolent," while showing insight, are not fully connected back to the idea of competition. In the following paragraph, the writer also does not make clear the relationship between the narrator's observations of Zenobia and the desire to compete with her. The statement *Perhaps, even, the narrator sees themselves as possessing such a weakly character* hints at the connection, but the idea is not investigated further. **Remember:** if you introduce a point, you must analyze it!

Sophistication: 1/1

Although the writer does not always effectively connect the evidence from the passage back to the thesis, the essay nevertheless earns the "Sophistication" point because it demonstrates a nuanced understanding of the dynamic between the narrator and Zenobia. Throughout the essay, the writer repeatedly calls attention to the conflicting impulses behind the narrator's reactions, and statements such as *the narrator is hard-pressed to ascertain Zenobia's true nature,* reflect an understanding of the ambiguity of the characters' relationship.

Passage 2
(From *The Rise of Silas Lapham* by William Dean Howells, 1885; 2019 exam)

They were not girls who embroidered or abandoned themselves to needle-work. Irene spent her abundant leisure in shopping for herself and her mother, of whom both daughters made a kind of idol, buying her caps and laces out of their pin-money, and getting her dresses far beyond her capacity to wear. Irene dressed herself very stylishly, and spent hours on her toilet every day. Her sister had a simpler taste, and, if she had done altogether as she liked, might even have slighted dress. They all three took long naps every day, and sat hours together minutely discussing what they saw out of the window. In her self-guided search for self-improvement, the elder sister went to many church lectures on a vast variety of secular subjects, and usually came home with a comic account of them, and that made more matter of talk for the whole family. She could make fun of nearly everything; Irene complained that she scared away the young men whom they got acquainted with at the dancing-school sociables. They were, perhaps, not the wisest young men.

The girls had learned to dance at Papanti's; but they had not belonged to the private classes. They did not even know of them, and a great gulf divided them from those who did. Their father did not like company, except such as came informally in their way; and their mother had remained too rustic to know how to attract it in the sophisticated city fashion. None of them had grasped the idea of European travel; but they had gone about to mountain and sea-side resorts, the mother and the two girls, where they witnessed the spectacle which such resorts present throughout New England, of multitudes of girls, lovely, accomplished, exquisitely dressed, humbly glad of the presence of any sort of young man; but the Laphams had no skill or courage to make themselves noticed, far less courted by the solitary invalid, or clergyman, or artist. They lurked helplessly about in the hotel parlors, looking on and not knowing how to put themselves forward. Perhaps they did not care a great deal to do so. They had not a conceit of themselves, but a sort of content in their own ways that one may notice in certain families. The very strength of their mutual affection was a barrier to worldly knowledge; they dressed for one another; they equipped their house for their own satisfaction; they lived richly to themselves, not because they were selfish, but because they did not know how to do otherwise. The elder daughter did not care for society, apparently. The younger, who was but three years younger, was not yet quite old enough to be ambitious of it. With all her wonderful beauty, she had an innocence almost vegetable. When her beauty, which in its immaturity was crude and harsh, suddenly ripened, she bloomed and glowed with the unconsciousness of a flower; she not merely did not feel herself admired, but hardly knew herself discovered. If she dressed well, perhaps too well, it was because she had the instinct of dress; but till she met this young man who was so nice to her at Baie St. Joan, she had scarcely lived a detached, individual life, so wholly had she depended on her mother and her sister for her opinions, almost her sensations. She took account of everything he did and said, pondering it, and trying to make out exactly what he meant, to the inflection of a syllable, the slightest movement or gesture. In this way she began for the first time to form ideas which she had not derived from her family, and they were none the less her own because they were often mistaken.

Prose Essay #3

In the 1885 novel, The Rise of Silas Lapham, **Howells reveals the complex experience of the two sisters within their family and society through the use of details, tone, and juxtaposition of the family with society at large.** Through his writing, he paints a picture of two sisters in a comfortable and tight knit family at the periphery of New England high society. The family is interdependent and content; but towards the end of the passage, independence is sparked in Irene through an encounter with a young man.

Howells uses carefully selected details to offer us a glimpse into the sisters' family lives and relationship with society. He begins by showing the reader details about the sisters which show us their role in the family. "Irene spent her abundant leisure in shopping for herself and her mother..." (4) while "The elder sister went to many church lectures... and usually came home with a comic account of them." (14) These details present the family as caring and amicable, enjoying spending time together. Howells also uses detail to show how the family is on the cusp of high society, yet not fully accepted into it. "The girls had learned to dance at Papanti's; but they had not belonged to the private classes. They did not even know of them..." (22) This crucial distinction reflects the families apathy and ignorance towards the society they border. Near the end of the passage, cracks begin to appear in this ignorance and isolation, as Howells reveals through details in Irene's interaction with the young man: "She took account of everything he did and said, pondering it, and trying to make out exactly what he meant, to the inflection of a syllable..." (64) Although Irene is intrigued by the man, the fact that she cannot grasp his intentions, despite paying close attention to his behavior, emphasizes her innocence and lack of knowledge of the world beyond her close-knit household.

Furthermore, Howells' shifts in tone throughout the passage reinforce the evolving relationship between the three women. For example, at the beginning of the passage, he states, "They all three took long naps every day, and sat hours together minutely discussing what they saw out of the window." (10) Here, Howells uses a languid, homely tone to introduce the sisters' dynamic with their family as intimate and comfortable. Later on in the passage, Howells takes this close knit relationship further, using an singular tone to convey the family's insular nature: "...they dressed for one another; they equipped their house for their own satisfaction; they lived richly to themselves..." (45) Near the end of the passage, however, Howells uses a poetic tone to convey the transformation Irene begins to go through, comparing her to a flower. "When her beauty, which in its immaturity was crude and harsh, suddenly ripened, she bloomed and glowed with the unconsciousness of a flower..." (54) This image of unfolding makes it clear that she is becoming a person far different from the one who spent days lounging with her mother and sister. The lushness of the language emphasizes Irene's metamorphosis.

Lastly, Howells juxtaposes the family next to society to show their peculiarly insular qualities and cluelessness of high society. "...multitudes of girls, lovely, accomplished, exquisitely dressed... but the Laphams had no skill or courage to make themselves noticed." (33) This quote shows how while the Laphams go to the same places as the prominent in society, they lack the knowhow or drive to break into the society. This is magnified in the following quote: "They lurked helplessly about in the hotel parlors, looking on and not knowing how to put themselves forward." (39) By putting the Lapham's right in the middle of high society, Howells draws attention to the family's isolated nature, emphasizing the distance that Irene must travel to become an independent person, as well as the strength of character necessary for her to break away. Even the fact that Irene's ideas were "often mistaken" (line 70) cannot be interpreted as a criticism. Rather, the very fact that she is able to formulate her own ideas testifies to the force of her blossoming independence.

In conclusion, Howells uses details, tone, and juxtaposition to portray two sisters' experience in a closed off family on the edge of society, and how one sister begins to take tentative steps toward breaking away.

Score: 6/6

Thesis: 1/1

This essay earns the "Thesis" point because it opens with a clear and defensible claim (*Howells reveals the complex experience of the two sisters within their family and society through the use of details, tone, and juxtaposition of the family with society at large*).

Note that in this case, the writer essentially rephrases the prompt itself (students were asked to analyze the author's portrayal of the "complex relationship" of Irene and her sister, Penelope, in the context of their family/society) in order to devote maximum time to writing the essay. While this can be a risky strategy, leading to an overly generalized thesis that is difficult to support effectively, the writer makes it work here by establishing upfront the specific techniques by which Howells conveys this relationship and then devoting a complete paragraph to each one. The presentation of the essay's structure in the introduction allows the reader to feel oriented within the argument from the start.

Evidence and Commentary: 4/4

Each of the body paragraphs makes extensive use of quotations that clearly support the point of the section. Throughout the essay, quotations are consistently commented on and related back to the thesis, e.g., *"The girls had learned to dance at Papanti's; but they had not belonged to the private classes. They did not even know of them..." (22) This crucial distinction reflects the families apathy and ignorance towards the society they border* and *"She took account of everything he did and said, pondering it, and trying to make out exactly what he meant, to the inflection of a syllable..." (64) Although Irene is intrigued by the man, the fact that she cannot grasp his intentions, despite paying close attention to his behavior, emphasizes her innocence and lack of knowledge of the world beyond her close-knit household.*

Notice that this essay is much easier to follow than the previous two. The commentary flows naturally from the quotations and is unobstructed by the kind of distractingly flowery language found in the other essays. As a result, the reader is free to focus on the writer's ideas.

That is not to say that the analysis is flawless. In the third paragraph, for example, it is not entirely clear what the writer means by a "singular" tone; however, this minor issue is outweighed by the overall strength of the analysis.

Sophistication: 1/1

The essay earns the "Sophistication" point because it effectively explores the tension between the insular, self-focused Lapham women and the larger society from which they are largely excluded, as well as the significance of Irene's first cautious step toward breaking away from her family. At each point, the discussion is centered on a specific technique that is discussed in detail.

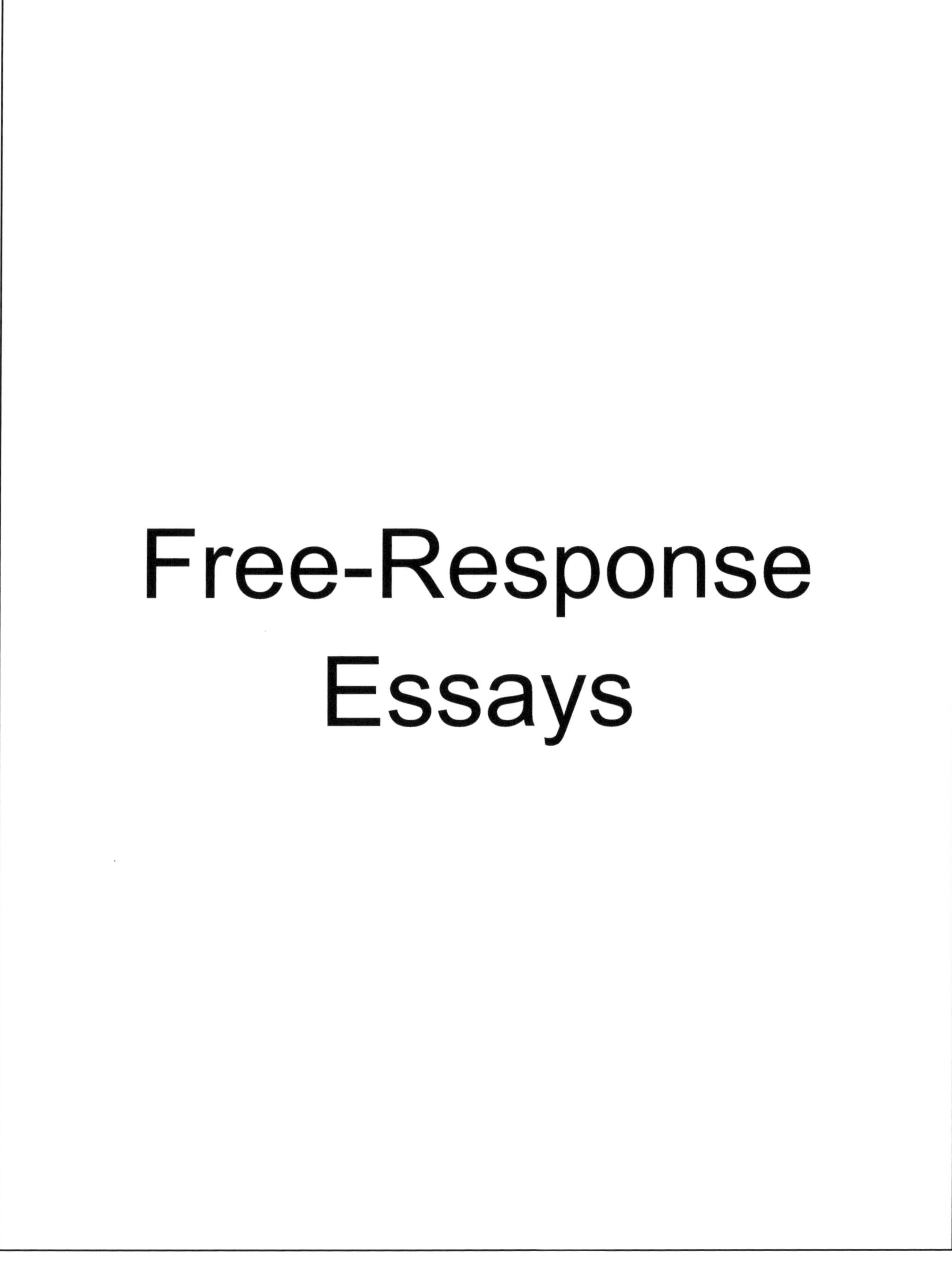

Free-Response Essays

Free-Response Essay #1

Prompt: Analyze a central question raised by a work and the extent to which it offers answers. (2004)

"'People who try to hold on to their individuality always come to a bad end'" (III.4). Such are the fateful words of Berenger, the lone survivor of the rhinoceritis epidemic in Eugène Ionesco's absurdist allegory, *Rhinoceros*. The horned mammals in his play are symbolic in many ways, historically representing fascists during The Second World War, more morbidly embodying death itself, and even capturing the alluring juggernaut of conformity, a rampaging beast which stamps out all vestiges of individuality. **Ultimately, Ionesco's *Rhinoceros* questions our capacity to remain devout to our own beliefs, and suggests to a large extent, through mirrored structures and irony, that we are bound to converge towards conformity.**

Throughout the work, Ionesco mirrors phrases, introducing them in one scene and then echoing them in another to reaffirm our inevitable inclination to conform. Upon first meeting in the play, Jean remarks that his friend Berenger is late as always. Initially, Jean's comment appears as a mere aspect of Berenger's personality, indicative of his tendency towards tardiness. However, in the final scene of the play, the true extent of Jean's earlier statement is revealed when Berenger laments that it is "too late" for him and that he has gone past changing. By echoing the earlier remark of his past friend, Berenger reveals that his lateness goes beyond being a simple surface quality—that he is late not just to physical rendezvous, but also ideological movements—namely, late to conform, metaphorically depicted as "'changing'" into a rhinoceros. By describing Berenger's failure to conform as a flaw in his personality through his tardiness, Ionesco conveys that Berenger is the sole outcast in an otherwise natural society of uniformity.

Moreover, Ionesco implements cases of situational irony in his play to further affirm our natural tendency towards conformity. In the beginning of the play, Berenger grieves that he always felt out of place in this world, that he didn't belong. In response, his former friend Jean suggests to him that he visit museums, attend concerts, and subscribe to literature in an effort to become more in tune with the times. Heeding Jean's advice, Berenger successfully masters his will, becoming a cultured man of society. However, just as he begins to become more synchronized with the culture of his contemporaries, the people around him begin to change and adopt a new culture—the primeval, bestial culture of the pachyderm. By the end of the play, Berenger anguishes that his English sounds foreign and meaningless, inferior the beautiful, guttural tones of the horned creatures all around him, that his "white, hairy body seems flabby and weak," while the lustrous green hide of the beasts appear strong and supple when naked.

Through Berenger's transformation, Ionesco illustrates the ultimate irony—that to be cultured and self-disciplined is now out of place, even futile, whereas just moments ago it had been valued most highly by society. Ionesco's use of irony suggests that regardless of how virtuous or appealing we find our own ideals to be, in the end, we will always attempt to abandon them in favor of the set of uniform ideals favored by the masses.

In effect, we are ceaselessly compelled to shed the soft, fleshy skin of our own cradled beliefs and capitulate instead to the impenetrable iron hide of conformity, and those who do not, as Ionesco describes, appear unnatural in society.

Score: 6/6

Thesis: 1/1

The essay presents a clear, defensible, and nuanced argument at the end of the first paragraph (*Ultimately, Ionesco's Rhinoceros questions our capacity to remain devout to our own beliefs, and suggests to a large extent, through mirrored structures and irony, that we are bound to converge towards conformity*) and easily earns the "Thesis" point. It also effectively previews the essay's structure: the two body paragraphs correspond to the two main devices analyzed (mirrored structures and irony).

Evidence and Commentary: 4/4

Each body paragraph corresponds to a single main idea, which is developed through the use of specific examples from the text and then commented on. In the second paragraph, for example, the writer provides an example of a statement that is uttered early in the play and then "mirrored" at a later time and comments on its altered significance (*By echoing the earlier remark of his past friend, Berenger reveals that his lateness goes beyond being a simple surface quality – that he is late not just to physical rendezvous, but also ideological movements – namely, late to conform, metaphorically depicted as "'changing'" into a rhinoceros.*). Likewise, in the third paragraph, the description of Berenger's social evolution is effectively used to illustrate the point about situational irony.

Sophistication: 1/1

Throughout the essay, the writer consistently conveys how the use of mirrored structures and irony illustrates Ionesco's larger point about conformity, consistently using the specifics of the text to comment on the meaning of the work as a whole. In particular, the situation of *Rhinoceros* in its historical context in the introduction and the discussion of irony in the third paragraph and the conclusion demonstrate an understanding of the work's context and complexity. The writer also uses challenging vocabulary (*juggernaut, supple, primeval*) appropriately and precisely. The result is a coherent, focused, and nuanced analysis that easily earns the "Sophistication" point.

Free Response Essay #2

Prompt: Analyze a character's idealism and its consequences, both positive and negative. (2019)

F. Scott Fitzgerald's 1925 novel *The Great Gatsby* entrances the reader with The Roaring Twenties' glamor, a mysterious, rich, and love splendored era that perpetuates perfection and idealism. No one better upholds the ability to idealize something—some*one*—than Jay Gatsby, the protagonist. **Jay Gatsby holds an ideal view of the world because he feels that as long as he matches up to a standard self-applied, that he can regain the love of his life. Yet this level of unmatchable idealism merely complicates his understanding of reality, never allowing him to realize his efforts are in vain.**

Jay Gatsby's idealism makes him do many things for love—so he thinks. He buys a house across the bay from Daisy, a woman engaged to another who, although he found her *first,* could not hold onto her during World War I. Thus, the reality of war complicated his fantasy of love. He holds lavish parties of grandeur and exquisite taste that attract everyone from East Egg and West Egg—rarely Daisy—using his money and time on a girl who barely realizes he is there. This makes him waste resources and forget about making real connections. Thus, although Gatsby believes that he acts as an ideal suitor, his ideal view of the world is not realistic for his circumstances—and Daisy's.

Daisy is the ideal woman for Gatsby, the person for whom he posits this ideal view of the world. Thus, as long as Gatsby believes he can be with Daisy, he views the world through rose-colored glasses. This disables him from acknowledging Daisy's marriage to Tom and from realizing he is engaged in poor business decisions. It also prevents him from realizing he is in danger at the end of the novel, before he is shot. When Gatsby dies, he dies alone, for his ideal view of the world was grand enough for everyone to enjoy his façade, but never the real man. Therefore, it becomes problematic but part of the cautionary message of the novel: excessive idealism can lead to tragedy.

Fitzgerald's portrayal of this idealism illuminates the meaning of the work as a whole because it shows how in all of Gatsby's riches, the perfect picture of his own life, he was never satisfied and the outsider looking in would take his life to be ideal even though he wouldn't. This irony asserts that nothing is what it seems, and no one is ever satisfied. Once the idea of perfection comes into play, someone so compelled to fight for what they believe is not easily distracted nor changed. This becomes problematic for the man behind the myth is shown to have been living in his fantasy the entire time.

Ultimately, Gatsby's ideal view of the world in *The Great Gatsby* is more sad than fantastic. He *wants* to have everything perfect but doesn't realize that his efforts go above and beyond what is needed or wanted. He works toward an unattainable goal, but he never veers from the course since that goal is doused in perfection. This brings his downfall as the idealism of the world blinds him to the reality of his situation.

Score: 4/6

Thesis: 1/1

As in the previous example, this essay contains a fairly complex, multi-part thesis: *Jay Gatsby holds an ideal view of the world because he feels that as long as he matches up to a standard self-applied, that he can regain the love of his life. Yet this level of unmatchable idealism merely complicates his understanding of reality, never allowing him to realize his efforts are in vain.* Here again, the argument is coherent and debatable, allowing the writer to earn the "Thesis" point.

Evidence and Commentary: 3/4

The essay makes solid use of textual support, particularly in the second and third paragraphs, where the writer cites various plot specifics (Gatsby's wasting money on lavish parties, his engagement in poor business decisions) to illustrate the emptiness that lies behind Gatsby's idealism and the tragedy that it brings about. In the fourth paragraph, however, the discussion becomes overgeneralized (e.g., *Once the idea of perfection comes into play, someone so compelled to fight for what they believe is not easily distracted nor changed.*), and the argument loses some of its focus. As a result, the essay loses a point in this category.

Sophistication: 1/1

Although the analysis is less specific than it could have been toward the end of the essay, the writer nevertheless offers a solid analysis of the novel's central paradox—namely, that Gatsby's attachment to an idealized lifestyle leads to his demise—and demonstrates a sophisticated understanding of how the tension between ideals and reality drive the plot. As a result, the writer earns the "Sophistication" point.

Free-Response Essay #3

Prompt: Analyze a character's idealism and its consequences, both positive and negative. (2019)

The protagonist of George Bernard Shaw's Man and Superman, Jack Tanner, is a highly idealistic man who is portrayed as an iconoclast with revolutionary ideas. His views are most thoroughly elaborated in an appendix to the play entitled The Revolutionist's Handbook, which is presented as a political treatise authored by Tanner. In it, and throughout the play, he describes his hope that mankind will transcend its limitations through breeding a race of Supermen. **While Tanner's idealism has positive effects in the sense that it leads him to rebel against the restrictions of nineteenth-century British society, it also has negative consequences that illustrate an overall theme of the work, specifically the limits of an overly theoretical approach to life.**

Tanner is against marriage, which he believes has degenerated into an institution that caters to desire and sentiment instead of facilitating good breeding. In his treatise, he critiques monogamy and endorses free love. Tanner, whose name is an anglicization of Juan Tenorio (Don Juan's full name), is an enlightened version of Don Juan. He is a committed bachelor who refuses to marry, engaging instead in philosophical pursuits. Tanner's ideals scandalize his Victorian contemporaries, demonstrating the positive consequences of his idealism. His defiance of tradition exposes the stuffiness and hypocrisy of Victorian conservatism. He also comes to the defense of a female character, Violet Robinson, who is believed to be pregnant out of wedlock (which would have been scandalous at the time), and praises her for following her instincts and not adhering to convention.

There are limitations to Tanner's idealism, however. His political ideals do not translate to real-world actions. He is a stereotypical member of the "idle rich" whose revolutionary ideals are confined to the realm of fantasy. He cannot be said to be a Superman because he cannot convert thought to action. And unlike the Superman, who knows what he wants and pursues it, Tanner's feelings about Ann Whitefield, the central female character in the play, are conflicted. His attempts to come across as intellectual sometimes fall flat; for instance, he misattributes a quote to Voltaire and is corrected by a mechanic. In some ways, Ann manifests the ideals of the Superman more than Tanner does. Her determined pursuit of Tanner (which involves outright stalking) is a manifestation of the "Life Force," the power and energy with which the Superman is imbued. In her case, this takes the form of a desire to marry and bring forth children.

One of the many ironies in this play is that despite Tanner's denunciation of marriage, it is his union with Ann that unites him with the Life Force. He condemns marriage as an institution that hinders mankind's evolution into Supermen, but the combination of Tanner's philosophical mind—represented by his idealism—and Ann's vitality would yield a Superman. Idealism is ineffectual unless it is paired with action.

Score: 5/6

Thesis: 1/1

This essay earns the "Thesis" point because it contains a debatable claim: *While Tanner's idealism has positive effects in the sense that it leads him to rebel against the restrictions of nineteenth-century British society, it also has negative consequences that illustrate an overall theme of the work, specifically the limits of an overly theoretical approach to life.* Although the thesis is quite complex, it is also very clear and provides an effective preview of how the writer's argument will be organized.

Evidence and Commentary: 3/4

The body of the essay is well structured, with the second paragraph focusing on the positive effects of Tanner's idealism and the third paragraph focusing on the negative effects. Each of these paragraphs illustrates the relevant consequences through specific examples (positive: Tanner *exposes the stuffiness and hypocrisy of Victorian conservatism* and comes to Violet Robinson's defense; negative: he is *a member of the "idle rich"* who *cannot convert thought to action*). However, the mention of the fact that Tanner's attempts at sounding intellectual *fall flat* seems somewhat off-topic—it is unclear how this relates to the character's difficulty converting thought into action, and the idea is not developed. The shift to the discussion of Ann Whitfield as a counter-example to Tanner is slightly awkward but adds depth to the analysis, which remains generally strong overall.

Sophistication: 1/1

Despite the slight lack of focus in the third paragraph, this essay earns the "Sophistication" point because it emphasizes the irony of Tanner's position, showing how his attachment to an "ideal" form of life causes him to act in ways that in fact show weakness and entitlement. At the end of the essay, the writer's focus on the contrast between Tanner and Ann, as well as the tie-back to the thesis in terms of their relationship (*the combination of Tanner's philosophical mind – represented by his idealism – and Ann's vitality would yield a Superman. Idealism is ineffectual unless it is paired with action*), provides an additional layer of complexity.

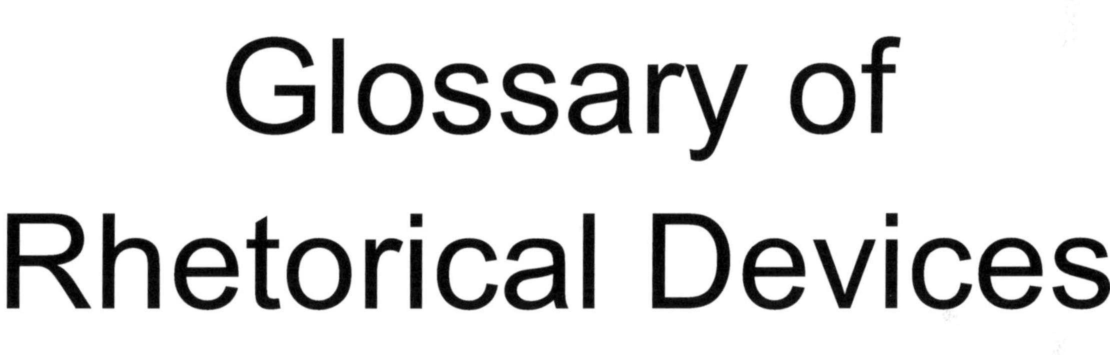

Glossary of Rhetorical Devices

Glossary

Literary and Figurative Language

Abstract Language – Vague and generalized speech, full of references to intangible concepts

Example: She felt a **tremulous need** to throw her **liberty** and her **leisure** into the things of the **soul**—the **most beautiful things** she knew. She found them, when she gave time to seeking, in a hundred places, and particularly in a **dim and sacred region**—the region of **active pity**—over her entrance into which she dropped curtains so thick that it would have been an impertinence to lift them.

Allusion – (Indirect) reference, usually to a literary/artistic work, character, or event

Example: Imogen saw a woman of immense stature, in a very short skirt and a broad, flapping sun hat, striding down the hillside at a long, swinging gait. The refugee from **Valhalla** approached, panting. Her heavy, Teutonic features were scarlet from the rigor of her exercise, and her hair, under her flapping sun hat, was tightly befrizzled about her brow.

In Norse mythology, Valhalla was a great hall ruled over by the gods, where slain warriors were sent after falling in combat. Note that if a passage contains a reference that high school students are not expected to know, a footnote will generally be provided.

Aside – Parenthetical remark used to offer commentary or address the reader directly

Shortcut: Parentheses and dashes

Example: Mary and I were brought up in the strictest seclusion. My mother, being at once highly accomplished, well informed, and fond of employment, took the whole charge of our education on herself, with the exception of Latin—**which my father undertook to teach us**—so that we never even went to school; and, as there was no society in the neighbourhood, our only intercourse with the world consisted in a stately tea-party, now and then, with the principal farmers and tradespeople of the vicinity **(just to avoid being stigmatized as too proud to consort with our neighbours)**, and an annual visit to our paternal grandfather.

Cliché – Trite saying that expresses a common or banal idea

Example: A troop of newly arrived students, very young, pink and callow, followed nervously, rather abjectly, at the Director's heels. Each of them carried a notebook, in which, whenever the great man spoke, he desperately scribbled. **Straight from the horse's mouth.** It was a rare privilege.

Dry/Wry Humor, Irony – Form of subtle, sometimes dark, humor, frequently based on wordplay or violation of the reader's expectations

Example: Being pretty well aware of what sort of **joy** you must both be feeling, I have been in no hurry with my congratulations; but I hope it all went off tolerably well. How did you all behave? **Who cried most?**

In most cases, one does not ask people feeling joy about how much they cried. Although the example above is taken from a discussion of a wedding—a happy event at which people do often cry—the unexpected juxtaposition between a positive emotion and a response typically associated with sadness creates a humorous moment.

Euphemism – Replacement of an offensive, crass, or unpleasant word with a milder one

Example: The good old office, now extinct in the State of New-York, of a Master in Chancery, had been conferred upon me. It was not a very arduous office, but very **pleasantly remunerative**.

Here, the narrator uses the refined phrase *pleasantly remunerative* as a roundabout way of indicating that he earns a lot of money.

Hyperbole (Exaggeration) – Overstated or over-the-top language employed for dramatic or humorous effect

Example: She moped: **no grown person** could have performed that uncheering business better; **no furrowed face** of adult exile, longing for Europe at Europe's antipodes, **ever** bore more legibly the signs of homesickness than did her infant visage.

Imagery – Rich, descriptive language that appeals to the senses

Example: The sun shone with a **warm yellow light** on the Upper Town, with its **girdle of gray wall**, and on **the red flag that drowsed** above the citadel, and was a **friendly lustre** on the tinned roofs of the Lower Town; while away off to the south and east and west **wandered the purple hills and the farmlit plains in such dewy shadow and effulgence** as would have been enough to make the heaviest heart glad.

Metaphor – Comparison that does not state that *x is like/as y*, but rather than *x is y*

Example: For a few moments **I was turned into a pillar of salt**, standing at the head of my seated column of clerks.

Metonymy – Replacement of a literal word or phrase by a closely related one

Example: While Captain Delano was thus made the mark of all eager **tongues**, his one eager glance took in all faces, with every other object about him.

Pathos (Appeal to Emotion) – Use of strong or highly charged language to elicit an emotional response

Example: What an excellent example of the power of dress, young Oliver Twist was! Wrapped in the blanket which had hitherto formed his only covering, he might have been the child of a nobleman or a beggar; it would have been hard for the haughtiest stranger to have assigned him his proper station in society. But now that he was enveloped in the old calico robes which had grown yellow in the same service, he was badged and ticketed, and fell into his place at once—a parish child—the orphan of a workhouse—**the humble, half-starved drudge—to be cuffed and buffeted through the world—despised by all, and pitied by none**.

Personification – Attribution of human characteristics to an inanimate object

Example: **Five-fingered** ferns hung over the water and dropped spray from their fingertips... The high mountain wind coasted, **sighing** through the pass and **whistled** on the edges of the big blocks of broken granite.

Rhetorical Question – Question asked without expectation of response, usually for dramatic effect or to emphasize a point

Example: I stood gazing at him awhile, as he went on with his own writing, and then reseated myself at my desk. This is very strange, thought I. **What had one best do?**

Speculation – Wonder about, come up with a possible explanation for

Shortcut: Maybe, perhaps, question marks

Example: As the train neared Tarrytown, Imogen Willard began to wonder why she had consented to be one of Flavia's house party at all. She had not felt enthusiastic about it since leaving the city, and was experiencing a prolonged ebb of purpose, a current of chilling indecision, under which she vainly sought for the motive which had induced her to accept Flavia's invitation. **Perhaps** it was a vague curiosity to see Flavia's husband, who had been the magician of her childhood and the hero of innumerable Arabian fairy tales. **Perhaps** it was a desire to see M. Roux, whom Flavia had announced as the especial attraction of the occasion. **Perhaps** it was a wish to study that remarkable woman in her own setting.

Synecdoche – Use of the part to represent the whole

Example: The enormous room on the ground floor faced towards the north. Cold for all the summer beyond the **panes**, for all the tropical heat of the room itself, a harsh thin light glared through the windows, hungrily seeking some draped lay figure, some pallid shape of academic goose-flesh, but finding only the glass and nickel and bleakly shining porcelain of a laboratory.

In the above example, the word *panes* is used as a stand-in for *windows*.

Understatement (Litotes) – Use of excessively restrained language; opposite of hyperbole

This is a form of irony and dry/wry humor, often used to satirize or mock.

Example: [T]he civilest…of men in the morning, yet in the afternoon he was disposed, upon provocation, to be **slightly rash** with his tongue, in fact, insolent.

The word *insolent* (extremely rude) at the end of the sentence indicates that the individual in question was much more than "slightly" rash.

Wordplay – Verbal wit or punning, often involving double meanings of words

Example: They seemed to think the opportunity lost, if they failed to **point** the conversation to me, every now and then, and stick the **point** into me.

Comparing and Contrasting

Antithesis – Use of parallel structure to set opposing ideas in contrast to one another

Example: Winter and summer, then, were two hostile lives, and bred two separate natures. **Winter was always the effort to live; summer was tropical license**.

Comparison – Description of the similarities between two people or things

Example: Marianne's abilities were, in many respects, **quite equal** to Elinor's. She was sensible and clever; but eager in everything: her sorrows, her joys, could have no moderation. She was generous, amiable, interesting: she was everything but prudent. The **resemblance** between her and her mother was strikingly great.

Contrast, or Juxtaposition – Description of opposing qualities

Example: …beyond [the den] was the **luxurious bathroom**, **a modern miracle of enamel tiling and shining glass**. Across the sun-flooded back of the house [was] Alice's little bedroom, **nunlike in its rigid austerity**.

Extended Analogy is an analogy that continues beyond a single comparison, lasting for several sentences or even a paragraph

Example: At first Bartleby did an extraordinary quantity of writing. As if long **famishing** for something to copy, he seemed to **gorge himself** on my documents. There was no pause for **digestion**. He ran a day and night line, copying by sun-light and by candle-light.

Oxymoron – Two contradictory terms placed next to one another for contrast

Example: Parting is such **sweet sorrow**.

Paradox – Statement that appears contradictory but that may reveal an underlying truth

Example: There was only one catch and that was Catch-22, which specified that a concern for one's own safety in the face of dangers that were real and immediate was the process of a rational mind. Orr was crazy and could be grounded. All he had to do was ask; and as soon as he did, he would no longer be crazy and would have to fly more missions.

Simile – Comparison using *like* or *as*

Example: In the morning, one might say, his face was of a fine florid hue, but after twelve o'clock, meridian—his dinner hour—**it blazed <u>like</u> a grate full of Christmas coals**.

Repetition

Alliteration – Repetition of the same sound at the beginnings of multiple words

Example: [H]alf-a-dozen **four-footed fiends**, of various sizes and ages, issued from hidden dens to the common centre.

Anadiplosis – Repetition of a word at the end of one statement and the beginning of the following one

Example: For me it is a misfortune. A misfortune, everyone knows what that is...

Anaphora – Repetition of a word or phrase at the beginning of a series of consecutive sentences/parts of a sentence

Example: [H]e **had** stolen away from every one alike, **had** kept no appointment and renewed no acquaintance, **had** been indifferently aware of the number of persons who esteemed themselves fortunate in being, unlike himself, "met," and **had** even independently, unsociably, alone... given his afternoon and evening to the immediate and the sensible.

Assonance – Repetition of a vowel sound within a group of words

Example: The sp**i**der skins l**ie** on their s**i**des, translucent and ragged...

Parallel Structure – Repetition of the same construction with a sentence or paragraph

Example: He had spent some such good hours there, had forgotten, in her warm, golden drawing-room, **<u>so much of the</u> loneliness** and **<u>so many of the</u> worries of his life**, that it had come to be **<u>the immediate answer</u> to his longings, <u>the cure</u> for his aches, <u>the harbour</u> of refuge from his storms**.

Polysyndeton – Repeated use of a conjunction to join multiple clauses or parts of a sentence

Example: It was four o'clock in the afternoon **and** the kitchen was square **and** gray **and** quiet.

Answers: Thesis Quick Check

1. 0 points

2. 0 points

3. 1 point

4. 0 points

5. 1 point

Recommended Resources

All of the AP English Literature essay prompts since 1999, along with sample responses and scoring analyses, can be found on the AP Central section of the College Board website:

https://apcentral.collegeboard.org/courses/ap-english-literature-and-composition/exam/past-exam-questions?course=ap-english-literature-and-composition

Reprints and Permissions

Austen, Jane. *Pride and Predjudice*, 1813. Chapter 1. http://www.online-literature.com/austen/prideprejudice/1/

-------*Emma*, 1815. Chapter 43. http://www.online-literature.com/austen/emma/43/

Booth, Matthew. "The Tragedy of Saxon's Gate," *Sherlock Holmes: The Game's Afoot*. London: Wordsworth Editions Limited, 2008. p. 157. https://books.google.com/books?id=js5Q48-JpWEC

Brontë, Anne. *Agnes Grey*, 1847. http://www.online-literature.com/brontea/agnes_grey/

Christie, Agatha. *The Mysterious Affair at Styles*, 1920. Chapter 1. http://www.online-literature.com/agatha_christie/mysterious_affair_styles/1/

Dickens, Charles. *Nicholas Nickleby*, 1839. http://www.online-literature.com/dickens/nickleby/

-------*Hard Times*, 1854. Chapter 2. http://www.online-literature.com/dickens/hardtimes/3/

-------*The Pickwick Papers*, 1836. Chapter 5. http://www.online-literature.com/dickens/pickwick/5/

Dickinson, Emily. "As If Some Little Arctic Flower," 1860. http://bloggingdickinson.blogspot.com/2012/02/as-if-some-little-arctic-flower.html

Dings, Fred. "Migratory Flight," *Poetry*, May 1995, p. 102. Reprinted by permission of the author.

Donne, John. "The Bait," 1633. https://www.poetryfoundation.org/poems/44094/the-bait-56d2230bf176d

-------"I Am a Little World Made Cunningly" (Holy Sonnet V), 1635. https://www.poetryfoundation.org/poems/44108/holy-sonnets-i-am-a-little-world-made-cunningly

-------"The Good-Morrow," 1633. https://www.poetryfoundation.org/poems/44104/the-good-morrow

Dove, Rita. "Reverie in Open Air," *American Smooth*. New York: Norton, 2004. p. 118.

Eliot, Geoge. *Adam Bede*, 1859. Chapter 2. https://www.gutenberg.org/files/507/507-h/507-h.htm#link2HCH0001

-------*Middlemarch*, 1871-2. Chapter 3, Chapter 69. http://www.online-literature.com/george_eliot/middlemarch

Emerson, Ralph Waldo. "The Snow-Storm," 1835. https://www.poetryfoundation.org/poems/45872/the-snow-storm-56d22594aa595

Erdrich, Louise. *The Beet Queen*, Harper Collins, New York, NY: 1986, p. 27.

Espaillat, Rhina. "Prosody." 1999 https://www.poemtree.com/poems/Prosody.htm

Forster, E.M. *Howards End*, 1910. Chapters 2 and 3. http://www.online-literature.com/forster/howards_end

Frost, Robert. "After Apple Picking," 1914. https://www.poetryfoundation.org/poems/44259/after-apple-picking

Hardy, Thomas. *The Mayor of Casterbridge*, 1886. Chapter 1. https://www.gutenberg.org/files/143/143-h/143-h.htm

Hawthorne, Nathaniel. *The Blithedale Romance*, 1852. http://www.online-literature.com/hawthorne/blithedale_romance/

Howells, William Dean. *The Rise of Silas Lapham*, 1885. http://www.online-literature.com/william-dean-howells/silas-lapham/

Ishiguro, Kazuo. *A Pale View of Hills*, New York: Random House, 1982. p. 23.

-------*The Remains of the Day*, New York: Random House, p. 133.

James, Henry. *The Ambassadors*, 1903. Chapter 1. http://www.online-literature.com/henry_james/ambassadors/1/

-------*The Portrait of a Lady*, 1881. Chapter 1. http://www.online-literature.com/henry_james/portrait_lady/1/

Jonson, Ben. "Slow, Slow, Fresh Fount," 1600. https://www.poetryfoundation.org/poems/50680/slow-slow-fresh-fount

Keats, John. "To Autumn," 1819. https://www.poetryfoundation.org/poems/44484/to-autumn

-------Sonnet X ["To one who has been long in city pent"], 1817. https://www.poetryfoundation.org/poems/44486/to-one-who-has-been-long-in-city-pent

-------"To a Friend Who Sent Me Some Roses," 1817. https://poets.org/poem/friend-who-sent-me-some-roses

Lahiri, Jhumpa. "When Mr. Pirzada Came to Dine," *Interpreter of Maladies*. New York: Houghton Mifflin Harcourt, 1999. pp. 27-28.

Lawrence, D.H. *Women in Love*, 1922. Chapter 1. https://www.google.com/books/edition/Women_in_Love/f1JAAQAAMAAJ?hl=en&gbpv=1&dq=women+in+love&printsec=frontcover

Lewis, Sinclair. *Babbitt*, 1922. Chapter 7. https://www.gutenberg.org/files/1156/1156-h/1156-h.htm

-------*Main Street*, https://www.gutenberg.org/files/543/543-h/543-h.htm

Longfellow, Henry Wadsworth. "Hymn to the Night," 1839. https://www.poetryfoundation.org/poems/44633/hymn-to-the-night

McEwen, Ian. *The Atonement*, New York: Random House, 2002, pp. 4-5.

Melville, Herman. *Israel Potter*, 1855. Chapter 1. http://www.online-literature.com/melville/israel-potter/1/

Naylor, Gloria. *The Women of Brewster Place*. Penguin: New York, NY, 1982. p. 19.

Piercy, Marge. "Fox in the Morning," *Superstition Review*, Issue 7, Spring 2011. Reprinted by permission of the publisher. https://superstitionreview.asu.edu/issue7/poetry/margepiercy

Pope, Alexander. "An Essay on Man," 1734. https://www.poetryfoundation.org/poems/44899/an-essay-on-man-epistle-i

Rossetti, Christina. "A Daughter of Eve," 1890. https://www.poetryfoundation.org/poems/44993/a-daughter-of-eve

Shelley, Mary Wollstonecraft. *Matilda*, 1820. https://www.gutenberg.org/files/15238/15238-h/15238-h.htm

Shelley, Percy Bysshe. "Ode to the West Wind," 1819. https://www.poetryfoundation.org/poems/45134/ode-to-the-west-wind

St. Vincent Millay, Edna. "Song of a Second April," 1921. https://poets.org/poem/song-second-april

-------"Love Is Not All," 1931. https://poets.org/poem/love-not-all-sonnet-xxx

Tan, Amy. *The Bonesetter's Daughter*. New York, Ballantine Books: 2001. Chapter 1.

Tennyson, Alfred Lord. "Ulysses," 1833. https://www.poetryfoundation.org/poems/45392/ulysses

Toomer, Jean. "Karintha," 1923. https://scalar.lehigh.edu/jean-toomers-cane-1923/karintha-by-jean-toomer

Twain, Mark. *Life on the Mississippi*, 1883. https://twain.lib.virginia.edu/solr-home/html/TwaLife.html#TwaLifed1e1113

------*Personal Recollections of Joan of Arc*, 1896. Chapter 23. http://www.online-literature.com/twain/recollections-joan-of-arc/31/

-------*The Gilded Age*, 1873 Chapter 1. http://www.online-literature.com/twain/gilded-age/1/

-------*The Tragedy of Pudd'nhead Wilson*, 1894. Chapter 2. http://www.online-literature.com/twain/puddnhead_wilson/2/

Vaughan, Henry. "The Waterfall," 1655. https://www.poetryfoundation.org/poems/45433/the-water-fall

Wharton, Edith. *The House of Mirth*, 1905. http://www.online-literature.com/wharton/house_mirth/

Whitman, Walt. "A Noiseless, Patient Spider," 1868. https://www.poetryfoundation.org/poems/45473/a-noiseless-patient-spider

Woolf, Virginia. "Kew Gardens," 1919. http://www.online-literature.com/virginia_woolf/862/

Wordsworth, William. "A Complaint," 1806. https://www.poetryfoundation.org/poems/45513/a-complaint

About the Author

Erica Meltzer earned her B.A., *magna cum laude,* from Wellesley College and spent more than a decade tutoring privately in Boston and New York City, as well as nationally and internationally online. Her experience working with students from a wide range of educational backgrounds and virtually every score level gave her unique insight into the types of stumbling blocks students often encounter while preparing for standardized reading and writing tests.

She was inspired to begin writing her own test-prep materials in 2007, after visiting a local bookstore in search of additional practice questions for an SAT Writing student. Unable to find material that replicated the contents of the exam with sufficient accuracy, she decided to write her own. What started as a handful of exercises jotted down on a piece of paper became the basis for her first book, the original *Ultimate Guide to SAT® Grammar,* published in 2011. Since that time, she has authored guides for SAT reading and vocabulary, as well as verbal guides for the ACT®, GRE®, and GMAT®. Her books have sold more than a quarter-of-a-million copies and are used by students around the world. She lives in New York City, and you can visit her online at www.thecriticalreader.com.

Made in United States
Orlando, FL
23 February 2024

44026747R00120